Information System
Business Management

Martin Combs

School of Computing and Information Systems
University of Humberside

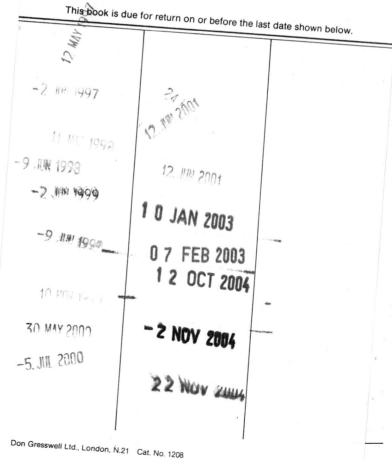

PITMAN
PUBLISHING

PITMAN PUBLISHING
128 Long Acre, London WC2E 9AN

A Division of Pearson Professional Limited

First published in Great Britain in 1995

ISBN 0 273 60145 8

British Library Cataloguing in Publication Data
A CIP catalogue record for this book can be obtained from the British Library

10 9 8 7 6 5 4 3 2 1

Typeset by Land & Unwin (Data Sciences) Limited
Printed and bound in Great Britain by Clays Ltd, St Ives plc

The Publishers' policy is to use paper manufactured from sustainable forests.

CONTENTS

PREFACE

When this book was originally discussed with the publishers I suggested that I might write a text that no one wanted to read. I believed that both typical management professionals and students are too busy to *want* to read a text on information systems for business management. My priority has therefore been to try and communicate ideas and principles as simply and clearly as I can. Where possible I have:

- briefly bulleted or highlighted principles and ideas
- given examples of their relevance
- explained the examples.

The development and structure of the book perhaps needs some explanation. Chapter 1 starts with a consideration of business principles as implied by the idea of a 'business plan' and a 'business review' (or what I call a 'business health check'). There may be many ways in which we can view or evaluate a business but, certainly for lending institutions and other investors with working knowledge of business, the 'plan' or 'review' is seen as identifying areas of key significance for its success or failure. The kinds of information required in a plan or review are similar to those required regarding a company's performance on an ongoing basis; thus we begin with what motivates us to want business information.

Chapter 2 considers how management have typically structured their companies with respect to the exercise of authority and responsibility. A discussion of the integration of technology into business and management provides additional background for the contexts in which management decisions are made and the information products intended to support them. The chapter concludes with a focus on the characteristics of decision making at different levels of management.

The theme of management is continued in Chapter 3, where the focus is specifically on the aspect of management control. The relationship between the exercise of management control and the need for appropriate knowledge, information and data is emphasised. Information systems are introduced at this point and further consideration is given to their role in providing information to support management action rather than contextually inappropriate data.

In Chapter 4, systems principles are presented as a set of thinking tools to encourage critical thinking to aid the understanding of better management behaviour and practice with respect to goal-orientated activities. I should mention here that goal-orientated activities are perhaps the exception rather than the rule in management practice; much of a manager's time and energy has to be spent attending to human relationships and interaction related to systemic aspects of management (e.g. fundamental psychologically and sociologically driven motivational behaviour patterns) that are more relationship and process-orientated than goal-orientated. The treatment of systems ideas has been expanded, on the one hand, to include the possibility, indeed the advisability, of including the consideration of inevitable interaction between different types of systems – the context in which information systems function. On the other hand, the systems language has been constrained so that it is possible to map reasonably between the need to monitor business performance and the relatively precise world of information systems. Information systems, by their very nature, are structured and limited in terms of the worlds about which they can deliver information and by the practical limitations of the technology in which they are implemented. By contrast, the scope of managerial tasks and experience extends far beyond purely goal-orientated behaviour that is based solely on achievement of business performance.

In Chapter 5 there is an outline of the characteristics of a relational database management system, which is currently the most common type of technology used by business information systems. The database, as a provider of business information, is introduced at this point so that the subsequent chapters on business data and process modelling can be understood within both the business and technological contexts which affect our understanding, the purpose and results of analysis and modelling.

Chapters 6 and 7 explain the principles and practice of top-down (entity relationship) and bottom-up (normalisation) data modelling. The treatment of these topics is kept at a relatively simple level with the emphasis on developing a sound understanding of the basics which can be built upon in more advanced courses or in practical systems development. Perhaps more significant is the approach taken in these chapters and in Chapter 8 on business process analysis and modelling. The approach is partly based on experience in other systemic fields and it is suggested as a practical, and revealing, alternative to some of the more traditional methods. The approach is also based on management-orientated 'diagnostic' requirements for information and enables the analyst to understand and control the investigation more effectively. The principal difference consists of building or synthesising a model from meaningful and carefully chosen diagnostics into a more complex system instead of reducing a complex system into simpler components or sub-systems. The advantage is that the analysis proceeds from a well understood base rather than from the less well understood, supposedly 'holistic', viewpoint which says that the analysis begins by 'producing a context diagram representing company X as a system'. The analytical products resulting from the application of the method used here probably differ little, if at all, from the more standard methods but the hope is that the novice analyst will have a better understanding of the business systems to which the method is applied.

Chapter 9 consists of an intelligent layman's guide to some of the essential characteristics of information technology that are commonly used for information systems. The main concern of the chapter is to focus in a non-technical way on those aspects of the technology that have to be taken into account by managers when they plan for its use in business.

Finally, Chapter 10 explores the case study. As an approach to learning, the case study has tremendous potential for students to acquire new material and become mature problem solvers. However, it is not always fun or as positive an experience as it ought to be. How to tackle and work through case studies in information systems is the subject of Chapter 10. A case with sample questions is included, and partially worked through, in order to illustrate the sort of approach that is expected by many lecturers.

CHAPTER 1

An introduction to business

1.1 INTRODUCTION

We start with an introduction to business, because, first, it is important to remember that business is the context in which the application or use of computer-based information systems is being considered. Second, it is also important to remember that the goals for which businesses strive are business goals, even though computers may be used to help businesses achieve those goals. Third, even if you are a business student or a student of computing in business, despite the many business options available, a succinct statement of key concerns to business may be useful.

The focus will be on issues that matter to the business community, and most of these change little over time. The aim is to give an overview which generates the questions that will form the basis of a diagnostic exploration of a business or, indeed, any kind of organisation that has to account for its performance and is responsible for how its resources are used.

One of the functions of management is to *structure the business* so as to fulfil its goals. Another function is to provide a context in which employees can give of their best and in which the performance of the business is effectively monitored; this management function is expressed as a *management approach*. The relationship between decision making and information is also considered along with the principle of control, i.e. how to monitor business performance.

The primary aim of this book is to communicate, as simply and as clearly as possible from a business management point of view, the principles that lie behind the development of information systems in a business context. The explanation and development of systems-based analytical thinking and modelling techniques can, and should, lead to greater insight into business activities and management, as well as providing a principled basis for understanding information systems.

Good theory should, where possible, be put into good practice, and throughout this book the importance of successfully implementing the ideas presented is not forgotten. With this in mind, the normal pattern of presentation is to give a principle and then an example to indicate what the idea means in a business context. This approach is strengthened by giving step-by-step worked examples which have already proved to be of value to business students, on introductory and intermediate level modules, in systems analysis and design. Throughout this book, the business dimension is kept alive because the success of information systems development depends at least as much on a good grasp of the business and management issues as it does on technical expertise.

1.2 A FIRST LOOK AT BUSINESS

Some essential business concerns are introduced in sufficient detail to demonstrate that we are interested in the real world, but do not want to become so detailed that attention is taken away from the main issue, that is to say the business as a whole. A starting point for a serious consideration of business is the business plan.

When someone wants to start a new business venture from scratch; this person will need a *business plan*. Creating a new business involves asking important questions, the answers to which a bank manager or potential investors will examine very carefully. Sometimes, when a business seeks further investment, or trading results suggest a health check is required, it is time to take stock and examine the ability of the business to survive and succeed within the business world. These questions have been chosen because it is important to appreciate what kinds of questions are significant to key players within business, that is to say, the people who aim to make a success of business by running it well, and those who provide the financial backing and investment in businesses with potential. Management decisions and actions will be very much concerned with the kinds of issues identified here. Computerised information systems play a significant role in modern businesses by monitoring business activities, thus providing information that can form the basis for management actions or decisions.

1.3 THE BUSINESS PLAN

No professional business investors will consider putting their money into a new venture without first seeing, and approving, a business plan. The business plan should force the entrepreneurs to consider carefully whether they have all that is necessary (within their control) for the business to be a success. The kinds of questions that have to be asked can be grouped under four main headings:

- purpose
- things
- finance
- market.

1.3.1 Purpose

Determining the purpose of a business, simple and straightforward as it seems, is nevertheless a crucial first step. The new venture should have a clear purpose, or reason, for coming into existence. The business may, on the one hand, provide products or services, for example, the manufacture of components, the retailing of certain kinds of products, the provision of a distribution, maintenance or repair service for certain kinds of products. On the other hand, a business may aim to sell products and have a repair service too.

1.3.2 Things

Things can include people, places, physical resources and products. Does the prospective business have the right people with the right skills and abilities available to it? Does the prospective business have suitable premises available, for example, a site for building a factory, or existing premises or a retail unit of the right size and in the right place? Will the business have suitable machinery and/or transport available? Will the business be able to obtain raw materials or other supplies of suitable quality and within reasonable time spans?

1.3.3 Market

There is no use producing goods or services unless there are people who want to buy them. Market analysis has to be undertaken to ensure there is a realistic expectation of custom. Careful attention has to be given as to how existing businesses of a comparable type exploit the market and to the potential for existing businesses to respond to new competition. Factors to consider are pricing, quality of comparable products or services, ability of potential opposition to adjust these factors to the detriment of new competition or to affect supply, to jeopardise future prospects, such as copying a new idea and marketing it more cheaply than the originator!

1.3.4 Finance

Finance is an area which touches many business activities. Finance is a factor, directly or indirectly, in most aspects of the business plan and as far as investors are concerned they will see most aspects of the plan in terms of financial costs and benefits.

Under the heading 'things', there are questions that relate the intrinsic value of the 'things' themselves to the business, for example, whether an engineer has the appropriate engineering skills to do the job required of him, or whether the intended premises are the appropriate size. Each of the things of importance to the company comes with a price tag. How much will the engineer need to be paid? How much will the business have to pay in National Insurance contributions, pension, etc., in addition to the salary the engineer receives? How much will the equipment cost? How much will the rent of the premises be? How much will it cost to maintain and eventually replace equipment, etc? All of these, and many more questions, have to be answered *before* they come as a devastating shock to the new business.

Marketing provides potential benefits to the business, but it has to be paid for. For example, what will be the cost of the time and expertise of those who conduct the market research or develop informational and promotional literature for the products or services, etc?

Not only will a business plan have to demonstrate that the benefits and the financial costs of the new business are well understood and planned for; management and financial control also provide benefits at a cost.

1.3.5 Reflecting on the business plan

Only a simplified view can be given here of the kind of considerations that tend to be included in business plans, but it should be clear that the process involves asking many pertinent questions and ensuring that there are satisfactory answers for them all. Some questions relate to the characteristics of the 'things' or resources that, together, contribute to the success of the business, while other questions relate to the cost to the business to use or produce those things. Clearly what helps a business survive is its ability to generate an income sufficiently greater than its outgoings. It is of critical importance, therefore, for management to know what questions should be asked to ensure the business has a good chance of success; trusting to luck is a poor substitute. Managers need to know what information is necessary and also where and how to get it for the business to survive and succeed.

1.4 THE BUSINESS HEALTH CHECK

A review of an existing business is a more complex process than developing the business plan. While many of the questions in the health check will be similar, in essence, to those asked in the business plan, many of the questions will relate to the ways in which the business *currently* functions. The health check identifies critical areas of business activity and asks what management is doing about them; it does not pay attention as to how effectively or efficiently the business manages them.

Fundamental business principles have not changed much over the centuries; some of the earliest written records relate to the recording and monitoring of business activity. Businesses operate in dynamic market conditions and successful businesses will create and modify their business strategies in response to changing market conditions, opportunities and experience.

Business is like an organic entity, which reacts and adjusts to its environment. Markets and consumer tastes change over time and businesses need to change in response to market trends, technological developments, etc. Not all changes within a business are planned and many changes are only partially planned. For example, suppose one business takes over a smaller rival; the larger business may gain outlets, extra capacity or even patent rights that allow beneficial modifications to its lead product. It may be faced with additional ranges of products or services which had not been part of the long-term strategic plan of the larger business. Some of the 'new' lines may show a better profit than older lines. Eventually, the shape and organisation of the business may change. Many factors lead businesses to the point where they should undertake a thorough review.

The right questions need to be asked if an accurate diagnosis of the current fitness of the business is to be made. A typical business review might include the following diagnostic categories:

1 developing a mission statement;
2 setting strategic objectives;
3 reviewing the main business functions;
4 developing action plans;
5 evaluating and refining the action plans (in the light of the mission statement and strategic objectives).

1.4.1 Developing a mission statement

The mission statement should express the main purpose of the organisation. A shift in demand and the success of new products over a long period of time may result in a business which puts more emphasis on its traditional products and/or services rather than ones which should be taking it into the future. The potential of new and successful products or services can remain unrecognised in an effort to cling to past strengths.

EXAMPLE

In the past the computer giant, IBM, had gone through a very traumatic period; a few years ago IBM was considered by many to be the largest and most successful computer manufacturer of all time. Few would have predicted the collapse of this world renowned company. IBM had to rediscover their mission: the world had changed. IBM seemed blind to the revolution in computing that they had initiated in the early 1980s with the introduction of their Personal Computer (PC). Still thinking of themselves as a manufacturer of 'serious' business machines, that is to say mainframes, they failed to adjust to customer demands and buying policies. The business health check required drastic remedies: to survive and succeed, the loss of thousands of jobs, the development of a new mission statement and the search for a new way forward were necessary.

In order to discover whether a business has a relevant and contemporary mission statement, questions have to be asked. It would not suffice to say, 'Yes, we have a main purpose'. Such a statement would need to be tested against hard facts gained from an honest appraisal of the market and product/service strengths of the business.

1.4.2 Setting strategic objectives

Strategic objectives are specific, measurable goals which should take the business towards greater success. The objectives are normally long-term and should be in line with the mission statement. These objectives are usually closely tied to the main functional areas of the business. Clearly, if a company has such objectives, then in the review the questions to ask are *what* are they and *how* are they to be measured? Are they in line with the mission statement? Do they really qualify as strategic objectives? What gains are they meant to bring and at what cost, etc? A business strategy usually involves a major commitment of resources in order to achieve the stated objectives. Strategy, therefore, has to do with long-term planning and the direction the business is to take. Strategic objectives should not, however, be confused with overall objectives. A business would normally have an overall objective of making profit just as a general might have the overall objective of winning the war or a chess player might have the overall objective of winning the game, but strategy has to do with *how* these overall objectives might be achieved. If a business decided that its strategic objective was to make more profit for the following year, it would make no more sense than for a general to say that his strategic objective was to win the war. There would be no strategy involved.

If a local bakery business decided to embark on a new venture and set a strategic objective of capturing the market for fresh sandwiches and rolls in the area, it would have to look carefully at how it might achieve the objective. How many staff would it take to give quick and efficient service? What range of fillings would bring most customers? Would it have to have fresh joints of roast beef and/or roast its own chickens, etc. to attract the sort of customers it wants? To a small business, there may be new and difficult decisions to spend money in order to make money. Some of the costs might include extra staff, spit-roasters, hotplates or buying a range of fillings, etc. The risk factor may be quite high, but the success (or not) would be measurable – perhaps in terms of incremental short-term goals.

1.4.3 Reviewing the main functions of the business

At the mission statement and strategic objectives level, decisions and questions tend to have long-term consequences and importance for the business as a whole (the time scale might cover a span of a few years). A review of the main functions of the business considers decisions and questions that relate more to tactical issues with a shorter operational span of, perhaps, a year. The reason for this is that each main function of the business needs to have specific measurable objectives and should make plans in order to meet them. As is often the case in business, any kind of achievement entails investment of some kind and functional areas of the business are not exempt; fulfilling their goals may be costly. Such investment has to be budgeted for as part of the financial control or resource management.

It is convenient to consider the major functional areas within the business under major headings, but it should be remembered that each of these areas is interdependent; many activities within the business are interdependent and therefore interact with more than one functional area. We will examine each of the following areas in order to build up a better understanding of why they are important and what kinds of questions they provoke:

1 marketing;
2 production;
3 people;
4 finance.

Marketing and production are modular functions in that their goals are specific to their areas, but people and finance are systemic functions in so far as their goals are to serve and improve the effectiveness and efficiency of all functional areas, even though they will also have their own structures.

1.4.3.1 Marketing

One of the main concerns of marketing is to ensure that the business is scratching where it itches, that is to say, the marketing departments should be very interested in what the customer really wants. Sometimes marketing attempts to have a role in creating demand, but for the most part the customers' demands and interests are the interests of marketing. Marketing, therefore, concerns itself with customers, what they want and why they want the things they do. Marketing specialists try to identify products and services that provide what the customer wants. They are also typically involved with the selling or communication of product information to the customer in such a way as to encourage the customer to buy.

If the marketing specialists get it wrong, the business may provide the wrong products or services. To develop new products or services can be a costly process, thus the importance of this business area. How do marketing specialists know, or at least think they know, what the customer really wants? They have to bring together several types of marketing research and hope they have the right combination of factors, in the right proportions, to identify the products or services most sought after by the customer.

Whether the company is fully aware of the performance of its products, whether it has adequate explanations for poor performance and plans for achieving performance targets should be questioned. Does the marketing component provide relevant information about customers, buying behaviour, the competition and any advantages or disadvantages of significance?

Market research consists of gaining market intelligence, which includes finding out about customers, buying behaviour and external socio-economic factors, such as those relevant to recession or recovery. Marketing specialists need to know how customers use and view the relevant products or services; also competing products' features, quality and prices need to be known. Distribution channels, promotional opportunities, etc. are additional factors about which marketing people have to consider and make part of their research.

1.4.3.2 Production

Production is the means by which a company generates its products or services. Products are 'things' that people or organisations purchase for their use. Sometimes the word 'product' is given a wider meaning and may be used for 'people', for example, graduates of a training scheme or a university. Services are less tangible items that are viewed as being consumed as they are being offered. Examples of this might be the service provided by doctors, transport companies such as British Rail, car mechanics, local councils or members of parliament.

The results of the production process or service are what the customer pays for, and the products or services are the means by which the business gains its income; in order to produce anything, a business has to draw on resources. Production is sometimes modelled as a process which has inputs and outputs, but business cannot view complex activities like production as a simple mechanical process in which inputs and outputs are neatly paired. Typical production inputs include raw materials, labour, energy and capital, while typical outputs would include the products or services.

The business will need to ask many questions in its review concerning production. It will need to examine its existing production processes and what they involve. In particular, a manufacturing company should not only ask what processes it uses, but also what alternative processes exist and how the existing approaches or processes compare? A primarily service-based business should consider how it goes about providing the services it does, what alternatives might exist and how they compare.

The issues have, so far, related to the *processes* involved in production. Other issues relate to *things*, in a broad sense. Questions could be asked about the raw materials used by the production process such as, how much is kept in stock? How much wastage is there? Are there storage or supply issues of interest, etc? Questions could be asked about other physical resources such as the appropriateness of the buildings (e.g. factory, offices or hotel) in terms of their ability to fulfil what is required of them, or the adequacy of the plant (e.g. machinery or kitchen equipment) to support the processes or about the staff numbers and skills. All these matters are relevant to whether or not the business can provide quality products or services to its customers, both now and within the time frame assumed in its strategic plans.

1.4.3.3 People

How people are regarded in a particular business often depends upon the prevailing management philosophy, but the basic issues relate to whether the skills needed by the business are actually possessed by the people it employs. A company skill profile should embrace those skills needed for policy and strategic decision making as well as those required for day-to-day operations. Consideration should be given to the number of people with the appropriate skills necessary for the business to function efficiently, effectively and to produce quality products or services. *Efficiently* in this context means producing something at the lowest possible cost, whether measured in time or money. *Effectively* means doing something in a way that best produces the desired result. Neither word implies the other.

Accepting that change is part and parcel of business culture, it is therefore reasonable to assume that the profile of the skills needed by the business will change as it changes. Ignoring some of the more provocative questions that this might raise, it would be more productive to concentrate on the question of whether the business actually has a people policy; people are often the single largest expense the business has to meet. Understanding and managing this resource is one of the most challenging, difficult and important areas of management. We are thus concerned whether the business actually has a plan to ensure that it has the people with the appropriate skills to deliver quality products or services. The kinds of questions that arise then are:

- Have the skills, abilities, etc. that are required for the specific products or services been identified?
- Have realistic estimations of workloads, and by implication, staffing levels been worked out?
- How does the business maintain an up-to-date knowledge of the skills, interests, and abilities of its employees and management?
- Does the business have a method of career/work appraisal?
- Does the business have a clear and effective approach to recruitment?
- Does the business have a clear policy or approach to the development and maintenance of a positive 'work culture'?
- Does the business encourage the exploration or development of new ideas by its people?
- Does the business have a policy for staff development such as for enhancing skills and thus potential effectiveness of employee performance?

- Does the company invest in updating and improving the skills base of employees so as to meet and capitalise on changes the business will have to embrace in order to be competitive?

1.4.3.4 Finance

The financial dimension is a significant factor in all areas of the business. Money is both consumed and produced by the business selling its products and/or services. Businesses that fail to produce significantly more income than their outgoings over a period of time will sooner or later fail. It is not surprising then that well managed businesses place a high priority on understanding and monitoring the tremendous variety of activities that happen within the business each day. Businesses should know what their main activities or functions cost them and how to assess their value to the company.

Each of the functional areas of the business costs money; it is sometimes easier to find out how much they cost than it is to find out how much they contribute to the company's finances. Marketing costs money: marketing specialists have to be paid; market research and the use of on-line information systems have to be paid for. Advertising costs money: we need to know what the expenditure is in relation to the expected gains from advertising, or even in relation to the possible cost of not advertising when competitors are. It is hard to know how financially beneficial advertising is to a business and whether it is worth it.

Production is another part of the business that has to be costed; manufacturers and providers of services, such as hotels, have to invest heavily in the physical resources that are used to deliver their products or services. Machines get old, wear out and break down. Hotels similarly require maintenance, redecoration and items need replacing. Realistic financial provision has to be made for all these things, as well as staff costs, utilities, etc. Has the business a budget, or current forecast, for expenditure and maintenance, etc. over a given period of time? Are there adequate means of tracking actual costs?

Labour and people costs are often the highest costs for organisations and clearly this is an area of the business which should receive careful attention. The goal should be to gain the maximum benefit from one of the business's most valuable resources. It is because labour and people costs tend to be very high that it is often to here that businesses turn in times of economic difficulty. Only with good information about costs and income generation can a business really know whether it will actually benefit by cutting labour costs.

The external financial climate will determine how much of a business's income is eaten up by interest charges on money used for investment in resources; a loan needed for modernisation may be hard, or very costly, to obtain in uncertain economic times. The strength of the British currency vis-à-vis that of other nations may assist the exporter but hurt the hotelier. These and other financial factors are very much part of the reality of trading as a business.

The financial questions that need to be asked are whether the financial function in the business actually monitors its internal performance. Does it know and understand what each aspect of the business enterprise means in terms of financial costs? What financial and other business benefits are gained? To what extent are external factors and economic trends monitored and are there strategies in place to respond appropriately to such external economic intelligence?

Having taken a brief look at four major business functions and considered questions that would be appropriate for a business review, it would be useful to now turn to the next part of the business review – the development of action plans – which will take the business from where it is now, to where it needs to be in the future, if it is to meet its strategic goals and fulfil its mission statement.

1.5 DEVELOPING ACTION PLANS

If section 1.4 constituted a business health check, then this section constitutes the programme for business fitness which takes the diagnosis as the starting point. The aim of the business review is to identify strengths and weaknesses within the major functional areas. It is then possible to develop action plans for these areas so that the strategic objectives of the business can be met. It is important to remember that, although we can usefully think in terms of each of these areas having its own special place within the business as a whole, it would be foolish for each area to develop its own higher-level plans in isolation from the others.

The success of the business as a whole depends on the co-ordinated interaction and mutual support of all the functional areas, e.g. market research may recommend significant resources be channelled into the development of a particular product line; production depends upon this intelligence to guide its activity and the production of a quality product depends upon, perhaps, designers and engineers. Marketing depends upon the production function to deliver on time, in order to take advantage of the culmination of an advertising campaign. No individual functional area can achieve success for the company on its own.

Action plans can, therefore, be seen to rely on information. But what is meant by action plans? Who is meant to take which kinds of actions about what? An action plan means that decisions are made about things which need to be done or changed. Often it is not known what needs to be done without the information which states that it is necessary; decision makers depend heavily on high quality information if they are to make sound business decisions.

A business health check

Let us imagine the case of an ailing brewery. A traditional local brewery has been fighting a losing battle with larger regional breweries who are dominating the market through tied public houses and aggressive advertising. The owners of the local brewery thought that customer loyalty and their excellent products would be sufficient to keep their business flourishing. Desperate, they undertake a business review with the following results.

Mission statement
To further develop and maintain the company's reputation as a distinctive, traditional brewer of very fine ales.

Strategic objectives
To reduce their current wide range of beers to a restricted but distinctive range based on old family recipes. For this they can draw entirely on their large acreage of uniquely flavoured, quality hops.

Review of main business functions
- *Marketing* There has been no formal assessment of the competition and there is no knowledge of marketing strategies employed by the competition. Very little thought has been given to own marketing (though much attention has been given to the quality of the products which they naively think will sell themselves), etc.
- *Production* Much attention has been given to the quality of the products, but almost no attention given to the efficiency, or effectiveness, of the production processes.
- *People* Specialist skills are strong but management lacks appropriate skills to ensure business success in a hostile and competitive business climate.
  There is no plan for people development.
- *Finance* Accounting processes are basic, manual and adequate but financial management is very weak; there is no monitoring for different areas within the business.

Action plans
- *Marketing* A marketing function needs development. An examination of the marketing strategies used by the competition is to begin immediately, with a view to developing an effective presence as a niche competitor.
  Plans for local and regional advertising include ordering a run of distinctive sweatshirts featuring their brews and sending discount vouchers to clubs and major employers in the area.
  A reassessment of the strategic objectives in the light of market research is recommended.

▶

▶

Marketing could begin looking at getting a better return on the more than adequate reserves of fine, distinctive hops.

- *Production* A new set of effectiveness and efficiency criteria are to be developed through a series of meetings with all employees involved in the production process, with a view to encouraging a fresh sense of purpose and commitment.
- *People* The gravity of the business situation has encouraged a realism in the brewery so that weaknesses in competence at all levels are to be addressed. Management training consultants have been contacted to start a series of confidential interviews with all levels of staff and on that basis to either initiate training programmes or, in some cases, recommend reallocation of responsibilities.

  The consultants will also find solutions to meet identified weaknesses in the brewery's skills profile, e.g. to either recruit a marketing specialist or hire a marketing consultancy to support the brewery's new initiative.
- *Finance* The brewery is going to investigate some accounting packages and has decided, when one has been chosen, to send, initially, the office manager and one other employee on a course to ensure that best use is made of the new computer-based system.

1.6 PRINCIPLES AND ASSUMPTIONS BEHIND THE BUSINESS PLAN AND THE BUSINESS REVIEW

Only a sketch of the kinds of considerations that are included in business plans and business health checks has been provided, but it should be clear that the process involves asking many pertinent questions and making sure that there are satisfactory answers for them all. Some of the questions related to the characteristics of the 'things' or resources that, together, contribute to the success of the business. Other kinds of questions related to what it would cost the business to use or produce those things.

The processes of developing a business plan, or undertaking a thorough business health check, will only have real value if the principles and assumptions behind them are understood. There are many similarities between these two discrete processes. Both processes have a bottom line interest in whether or not the business can, or will, be financially viable, i.e. whether it has a good chance of making money. Both processes recognise that the cost of making money is usually high and that naiveté in business is a very serious threat to business survival; naiveté may lead to false expectations of income and/or unrealistic assessment of the extent of specific costs or of not planning for some costs at all. The other side of the naiveté coin is that both the business plan and the business health check depend on *knowledge* and *information*.

The processes of developing a business plan or undertaking a business health check make use of business knowledge in that the ingredients of success and causes of failure have been reasonably established, especially by those who make their money by risking it through investment. The risk takers have no wish to shorten their odds on a profitable return by ignoring lessons of the past; they have to ensure that the business, or prospective business, has addressed all the important questions. In both cases, if *business knowledge* identifies which questions need to be asked, then it is the *information* that is returned that provides the risk takers with the *foundation* for deciding whether the risk is worth taking.

1.6.1 Assumptions

It is assumed that the questions asked are the right questions. The questions wanted are those which will provide the best guide to whether a prospective business has a good chance of success, or what an existing business can or should do to improve its position within the market place. It must be assumed that, since the market place changes through time and, perhaps, business knowledge increases with improved technological resources, that business health checks should not be a once and for all exercise. Business health checks should be undertaken, perhaps, over fixed periods consistent with the rate of change within that particular business sector. It is also assumed that even if the questions asked are the right questions and that satisfactory answers are given, there are still factors that cannot be accounted for. External factors within the business environment, such as consumer demand, competitors' actions or unexpected interest rate increases, cannot be predicted with any certainty. Internal factors such as staff morale, other working environment problems or deviant behaviour on the part of trusted personnel cannot necessarily be identified by a business health check.

1.6.2 Principles

The principles summarised in Table 1.1 are themselves built on the deeper principles that, in order to achieve business success, we need *knowledge* to ask the right questions and appropriate *information* to answer the questions and provide a sound basis for making decisions and moving forward intelligently.

1.7 SUMMARY

In this chapter some aspects of business have been examined that are important enough for banks and other potential investors to ask questions about prior to committing their financial resources to a business seeking investment. It can only be concluded that these aspects are areas about which management needs information. If it doesn't collect and store information about these areas, management cannot exercise management

Table 1.1   The principles behind the business plan and business health check

Business Plan	Business Health Check	Principle
Purpose	Mission statement	To ensure that the business is quite clear about its purpose; its niche in the market
Things	Production People	These relate to the tangible resources available to a business. The raw materials, the products of manufacture, the physical buildings, machinery or other equipment, and the people who do all the work. The costs and benefits of all should be known or estimated.
Market	Marketing	The market for the products or services should be well researched and exploited if the business is to have competitive success.
Finance	Finance	The costs and benefits of the day-to-day running of the company, including its major functional areas, have to be well understood, predicted, and managed, as well as the costs incurred for planned developments, etc.

control where it is considered most significant by those who are among the most concerned about the success of the company.

The business plan and the 'business health check' provided the basic framework for our thinking and exploration of key areas of concern to management. The importance to a business of having a clear mission, and one which is in tune with changes and trends, has been discussed. Specific strategic objectives provide the challenges for which the major business functions have to be geared up and managed for success. Without reliable and up-to-date information about the performance or health of the key areas of the business, managers will not know how or whether goals are being met; investors will not have any encouragement to supply the capital required for a business to succeed or expand.

Chapter 2 takes a closer look at different ways in which management organises an organisation to meet its goals and the different styles that managers have of exercising their authority and control. One responsibility of managers that is interesting is that they make decisions; when they make decisions they usually need appropriate information to support them. The nature of decision making, how the level of management can affect the characteristics of the decisions and the kinds of information that tend to support them is also examined.

QUESTIONS

1 Explain why investors insist on the preparation of a business plan before risking their money on a venture.

2 Discuss some of the more obvious similarities and differences, as you understand them, between a business plan and a business health check.

3 Why is it important for a business to have a mission statement? Explain what a mission statement is and suggest what factors might be important to consider in its development.

4 Consider the idea of setting strategic objectives. Typically, businesses have associated strategy with long-term planning . . . an assumption made in this chapter. It could however be argued that, in a fast changing business environment, making long-term plans is a dangerous thing. Discuss the strengths and weaknesses of so-called strategic planning in the context of a business sector of your choice.

5 Marketing is one of the main functions of a business. Take a look at, or listen to, the media and identify what you believe to be a marketing initiative by a company. Consider what aspects of human behaviour the advertising is relying on and what criteria you would use if you were the marketing executive to determine whether the campaign is successful. Precisely what information would you need and where could you get it from?

6 Discuss the sorts of issues that a business manager would need to consider in the case of (a) a hotel that offers a service to its customers, and (b) a company that produces designer lighting solutions. Restrict your consideration to the issue of 'production'.

7 If 'efficiency' and 'effectiveness' are not the same thing then explain the difference and consider (with examples) how an approach to monitoring might differ if our concern was more for one than the other.

8 Explain the purpose of an 'action plan' and give an example of what it would mean for a company in the context of a 'business health check'.

BIBLIOGRAPHY West, A., *A Business Plan*, NatWest Business Handbooks, Pitman Publishing, 1995.

Your Business Success, The Employment Department, Moorfoot, (available through Durham Small Business Club Ltd).

CHAPTER 2

Management and decision making

2.1 INTRODUCTION

In Chapter 1 the key aspects of a business, particularly those of crucial significance to potential investors in a business venture, were considered in some detail. In this chapter the focus is on how management can create the conditions or environment to support quality decision making and thus facilitate the success that investors demand of the business. For the purposes of this text management will be considered to have two major functions: the first is the responsibility of management to organise or structure the business so that it will be able to meet its goals; the second is that, given the constraints (or possibilities) of the structure, management should exercise control and ensure that the various activities within the business operate effectively, that the activities are appropriately co-ordinated and that the goals are indeed met.

There are few constants in business, though it would be reasonable to take the aspects discussed in Chapter 1 as important issues of continuing interest to people seeking profit and success. One constant that all businesses can rely on is that of change. Markets, customers, business environments and resources all change over time. Businesses need to adjust, prepare for and take advantage of change. The problem is that change can be disruptive. The organisational design chosen for one set of circumstances may be unhelpful for another. A management approach which seemed successful in one era may be unacceptable in another. The human and technical resources available at one time will also have changed dramatically within a few years. Aside from this, a business may have merged with, or taken over, another and major parts of the company may have been gained or lost over time.

The evidence of change is virtually always present to some degree in established businesses. Market and other external conditions may cause the business to change its products or services, but the structures may have changed little, or in a piecemeal fashion only. Reasons for the resistance to change of management structures are beyond the scope of this book, but it is sufficient to say that anything more than small incremental changes may mean restructuring the business, involving changes of job definitions, skill requirements, responsibilities, etc. Change which is desperately needed by the organisation as a whole can be threatening to the individuals who work for it.

Management that has its eye on the ball will evaluate whether its current structures, management approach and resources still enable the most effective business responses to be made in a changing environment. Change is certain and, at this point in history, change can be rapid. Business success will depend on quality, often rapid, decision making, and it will depend on information to support those decisions. Technology, once the means to an end and supportive of business activities, is now seen in some industries as a determining factor in how business should be organised.

Modern approaches to management and organisational design tend to emphasise that organisational structure, management approaches and technological resources should enable, and support, all employees to exercise their unique abilities effectively and efficiently in the business. More than that, however, most modern approaches recognise that taking account of human and social factors is good management *and* good business. In this text awareness of the importance of the human and social elements is assumed, but the focus is on the enabling and supporting elements.

Assuming that a business has a clear set of goals or, in terms of the 'business review', a mission statement and some specific strategic goals, when starting or reviewing a business, a plan is needed to organise the business activities in order to achieve those goals. In a business review, the fact that changes may be necessary if we are to achieve a revised set of goals will need to be dealt with. The following are three key enabling and supporting factors:

- organisational structure
- management approaches
- technology.

2.2 ORGANISATIONAL STRUCTURE

Consideration of organisational structure may be done by looking at a small business, such as a single shop in which the owner does almost everything. Even if part-time assistants are employed for busy periods the business will still have a relatively simple structure. Nevertheless the business will still need to decide on:

- Should it advertise, and if so, where?
- What ranges of products should it sell, including colours, styles and sizes?
- What image should the shop have?
- Should it take Switch and major credit cards, etc?
- Is part-time or full-time help required?
- How much should it pay for the help and what would the overheads such as National Insurance be?
- What hours should employees work, and when?

- What tasks should it give them, and should it encourage them to 'learn the business'?
- Where can it acquire finance if the business needs it?
- How much finance does the business require?
- How much will it cost, etc?

We can see that even the owner of a small business has to be concerned with the major business functions, i.e. marketing, production, people, finance; the business needs to be organised to address them and to meet the business goals.

As businesses become larger, more products may be produced or sold, services may be expanded or offered to more people, suppliers may increase, volume of raw materials may grow and more employees are needed. With the increase in all these *things*, there has to be an increase in documentation and other means of recording or monitoring what is ordered, invoiced, actually delivered, sold to customers, etc. Employees need pay cheques and pay slips. All kinds of information are needed in order to know what is going on in the company. With this information, managers exercise control, take actions and make decisions. The organisational structures need to facilitate not only how the major business functions are to be implemented effectively and efficiently, but also how they are to be monitored to ensure they function as intended.

As the volume and scope of business activities increase, more and more human activity has to occur to keep the business going and growing. The larger the business, the more specialised jobs tend to be and the greater the opportunity and incentive for jobs to be complemented by, supported by or replaced by technological resources. Computers are inclined to be more efficient partners for people, or can be efficient replacements for people, when used for more specialised purposes, and larger companies can benefit more from technological changes. Despite this, however, many beneficial changes to a company can also come about from changes in organisational procedures and management style.

One of the keys to the success of a business is just how well top management design their organisational structures and processes to meet its goals, maximising the effectiveness of its resource base. Organisational design in business tends to follow a few standard patterns which are outlined below, but there is no single design that suits all business contexts.

2.2.1 The challenge of complexity

One of the most daunting problems for students of business, or information systems, and for many high-level managers when they want to understand or formally analyse a company, is the formidable complexity of medium-sized or large businesses. The degree of complexity in an organisation, or even a part of an organisation, can be inferred by three basic characteristics:

- the number of layers of management there are from top to bottom in a reporting structure
- the number of different reporting structures there are
- the relationship of the outputs or services of different activities or parts of the business to each other.

'Reporting structures' suggest that managers or specialists, responsible for activities or areas of activity within the business, are in some defined chain of command. The number of layers of management in a reporting chain indicates the depth of the business structure, while the number of different reporting chains or structures gives some sense of the breadth of activities within the business. In an organisation such as a hospital, the breadth can be quite extensive, encompassing many specialist units and activities. The relationships between activities or groups of activities within the business reveal a network of dependencies and inter-dependencies between them. The way in which the business is organised will have a significant impact on the degree of management complexity.

Organisational structures need to take into account what tasks or functions need to be carried out and how they need to be carried out. How is information about the tasks to be obtained and reported to the right individuals? How can the tasks be assessed and the results reported? How should the different tasks be grouped, related and co-ordinated with each other? On a human level, the structure may determine who has what authority and responsibility, including who reports to whom, how many subordinates can or should one manager be responsible for, how many managerial levels exist in a chain of command and how horizontal co-ordination is ensured. The different organisational designs can either ease or increase the burden of complexity. From a management perspective, failure to deal effectively with complexity usually results in a lack of understanding and a loss of control. Discovering the organisational design best suited to a particular business may be vital to its competitive success.

2.2.2 The functional design

The functional design is probably the oldest Western model of organisation; at first glance it seems the most obvious. The functional design is a direct structural answer to an organisation which grows; as the volume of business increases, responsibilities and tasks get broken down into more specialised ones and, perhaps, into very simple and very efficient high volume processes. The functional design focuses on areas of specialisation such as personnel, accounting, engineering or marketing. Expertise and interest become the basis of division between groups in the organisation, and 'expert' subcultures may result. For example, a person may set up a small business printing T-shirts and sweatshirts for special interest groups such as environmental campaigners and initially run it alone. The buying of the stock, monitoring of sales, selling the merchandise at big events and to specialist outlets, the processing of orders to suppliers, the paying of invoices, dealing with possible overdrafts from the bank, negotiating cuts for event organisers, storing of non-displayed items, etc. are all the responsibility and the tasks of the sole individual. If the business is successful then the sheer volume of work will require more time and energy than the person has available. It is likely that the owner would engage a new employee, perhaps to do the printing, while the entrepreneur would specialise in buying the shirts, marketing the products and keeping the paperwork under control, etc. As trade increases, so does the dependence of the business on the effectiveness of each of its functional areas.

Functional or work specialisation is, to some extent, inevitable because specialist knowledge in some areas is considered essential such as in finance, legal matters, engineering or marketing. In fact, specialisation is an inevitable response to complexity, both within the organisation and outside it. Companies are often obliged by law or customer expectations to employ or use the services of qualified people. But specialisation can be taken to extremes and this can happen when employers decide to organise the work environment so as to require specialisation at the lowest level of skill possible, the aim being to reduce the cost of production or services by going for simplified, specialised, high volume and repetitive worker tasks. This makes it quite easy for a single supervisor to monitor a relatively large number of workers in a factory environment – labour and supervision costs can be cut to a minimum.

Arguments for the functional approach include the idea of 'economies of scale', where duplication of expertise in different parts of the business would be eliminated in favour of functional specialisations which can be deployed more efficiently and effectively as common organisational resources. Also, some believe, that decision-making as it affects specific functional contributions to the organisation would be more centralised and consistent than would be the case otherwise. Specialisation as a natural product of the functional approach provides the benefit of expert responses to a range of relevant problems.

Disadvantages usually relate to human problems of communication. Vertical lines of communication may make reporting up and down the structure quite straightforward in principle, but it may also be quite cumbersome, leading to very poor response times and lack of flexibility. Specialisation may lead to specialist cultures within the organisation which are intolerant of other groups and high-level organisational goals may take second place to those of the functional specialists. Communication across the organisation may also be very difficult, leading to decisions being made for the wrong reasons, or without access to the full picture, disadvantaging the business.

2.2.3 **The product or service-based design**

Businesses may be structured according to a product or service focus, for example, a transport manufacturer may have separate divisions for domestic cars, goods vehicles and agricultural vehicles. Within these major product areas of the business, the organisation may be organised along functional lines. Geographical separation can coincide with product or service distinctions. It is not uncommon for different parts of the company to gear up to different customer bases, for example, some computer companies have distinct divisions for government, commercial and educational markets. The reasons are not difficult to find: customers in similar environments often have similar problems and expertise built up in solving such problems can benefit both the customer and the supplier in terms of delivering appropriate solutions. The sales and marketing functions are then more likely to be better targeted and the customer could feel more confident in the product or service offered by the business.

The advantages arise because the business is tuned to the needs of specific, and well understood, markets. The internal organisation of each part or division of the company is designed to deliver a superior product or service to its customers. Disadvantages result from the possible duplication of functional expertise or resources across different parts of the organisation. If major investment were needed for upgrading of physical plant, competition between company divisions could lead to conflict and disharmony.

The recent experience of one major computer manufacturer saw two of its divisions competing for the same business, each proposing a different answer to the customer's problem. The customer was left confused and uncertain as to which set of experts from the same company had the more appropriate solution. The need to generate new business had led each division to identify a common subset of potential customers – the computer company reorganised the two divisions into one. Convergence of technology made the old distinction between the divisions untenable. The organisational design of a company should be kept under review since market and other changes may turn yesterday's organisational design solution into tomorrow's problem.

2.2.4 **The matrix design**

The matrix design attempts to use both the functional and product-based structures together. The idea is that functional specialists are made available to product-based divisions on the basis of need. The services of functional specialists have to be negotiated between those responsible for the product/service division and between those responsible for the running of the functional area.

The gains which are sought for this design are efficient use of functional resources, the elimination of duplicated resources across product divisions and the tuned responses of product/service divisions. The management structure of a matrix would include the manager of the matrix and managers for the product divisions and managers of functional areas.

In order to achieve the efficient use of functional personnel, it is clear that a good deal of negotiation will be necessary. The functional personnel are a limited resource and the divisions generate a greater demand for their services. Unless the demand is regular and planned, the inevitable consequence is that there will be times of under and over supply of functional resources. Another difficulty of this approach is that functional personnel will often be answerable to two bosses – their functional manager and the product division manager. Depending upon personalities and other factors within the business, one or other dimension of the matrix will probably dominate, possibly to the detriment of the business as a whole.

2.2.5 The team design

This design is usually integrated into a more general functional model. One of the weaknesses of the functional design is its cumbersome chain of command structure, while another weakness relates to the absence of formal links with other functional areas, except at the top level. The team approach recognises both of these difficulties and sees the value of interdisciplinary teamwork. Teams can consist of managers and specialists who have an interest in a common problem, or in meeting a common goal. These structures may be beneficial at many levels of a business. Decision making within such contexts, whether they be executive decisions or recommendations passed upwards for higher management action, can be much better informed and lead to significant improvement of performance.

This design principle has been tried with success in various kinds of businesses, including hospitals. In one health region, teams met at ward or specialist unit level and participants included doctors, appropriate nursing and hospital management. Quality of care and co-operation were reported to have increased, together with improvements in morale.

The advantage of such an approach is that it tries to address the problems of communication across different reporting structures which can severely handicap the pure functional approach. If complex problems are identified through the process, then the investment of time, energy and resources by management necessary for implementing a solution could be resented or resisted.

2.2.6 The network design

The so-called 'network' approach to organisational design has fired the imagination of some management specialists. It is an attempt to use communications technology to exploit an international pool of business resources. The business actually consists of a business headquarters which specialises in logistics and business intelligence; virtually every major functional area is contracted out to other companies that can offer the most competitive services or products. The main role of the business is to identify the products for which there is demand and then co-ordinate all contracted-out services, from manufacturing to sales and distribution. Product design could be contracted in the UK, manu-facturing contracted to companies in the Far East, sales and distribution could be handled by companies in Europe and North America, accounting functions could be provided by a firm in the USA. The main company is the nerve centre of the entire operation.

There is a reluctance by some to think of this approach as a true organisational design, since the organisation itself really consists of the nerve, or logistics, centre. From an organisational point of view, such businesses are interesting in their heavy use of, and dependence on, communications technology and business intelligence. A major advantage claimed for this approach is that if the most competitive contractors are identified then products could be produced and marketed at the lowest possible cost. Another advantage is that the main business has minimal investment in physical and human resources and its administrative overheads are very low. The flexibility offered by the network design means that it may be easier for such a business to respond more readily to changes in the market. There are several serious weaknesses: the main business is critically dependent upon the contractors performing their functions exactly as arranged. The success of the network structure is only as secure as its weakest contractor – a contractor going out of business, producing items not up to specification or distribution services not delivering on time all lie outside the direct control of the main business. Contractors may have little loyalty to the main company and could decide to market a successful line more cheaply under a different label in competition with the original product. These advantages and disadvantages have all been experienced by network organisations.

2.3. MANAGEMENT APPROACHES

It would be a lot easier to manage a business if people were not involved: people are involved in the business at every level and at a certain level a management approach is practised, or advocated, which will affect the rest of the organisation. There are some recognised styles and philosophies of management which can be identified by their characteristics and be deliberately adopted by businesses. The organisational structures provide an environment in which management approaches may be practised. Who makes what decisions, how control is exercised and what information is needed for these purposes will be determined, to a greater degree, by the management approach. The essential characteristics of these management approaches are explored below.

First, a look at approaches that originated in the so-called 'classical' period, when managers and researchers began to examine more carefully the aspect of business life that had usually been taken for granted – *management*. More recently some 'modern' approaches to management have been proposed in order to take advantage of:

- developments in the understanding of how to motivate and treat people
- more informed approaches to business analysis
- the rapid pace of change (which management can either choose to resist, ignore or embrace).

2.3.1 The classical approaches to management

When writers refer to the 'classical approaches to management' they are referring to the period in the late 19th century and early 20th century, when it appears that managers and academics first began to reflect on management thinking and practice as something worth studying, meriting serious thought. It is not a coincidence that other social sciences such as psychology, anthropology and sociology were also emerging as disciplines that considered aspects of individual and group behaviour. Businesses and management saw opportunities in this new awareness to exploit some of the ideas for the greater financial gain that might result. The approaches discussed below vary considerably in the kind of value that they seem to attach to the most important resource available to business – its people.

2.3.1.1 The scientific approach

Frederick Taylor (1868–1924), an American, is credited with the first attempt to apply the rational thinking of science to the nature and management of work. Taylor was employed at a heavy engineering company and observed that shop-floor workers aimed to produce the minimum amount of work that management would accept, since the workers thought (rightly) if they worked harder, then the company would lay some of them off. The management had no specific expectations of the workers at that time because no one had a clear idea of what a worker could, or should, produce within a given time span. Time and motion studies were introduced by Taylor to determine what constituted optimum performance and conditions for different worker tasks.

The worker was regarded as a somewhat unreliable machine – a production unit. Taylor thought that the way to achieve higher worker productivity was by a combination of financial incentives and tight supervision. To facilitate this, work should be organised so that individual workers would have a narrow, if mundane, production job, eliminating the need for expensive craftsmen and allowing effective quantitative monitoring of the workers' output. Many workers were closely supervised, given production targets and paid a bonus for achieving 'above-the-average'. Supervisors' duties were to ensure that the targets were met; the only exceptions or problems that affected achievement being the substance of information reports that were passed to management. In this approach a control hierarchy is used to ensure that the business goals are met.

Other, and many would say, better management approaches have been tried since the early days of scientific management but this approach is still being practised in one way or another in many businesses today. The scientific management approach had a low-level operational management focus. The basic ingredients are knowledge of what constitutes optimal performance, setting of production targets that are based on such optimal performance, provision of financial incentives related to exceptional productivity and making sure that performance is closely monitored.

2.3.1.2 The administrative approach

The administrative approach to management is associated with Henri Fayol (1841–1925), a Frenchman. Fayol, a senior manager in industry, suggested a definition of management as well as a set of principles to guide the practice of management. Fayol has also been called the 'father of modern management', and advocated management practices which would compare well with the best management principles of today. Interest in Fayol is limited here to his observations relating to the issue of management and decision making.

First, Fayol provides criteria that identify and differentiate the management function from other major functions that he recognises, such as technical or financial. The function of management, according to Fayol, should entail:

1 planning;
2 organising;
3 commanding;
4 co-ordinating;
5 controlling.

Fayol's perspective is of a higher order than that adopted in the *scientific* approach. Whereas the *scientific* approach is very narrow in scope and mechanistic, the *administrative* criteria are wider in scope and are as relevant at the top level of the business as they are to lower levels of management.

Planning

In the context of the business as a whole, planning is a high-level activity that would normally be restricted to those who have authority and a perspective on the business as a whole. Planning means that decisions have to be made that require knowledge about the environment of the business and the performance of the business including its income, outgoings and all of its resources. Planning may focus on how to achieve strategic goals or it may suggest modifications of them, for example, a security firm may decide that it could maximise its use of its fleet of armoured vehicles and plan to extend its range of services by marketing a prisoner escort facility. The decision would have to take into account environmental factors such as potential demand, co-operation issues with official agencies and internal factors, including a full cost benefit analysis of running the new service. Since the plan would affect the company nationally, it is a high-level issue.

Organising

Making the best use of available resources in order to fulfil the plans involves organising and this will occur at various levels within a business. Managers should have appropriate authority and access to resources so as to organise them to meet the business goals for that functional area. In a large business there may be pressure to standardise organisational procedures. Top-level managers decide how the business needs to be organised to best achieve its goals. This decision will have a direct impact upon:

- Who has what authority?
- Who has what responsibility?
- Who makes which decisions?
- What information is needed?
- How prompt and accurate must the available information be, etc?

A highly vertically structured organisation, with many levels of management, provides many opportunities for information to be used, restructured, modified, frozen or ignored as it passes from top to bottom, or vice versa. A flat structure of organisation may have very few intermediate managers between high-level and low-level management.

Commanding

In order to implement decisions and co-ordinate activities within their area of responsibility, managers have commands, for example, a marketing director may issue instructions to the advertising manager and the regional sales managers for advertising and sales reps to co-ordinate their activities because of a planned promotion of product 'X'. A clerk receives a decision made by the credit manager in response to his query about a customer's account. The commands, if they are to be effective and relevant, would have to be based on good market intelligence and appropriate information received from without and within the organisation.

Co-ordinating

Co-ordinating is a relatively high-level task that means a manager requires knowledge, for example, of the way in which different activities, jobs or departments need to interact in order to produce a defined outcome. The person responsible for the outcome should have access to the necessary information, and have the authority to ensure the co-ordination can be obtained. For example, a production manager may have to co-ordinate deliveries of raw materials, the maintenance schedule for machines, the retooling of machines for different processes and arrange for storage of the finished products. The co-ordination may involve negotiation with colleagues, instructions/commands given to engineers, knowledge of the key factors for each of the parts and careful attention given to timing.

Controlling

Staff exercising responsibility to ensure that the activities entrusted to them are done well are exercising their control. The standard ideas of control are very simple: control in a business context means that many processes and situations in the organisation are monitored. The assumption is that there is a desired, or planned outcome or state, and the actual outcome is examined, so that what is observed is compared against what was wanted or planned. The difference between the two states may cause action to be taken, or some decision to be made, to deal with the situation.

A cosmetic house represented in a department store will set sales targets for their products; the counter staff have to try and meet those target figures. If they fail to achieve the targets then they, or a manager, will look for explanations and take actions to improve the situation by, for example, trying more eye-catching displays, ensuring sales techniques are the best or attracting custom through a sales promotion.

In another context, a chef in a top restaurant may periodically taste a dish being prepared; the monitoring of the flavour provides the information needed to ensure that the eventual combination of flavours will produce the perfection desired. The chef's remit is to manage the cooking process and is an instance of operational-level management.

Fayol would stress that all the management activities are inter-dependent. In many cases single individuals would exercise all of these functions, perhaps even for a single event. The management principles advocated by Fayol are certainly worthy of practice by any organisation today but, for these purposes, the functional activities considered above give enough insight into the administrative management approach.

2.3.1.3 The bureaucratic approach

Max Weber (1864–1920), a German sociologist, took a particular interest in the structure and functioning of organisations. For Weber, the idea of bureaucracy was a positive alternative to management that operated on the basis of privilege or personal charisma. Since these were abuses of position or power in Weber's eyes, he believed a well designed bureaucratic system would provide safeguards against such abuses, and a level playing field for all. Managerial positions, he thought, should be competed for on a fair and equal basis. Weber's solution was to introduce rules and controls which would ensure a person's privileged background or connections would not give them an organisational advantage or a fast track to the top.

Decision-making responsibilities would be tightly prescribed by the position of the decision maker in the structure. A defined management hierarchy would make it clear where responsibility lay. The organisational structure itself would limit the scope of responsibility by clear demarcation of specialist functions, including that of management. The integrity of this model had to be maintained through authoritarian and rigid enforcement at all levels of management.

This rule-bound method of managing is, therefore, motivated by what it guards against, rather than its positive characteristics. Despite its rather unattractive and negative appearance, this approach to management has been adopted widely by public sector institutions worldwide. The advantages and disadvantages of such an approach are outside the scope of this text, except to say that even Weber accepted that his 'ideal' bureaucratic organisation could not be found in practice. The human element should not be understated in any study of management or decision making, but there is a danger that bureaucratic management may find it preferable to ignore the significance of the human dimension in problem situations.

2.3.2 Modern approaches to management

Now that we are considering *modern* approaches to management, it does not mean that the classical ones are no longer considered or practised; this would not be true. *Modern* approaches have not automatically displaced the more classical approaches just because they are more modern. They tend to consider more carefully the human aspects of management because the real challenges are often found there, but such considerations increase the burden of management. Technology does not need motivating, has defined communications protocols and tasks and its performance can be readily monitored. In contrast, humans need motivating, have formal and informal communication networks, perform many kinds of tasks and not all activities can be monitored. Furthermore, humans think and feel, and can be unpredictable.

The scientific style of management is the most mechanistic of the earlier approaches and contrasts most with almost all of the subsequent views. The bureaucratic approach has not been widely adopted by businesses for obvious reasons. Except for Henri Fayol, the classical approaches largely ignore the human factor.

2.3.2.1 The human relations approach

Following the pioneering work of Taylor in gaining higher productivity through *scientific management*, and of Weber, in suggesting a *bureaucratic* route to better management, money was put into research on the relationship of the work environment to productivity. The research continued for some years, and followed the productivity theme begun by Taylor.

The research, known as the Hawthorne Studies (1924–1932), sought to discover the very best working environments and so find the working conditions that favoured the maximum possible output from workers. Experiments sought to relate factors such as different levels of lighting to levels of worker productivity. The studies, however, did not produce the expected results, but rather they eventually concluded that the best productivity occurred when:

- workers felt valued as people rather than treated merely as production units
- human relationships between workers were positive and supportive
- attitudes and job satisfaction were considered just as important as financial rewards.

From these studies we can see that a great gulf existed between how the management valued labour and how the workers valued themselves and the work that they did. The human relations approach thus began to explore the nature of this gulf and demonstrated that when management gave serious attention to their human resources, dramatic improvements in productivity could result, for example, in the lighting experiment, a group of workers was isolated from the rest in order for the experimenters to observe the effects of changes. As the lighting changed, the productivity went up, but never in relation to the amount of light. At last, the researchers saw that the special treatment, the freedom from close supervision, and being required to take more responsibility for their performance, etc. caused the workers to feel a lot better about themselves and their work. They themselves had accepted responsibility for their performance and good supportive working relationships developed between them.

The human relations approach to management stresses the importance of using insights into human behaviour gained from social science research. However, the cost of 'getting it right' may seem to exceed the potential productivity gains.

2.3.2.2 The systems approach

The systems approach to management has been borrowed from systems approaches in other disciplines. The study of biology has provided some of the clearest examples of working systems. Chapter 4 will expand more on systems in business, but here the focus will be on the main principles of this approach.

First, what is meant by the idea of a system needs to be clarified. Unfortunately, the word *system* is commonly used in the context of business and computing and it often refers to different things. Looking at some of the more familiar uses, it is possible to distinguish what is meant and what is not meant by 'system' in this particular context. We *do not* mean the following.

- **Computer systems** can refer to anything from a large *mainframe computer* that lives in a specially cool air-conditioned room, to a *desktop computer*, such as a PC. Quite often all the physical parts of the system – for example, *computer screens, keyboards, printers,* and pieces that link the parts together – as well as the *software* or *programs* that drive the physical parts and the *data* that the programs use.

- **Systems software** consists of *a suite of programs* that provide the ability to use the different kinds or numbers of computers, that may be linked in a network. If we consider the physical components of a computer system as a set of hardware resources, then the systems software provides us with the ability to manage and use those resources. Each kind of systems software has its own standard characteristics; the systems software used to run IBM PCs is called MS-DOS or DOS for short.

- **Information systems** is an expression that is usually intended to refer to computer systems that have been designed to provide business information for managers and other employees in a company. Such computer systems make use of a special computer resource called a database management system. Information systems and the technology which is typically at the heart of them will be looked at in more detail in Chapter 9.

When a 'system' is referred to in this context, what we *do* mean is *systems theory*. Systems theory refers to a number of key ideas that, together, give us a model, or valuable, perspective on what management of a business is about.

Some of the main assumptions and principles of this theory will be examined here. One assumption is that a model of the way biological systems manage themselves is an appropriate model for us to use in a business context. Biological entities such as plants and animals are, by and large, very successful systems capable of responding to a continually changing environment. From the examination of biological and other similar kinds of 'natural' systems, the following characteristics can be identified:

1 systems are assemblies of parts that are organised in a pattern or in a particular way;
2 the assembly of parts has an identifiable purpose and there is a reason for them being assembled in that way;
3 each part is affected in a particular way, or ways, by being in the system and if a part is removed its role or function is changed;
4 systems normally produce something, or at least have an effect;
5 systems have boundaries: what is internal should be under the system's control, but what is external is beyond its scope;
6 systems exist within an immediate environment which consists of a set of external influences or factors which can impact on the system, over which the system has limited, or no, influence.

Complex systems may have sub-systems, and sub-systems may have their own sub-systems. Each sub-system has the same basic characteristics as a system as a whole. How do these ideas relate to a 'systems approach' to management? Table 2.1 shows what happens when the idea of a system is applied to a small brewery, for example, in particular, the production function.

Table 2.1   A systems view (high-level) of the brewery's production function

Identifiable purpose	To produce a range of high quality beers.
Product/effect	Specific high quality beers.
Boundary	The scope of the beer production process.
Parts	The brewing equipment, brewing processes, brewing production workers, raw materials such as hops and yeast, etc.
Assembly of parts	All parts related in specific ways to meet the brewing production goals.
Environment	The immediate environment is the rest of the brewery, for example: • the marketing function gains more business which means the beer production has to increase; • the finance function puts a two month hold on money for a new fermentation container.

A high level view pays little attention to detail; the systems approach should identify the business characteristics which are relevant. If the production function as a system, the view is high level and only certain relevant characteristics of the system would be appropriate to that level. Starting at a lower level of the system would involve examining a specific part and identifying the relevant characteristics appropriate to that part, such as producing one specific beer, or fermenting a beer (*see* Table 2.2).

An example from biological life could be a duck; at a high level we see the complete animal. As a complete entity, it is designed to fly, walk and swim on the surface of water; its purpose is, perhaps, open to interpretation. Each part of the duck has a specific part to play and if a part were to be taken away from the duck, both the part and the duck would be different. The part would no longer have the same role as it had as part of the whole and the duck, without the part, might have some difficulty surviving. Note that we can distinguish two kinds of parts: first, there are the parts that seem the most obvious, such as legs, body, wings, head, feathers, etc. Second, there are parts that comprise of the less obvious, but vital, sub-systems, such as the skeletal system, the nervous system, the circulatory system and the digestive system. There is a complex interaction between these sub-systems, and also between the more obvious parts. It would be hard to understand much about a duck if we did not realise that it is composed of a set of different sub-systems with different purposes, yet no sub-system is isolated from the rest. If the duck were to become sick, a veterinary surgeon would rely on their knowledge of how the sub-systems work and interact to produce an accurate diagnosis of the duck's illness and to prescribe an appropriate cure.

Organic entities such as the duck have 'parts' that we can model as sub-systems, for example, its nervous system. This way of looking at the duck can be very useful but it raises significant questions which may not be easy to answer. The idea of a boundary, for instance, enables us to better define the context and bounds of our investigation; the boundary of a wing or webbed foot can easily be defined so as to distinguish one part from the other; the nervous system can only be defined in such a way as to exclude the wing or foot on the basis of the purpose of each sub-system, since the nervous sub-system is relevant to the performance of virtually all other sub-systems. Modular parts like the wing or leg, while easy to identify as parts suitable for dissection, must be understood to contain components of the circulatory, skeletal or muscular systems.

The principle of modelling a business as a system is not so different. Chapter 1 discussed functional areas, such as marketing or production, whose main purposes are defined by their special role in the company; these functional areas appear to be self-contained modules of activity. On the other hand, there are systemic functional areas, such as the financial or human, where every part of the company may be affected, for example, by financial policy such as whether modular parts of the company are regarded as cost centres, or by a policy to invest in regular updates of skills for staff of a certain type or level. As in the duck example, the systemic sub-systems have their own structure or organisation too, which usually interact with the modular sub-systems. The production function in the brewery may be judged inefficient in financial terms as a result of financial monitoring, but the policy to update skills for the production team might lead to well motivated improvements through the adoption of new techniques.

Table 2.2 A systems view (low-level) of a production process

Identifiable purpose	To ferment 'Granny's XXXX' traditional strong brew.
Product/effect	A vat of 'Granny's XXXX' at the right specific gravity.
Boundary	The scope of the process used to ferment the particular beer.
Parts	The vat, hydrometer, the unfermented liquid, the relevant brewery worker(s), the heater, etc.
Assembly of parts	The procedure for testing temperature, changes in specific gravity, etc. in which all the parts are used or have a role.
Environment	The immediate environment is the production function and in particular the other parts that immediately affect the fermenting process, for example, the process that mixes and prepares the unfermented liquid, anything that affects the fermenting environment, etc.

The fermenting process can be viewed as a system within a system (the production function). Within the fermenting process sub-parts or sub-processes can be identified that could be used as a model for (sub)systems too, for example, the process for monitoring the specific gravity or the process for adjusting the temperature.

The systems approach provokes analytical thinking and requires a clear sense of purpose wherever things are *being done*, at all levels of the business. While the basic systems approach is strongly analytical, one of the key principles is that each sub-system should serve its next higher system. This idea is the opposite of analysis, or breaking complexity down into simpler parts; it is concerned with synthesis, or seeing the parts as a whole. It is tied in with one of the major assumptions of systems theory, which is that *a whole is greater than the sum of its parts*.

This means that if a system is composed of various parts, including sub-systems, then the output of that system depends upon the contribution of all its resources and sub-systems to the system's overall purpose. For example, to produce the beer, the things that are needed will be the resources, that is, the ingredients, brewing equipment and the people who make it happen, plus the sub-systems or processes that together make it happen. Standards have to be set in the form of special recipes that have to be adhered to for each beer. Other standards include measures that have to be followed, such as the requirement that each batch has to be of a specific volume, and specific brewing times are determined for each kind of beer, etc.

Systems concepts will be examined in greater depth in Chapters 4 and 8 but, as a point of comparison with the classical approaches to management, the systems approach has particular appeal because it offers a set of analytical principles that have had proven value in studying complex, albeit natural, systems. Most businesses are complex in organisation and they contain a set of complex dynamic interacting (sub)systems. Systems ideas provide a way of better understanding business complexity but, where the classical and other 'modern' approaches to management build in assumptions about how people do or should act, the systems concepts are more abstract and mechanistic.

As an approach to management, it is difficult to see why many texts include 'systems' at all. The systems ideas do not prescribe *what* management should do or *how* it should do it. The ideas help us to think more clearly about how to *unravel* some of the complexity of organisations, but they do not tell us how to *manage* complexity. Systems ideas help us to think about, and understand, business complexity just as they help us to understand about the complexity of natural phenomena, such as the duck. Assessing the health of the duck or diagnosing its condition relies on a knowledge of the systems through which it maintains its condition and performance. Similarly, our ability to diagnose the condition of a business depends on our understanding of the systems through which it maintains its condition and performance. Information systems, with which this text will become increasingly concerned, are important (sub)systems in business that are akin to the nervous system in natural beings. It is through these systems that we become aware of information that tells us about the condition or performance of the organisation. A duck may feel hungry because its nervous system registers its need for food, while sales information in a business tells the management that some aggressive marketing is necessary to counter a downturn in demand.

2.3.2.3 The contingency approach

This 'modern', but not so new, approach to management contends that since all activities or areas of responsibility in a business are not necessarily of one kind, managers need to be aware of specific factors within their own business or sphere of responsibility that would indicate whether one management approach would be more appropriate than another. The contingency approach suggests that some types of situation are better managed using one management approach rather than another, and that not all activities in an organisation are necessarily of the same type. The type of task, the requirements of the management role, the human dynamics involved and how all the parts are organised to achieve the goals of the whole are all variables to consider in any one context. The contingency model advocates that elements of different management approaches may be integrated into an overall management strategy for the particular business.

Managing the activities of a large number of semi-skilled workers in a factory workshop will involve a very different set of factors from managing a professional football team, a legal practice or a department of academics at a university. In the real world, most managers have very little formal, or informal, training in management and tend to manage according to established expectations for the job. Progression up the company will probably mean progressing through different work contexts for which different management approaches might be more productive. An awareness of the strengths and weaknesses of the management approaches, and of the context being managed, at least allows the possibility that the full potential of individuals may be harnessed for the good of the company.

Critics say one weakness is that the differences in the underlying orientation of each management style may lead to potential conflicts within the organisation, but it is unrealistic to expect every part of a large or diversified business to be managed in the same way as every other part. It is common to find different management approaches being practised in different divisions or major parts of large companies and organisations.

2.3.2.4 The pursuit of excellence in management

To conclude this introduction, a consideration of recent attempts to discover the key to successful management in a rapidly changing and uncertain business climate follows.

Japanese domination in the consumer electronics and automobile industries eventually caused management elsewhere (initially in the USA) to ask how Japanese business has achieved such success. A number of factors can be identified; a significant factor is that Japanese manufacturing businesses have received very favourable treatment by their government. The environment in which Japanese business operates has therefore been relatively supportive. It appears there is a strong cultural element which emphasises group identity and, to some extent, collective responsibility. At a national level the government feels a responsibility to contribute to the success of its manufacturers because the success is shared by the nation as a whole. This paternalistic role of the government is reflected in the work practices of the businesses. Businesses have been committed to their workers and the workers have been committed to the goals of the company. A sense of pride at a national or company level, we can assume, is a strong social ingredient of the success experienced by Japanese business.

This environment supports a quality business culture: an expectation of excellence in attitude and management, as well as in excellent products and services. This cultural background provides fertile soil in which strategic ideas can be planted and cultivated to produce vigorous and sustained economic growth. The mechanisms for turning the strategic ideas into realities have been identified as:

- Decision making on a consensus basis in which involvement at all levels is sought
- Responsibility for success in all functional areas accepted by every participant
- Control relatively informal and implicit, since responsibility and desire for excellence is shared
- Slow, non-specialised promotion paths
- Holistic concern for all employees

In the USA, a management approach called *Theory Z* has attempted to take the best characteristics of the Western individual-centred management and the best of the Japanese team-centred management. It is easy to both simplify and distort the realities of management practice in either the West or Japan, but it is acknowledged that the social dimension and Japan's approach to its human resource has contributed significantly to its undisputed dominance in manufacturing and other businesses.

Recent studies of American management, such as those of Peters and Waterman in *In Search of Excellence*, indicate that successful American companies have made certain changes a priority:

1 the use of small organisational units to promote a sense of belonging;
2 the encouragement of individual initiative;
3 the encouragement of informal communication between key groups to spark off a creative synergy, through, for example, carefully sited company rest/eating/coffee drinking areas;
4 the trend towards flatter companies with fewer levels of management. Top-level managers tend to become more involved and aware of what happens at lower levels; communication is more effective and motivation enhances the performance of all employees as they are entrusted with greater responsibility and influence in the business.

These changes focus on the potential of each individual to make a positive difference to the business and on how to gain the greatest benefit from the unique combination of abilities each employee has. There is also recognition that the company *can* benefit immensely from the creative energy which may result if it meets some of the peculiarly human requirements for emotional and psychological support.

Other excellence criteria include the importance to the business of having:

(a) a clear mission or purpose that is consistent with the strengths of its resource base;
(b) a commitment to quality products and services; and
(c) the willingness to restructure the business with a view to creating a simpler and more responsive organisation.

2.4 TECHNOLOGY IN BUSINESS

Technology provides a special set of possibilities and problems for management. We take technology to include all the tools that are available to a business to transform inputs into outputs. In this text, because we are primarily interested in 'systems' that provide information (i.e. information systems) the outputs will be information products. Many activities within a business can be modelled as systems that produce outputs, but there are times when the activities are purely human and times when technology is used, for example, one of a manager's responsibilities may be to head up a project group which has to produce a feasibility report. The activity goal is to produce the report and the input consists of all the details which have to be assembled. The manager should know what needs to be included in the report and will assess the output, i.e. the actual drafts and final copy, against the criteria they, or senior management have set; this would be a purely human activity unless database technology had been used to store the original details and produce the information for the report. In manufacturing, technology may transform raw materials into finished products.

The possibility of having complex activities which contain sub-processes, etc. and technologies of different kinds to enable many of these processes to be carried out and/or monitored has already been discussed. For example, in a shop, a point-of-sale till is used in the exchange of cash for a product but it may also be the source of input for a database which contains details of the stock positions of products. In a drilling operation, electro-mechanical technology may perform the drilling and sensing components may send data to a computer which is programmed to monitor the task. The computer may then process the data which results in an instruction to change the speed of the drill or, perhaps, stop the drilling process. Thus we can see technology being used to do activities and also to assist in monitoring them. This distinction can be useful because, in this text, we are more concerned with the role that information systems have in monitoring and giving information on business activities.

In principle, even the most mundane implements, such as watches or pencil sharpeners, are technology but here the primary interest is in technologies that are directly related to enabling businesses to achieve their goals. In many cases technology has been used to do what humans would have done, but better and/or faster. Technology has also enabled humans to do what would otherwise be impossible to achieve. Perhaps the most significant technology is *computing* in its many different applications.

2.4.1 Management and technology

While it might be advisable to make a distinction between the computing technology that underlies most information systems, and the mechanical, or other technologies of industry and manufacturing, there are nevertheless some general principles to be taken account of.

Technology is not just used as a replacement for manually based activities and it cannot be evaluated solely on the basis of mechanistic advantages such as productivity gains. A British researcher, Joan Woodward, concluded that manufacturing technology should be classified according to its technical complexity. Technical complexity could be measured in terms of how many activities or processes in the company had been assumed by the technology. Woodward found a direct link between the performance of companies and whether their organisational structure was appropriate to the complexity of the technology.

Low-complexity technology can be found in low volume, but highly skilled, contexts such as joinery shops. Skilled craftsmen use specialist machines to do specific tasks. Monitoring of the tasks is usually the job of the individual craftsmen.

Medium-complexity technology can, typically, be found in factories. The bulk of the tasks are high volume, simple and repetitive. The level of skill required of workers has traditionally been low and the range of their responsibilities has been narrow. The relationship between each task in the assembly of the final complex product tends to be very tight and highly structured. Monitoring may occur in terms of measuring the number of units of output against targets and random checking of components or assembled units.

High-complexity technology can be found in contexts such as chemical plants where technology may be used to perform a number of co-ordinated continuous processes and, in addition, it would normally monitor and provide information about the processes and products. Database technology, which underlies most information systems and communications technology that allows people and information systems to communicate with each other, is also an example of high-complexity technology.

Woodward drew attention to the relationship between the use of technology to perform tasks and the role of management in monitoring the performance of tasks. If one goal of organisational design is to facilitate the effective and efficient achievement of all the activities that the business needs to perform in order to fulfil its mission and another goal is to design into the structures ways of monitoring the performance of the activities, from the lowest to the highest levels, then if a business moves from mainly people-based performance and/or monitoring of tasks to technology-based methods, the implications for organisational design are profound. Appropriate organisational design should ensure that tasks are being carried out as planned, that related tasks are effectively co-ordinated and that information about performance is getting to the right people at the right time. The skills, and thus costs, of employees and the type and scope of management supervision appropriate to each kind of context, would differ considerably. Different kinds of technology therefore tend to require different structural designs for optimal business performance.

When regarding the operations of business from a mechanistic point of view it may be tempting to ignore the human element but technologically-based monitoring is only capable of certain kinds of interaction with people and can only give certain types of information. Organisational design may become more complex if it is to monitor task performance, the motivation and well-being of employees and to relate task performance to the human factors that can affect it. Any changes in the use and/or types of technology affect the balance of factors that organisational design needs to take into account for optimum performance in the company.

2.4.2 Information systems

A business needs some way of knowing how it is performing, how many products it is selling, of what kind, to whom, etc. A hospital needs to be able to track what is happening to its patients and a credit card company needs to know the state of customer accounts, trends in spending, etc. Such questions represent only a fraction of all the possible ones that any company should be asking if it is exercising real control over its affairs. Information systems, whether manual or computerised, are essential for effective management and, therefore, effective decision making. The information systems are the nerve system of the business.

Changes in buying patterns, performance of suppliers, rising costs, etc. are all elements of vital intelligence for managers of a company. In a medium-sized or large business there may be thousands of activities occurring each day which are of potential interest to information systems.

The way that an organisation is designed, both to perform
needed to meet its goals and to enable effective monitoring
about them, is clearly a question of considerable rel
information systems. In principle, computerised information systems are
just a means to assist managers or decision makers; the better the
information, the better the quality of decisions. But just what information
does a particular manager really need in order to make decisions? It is
quite possible, even common, for decision makers to have too little, too
much or irrelevant information.

From an organisational perspective, the integration of information
systems into either the whole organisation or perhaps discrete parts of it
does not simply mean that there is a new and better way of providing
decision makers with information. Accepting that an information system
is an example of high-complexity technology, then many activities within
the organisation may be assumed by it, in the sense that people who
either had responsibility for information processing or who had the
power of controlling information, may be bypassed or deprived of those
roles. Indeed, management may find it advantageous to redesign or *re-engineer* the way the business is organised to make the best use of a new
system.

2.5 MANAGEMENT DECISION MAKING

However the business structure is designed, or whichever management
approach is adopted, different managerial contexts in which decisions are
made and the types of decisions that have to be taken within those
contexts can be distinguished. The contexts are defined on the basis of
the extent to which the decisions affect the organisation and the types of
decisions are defined on the basis of the complexity of the problem – the
control that the decision maker has over the factors involved, and the
decision outcome. (*See* Fig. 2.1.)

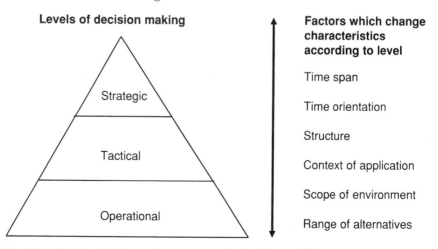

Fig. 2.1   Characteristics of management decision making

Decision making at each level can be affected by a number of factors. The reason for a continuum is that there is not necessarily a clear boundary between each of the levels. The factors involved in making decisions tend to have particular characteristics at the different levels: strategic, tactical and operational.

2.5.1 Factors in strategic decision making

Business strategy involves finding a way forward, often in a tough, competitive climate. Even though strategic decision making often affects the whole business, it does not mean that 'making more profit' or 'seeking competitive advantage' are considered strategic issues. Such desires are common to all businesses, and say nothing about how the business intends to achieve its success. Strategic decisions must always be expected to cost something, even if it means avoiding change. Because such decisions involve cost and risk, strategic decision making is usually made, or endorsed, by a board of directors or the equivalent.

Table 2.3   Characteristics of management decision making

Time span	Decisions tend to be for the long term.
Time orientation	Decisions are quite often forward looking.
Structure	Decisions may be relatively unstructured, i.e. they may not be based on hard facts, but to do with a sense of opportunity or the need for change. Unstructured decisions may be associated with a high level of risk.
Context of application	The decisions will often be significant for the whole business and could not sensibly be taken independently within some chain of authority or some segment of a company.
Scope of environment	The factors which have to be taken into consideration include internal and external intelligence. Information about competitors and other relevant factors in the company's trading environment are particularly important at this level.
Range of alternatives	Decisions almost always involve choice, even if one choice is to do nothing. Choice at the strategic level may not be between a set of similar options but where, perhaps, high-level managers have to try and assess the cost of doing nothing against the projected cost of a new development.

Strategic decision making is not about winning the war but about *how* to win the war.

EXAMPLE

In a small accountancy practice in which most of the preparation of accounts and other work is done by hand, the partners see their larger clients take their business elsewhere. To keep such clients and reverse their troubles the partners need a strategy. Some frank talks with ex-clients, and some investigation into their competition, reveal what the partners fear most: the major practices use computers for financial modelling and reports. The work of their competitors is more accurate, looks more professional and, what is worse, their rates are more competitive. Strategic decisions usually require external and internal intelligence; the ability to synthesise diverse business intelligence and to recognise emergent properties may be crucial. Tight-fisted as they are, the partners make a strategic decision to introduce computers and to become expert in their use in accounting. The decision will cost them time and money, but the alternative would, in the long term, be much more costly.

EXAMPLE

A major consumer electronics company produces high quality products and is known for innovation and reliability. One of its product ranges uses advanced and superior technology, but over a relatively short time its market share decreases. Competitors successfully dominate the market, although their products are comparable in price, and the technology is less advanced. The electronics company needs a strategy to overcome this difficulty. A careful look at the environment reveals that the use of the products depends on consumers purchasing other products to use with the technology. The supply of the other products to suit the competing technology was much greater and the conclusion is that consumers go for the technology which gives them the greatest flexibility of use.

As long as other companies can produce items on which their own technologically-based products depend, the electronics company is unable to reduce the financial risk involved in research and development. The electronics company may reduce the element of risk by buying, and thus controlling, companies on whose products it depends. This major investment would be a strategic decision made in the long-term interests of the business.

2.5.2 Factors in tactical decision making

Tactical decision making is concerned with the decisions a manager has to make to ensure that his or her part of the company is contributing effectively to meeting its targets or fulfilling its role in servicing the organisation. The manager's goals are determined in a more general sense by the goals of the organisation but more specific goals may be set by a high-level executive who co-ordinates the activities of a number of managers. Managers or other tactical decision makers also have to co-ordinate activities within their remit and handle exceptions and problems from lower level activities.

Table 2.4   Tactical decision making

Time span	Decisions tend to be for the short to medium term.
Time orientation	Decisions may take into account recent trends and often affect the near future.
Structure	Decisions usually quite structured, using knowledge of hard facts and available resources, therefore, the element of risk is quite low.
Context of application	These decisions are made up and down chains of command and across the business, usually affecting or determining the output of coherent groups or activities. A tactical decision made at the top of a chain of command may affect the levels below.
Scope of environment	The most obvious environment for a manager at any mid-point in an organisation consists of the influences that cannot be directly controlled and yet should have a real impact on the decisions made. Decisions and goals set by those higher in a chain of command or the performance of, or dependence, on closely linked activities in the company, perhaps in parallel chains of command, provide the manager's environment. Although, in theory, a manager may have responsibility for what happens in the chain below, much decision making has to do with handling exceptions and unplanned outcomes from below.
Range of alternatives	A manager may have the option of choosing one of a number of ways to achieve goals which have been set by more senior management. The organisational structure or the preferred managerial approach may limit the scope of action, however.

The manager's scope for making plans and deciding on ways of achieving desired performance will depend upon the level of the manager, the organisational structure and the management approach.

EXAMPLE

> If a merchandising manager discovered that in a range of summer shoes certain colours sold very badly, she might decide that it would be better to carry only the best selling colours and sell off the rest at a loss in an end-of-summer sale. In a bureaucratically designed management structure, the manager's idea would only be taken as an opinion to be passed up the chain of command. In an administratively designed structure, the manager may have been given authority to implement such decisions. In a team design structure, an advertising specialist on the team may point out reasons for the problem, with possible solutions, etc. The resulting, considered, tactical decision may be to invest in new advertising for the product, rather than reduce the price of the unpopular colours and lose money on them.

EXAMPLE

> A production manager is given a rush job to produce 10,000 of an item, for dispatch within 24 hours. He may decide to use one machine, but would have to run it through the night. If he decides on that alternative, he will have to include special rates for night shifts in the cost of the job. There is also a small risk that if the machine fails during the night, the maintenance response would be too slow to allow the job to finish on time. The manager could run two machines during the day, but each machine has a set-up and preparation period before use, and has to be cleaned directly after a run or series of runs. Thus although the hourly rate is less during the day, the total hours on the jobs would be more. The manager has to make a tactical decision which will satisfy all relevant criteria in the best way possible. There may be more than one alternative, but the advantages and disadvantages associated with each are well understood. The goal was set by a higher authority, and other parts of the business, for example, sales and distribution, are dependent upon the production area meeting performance criteria.

2.5.3 Factors in operational decision making

Table 2.5 Operational decision making

Time span	Decisions tend to be relevant to daily activities.
Time orientation	Decisions are usually about now, or the recent past.
Structure	Decisions are typically very structured, depending on current, hard facts. Straight-forward decisions based on well-known facts or criteria.
Context of application	Lower level, and supervisory management. Although this type of decision making can also occur at all levels of management. The context is usually activity specific, i.e. the decision affects only the activity of interest.
Scope of environment	The environment is bounded by the activity. Concern extends only to comparing actual output or performance with the goal or standard set for the activity.
Range of alternatives	In a business context, the range of possibilities for action or decision making are relatively limited and well understood.

Operational decision making is the kind of decision making that is confined to a particular activity.

EXAMPLE

A clerk in a government department can decide to send back an application for an official document because the right details were put in the wrong section, or she could decide to ignore the error and validate the application.

EXAMPLE

A production supervisor in a factory which produces DIY furniture kits discovers some pieces for a new chest of drawers unit have an unacceptably rough finish around drilled holes. He must decide whether the chipboard is of adequate quality and report the problem to his manager, or whether the drill bit is blunt and tears the chipboard. If it is the latter he must request the maintenance engineer to replace the bit.

EXAMPLE

> A high-level manager requests a demonstration of a new multi-featured video telephone system. The demonstration does not match the advertised performance, nor the manager's expectations. He can decide to see a competitor's product, or he can decide the technology is not mature enough and thus decide to wait, or he can look for another solution.

In all the above cases the facts are known, the decision choices are quite simple and the decisions relate solely to the task in hand. In this sense even the high-level manager is involved in operational decision making. If he decided to purchase the system for the company then the kind of decision would be of a different sort. Operational decisions are made independently of other factors.

2.6 SUMMARY

Top management have to decide how a business should be designed or structured in order to achieve its mission in the market place. Market conditions change and, as a business responds to the changes, it may be necessary to redesign its organisation. Reference was made to research which concluded that if the organisational design is well suited to a type of business, the business performance benefits. The issue of complexity and the need to control it through good design was discussed.

Different management approaches were considered, providing a backdrop against which management decision making could be considered. The scope individual managers have to make decisions is limited by their position within a structure, its design, the management culture, or the approach in which they function. Some management approaches focus on the mechanisms by which business activities and individuals can be monitored, ensuring aims are achieved. Other approaches focus more on motivation and understanding the human dimension in work, creating a climate in which people achieve closer to their potential. A third type of approach takes elements of the others to try and maximise the overall effectiveness of the organisation.

Technology was considered as not only an aid to management; as the technology becomes more and more complex, performing and monitoring many activities in the business, the business may have to adapt itself more to the technology, since the advantages the technology gives, may be important to the success of the business. Information systems are used extensively to help us monitor business activities.

Finally, the characteristics of the decision-making process at different levels within a business were looked at and it was recognised that the characteristics relate more to the context, or type of decision that has to be made, rather than the status of the manager or a specific level in a company. One of the key ingredients of good decisions is the quality and availability of information to support decision making. A distinctive role of management is that of making decisions and deciding who should make decisions about what. This chapter has introduced factors of significance in this process. In Chapter 3 a more detailed look is taken at what is meant by information – that essential part of all decision-making activity.

QUESTIONS

1 Most businesses are complex organisations simply because, whether they are large or small, the 'major business functions' will still reflect and be part of the experience of each enterprise. What, ideally, should the role of organisational structure be in addressing the issue of complexity from a management point of view?

2 Organisational structures can take many forms although they may be loosely classified. Compare and contrast what motivates the development of the different types of structure mentioned in section 2.2.

3 Subtly different from organisational structure is the approach that management may have towards delegating power and responsibility in the business. Section 2.3 explains some typical ways in which companies operate in this respect. In this context the term 'empowerment' is increasingly used; it is seen as a gift that managers are giving their employees to enrich their working lives. Let us assume that empowerment means giving employees:

(a) the right to make decisions;

(b) specifically the authority to make selected decisions;

(c) a say in decisions made at a higher level where the employees are affected by the decisions;

(d) the responsibility for following up on decisions they make;

(e) the training to develop appropriate decision-making skills and business knowledge; and

(f) the information needed to support their decision-making activities, etc.

Consider the different management approaches in section 2.3. and comment on what you consider the impact might be on each approach if the idea of 'empowerment' were taken seriously by management.

4 Management approaches, it could be argued, could be grouped into those which are more goal-oriented, rigid and mechanistic and those which seem more conscious of the human dimension.
   Comment on:

(a) which approaches you would put in which group and why; and

(b) whether you think any of the approaches embody your idea of 'good' management and why.

5 One of the important challenges that face an information systems department and management of a company is the integration of a new computer-based system into the work environment. Comment upon what challenges you see that are likely to arise out of the relative complexity of the work situation and the information technology which needs to be integrated into it.

6 Management decisions are typically classified into different levels according to generally accepted criteria. Consider each of the criteria mentioned in section 2.5. and think about what might be their implications for a small but successful toy and model shop in a large town, and a medium-sized business which imports fine wines and continental foods.

7 Consider a single product, say a line in children's pyjamas, then suggest how the interest in stock and sales information might change according to the level of management interest in the product.

8 Despite there being criteria that enable us to talk of tactical level management and decision making, explain why it is harder to maintain such distinctions in terms of job hierarchy than in terms of role.

BIBLIOGRAPHY   Bedeian, A. G., *Management* (3rd Edn), Harcourt Brace Jovanovich, 1993.

Bowman, C., *The Essence of Strategic Management*, Prentice Hall International, 1990.

Daft, R.L,. *Management*, Harcourt Brace Jovanovich, 1991.

Lucey, T., *Management Information Systems*, DP Publications, 1991.

CHAPTER 3

Management control, information and data

3.1 INTRODUCTION

Chapter 1 introduced some fundamental business principles, drawing attention to areas of a company that shrewd investors or senior business managers would want to know about if they had any interest in the company's prospects. In Chapter 2 the different ways in which a business may be structured so that it can fulfil its mission and meet its goals were examined as well as the different approaches management can take to exercise control and authority within the business. These aspects of management are important to recognise because they help us to understand some of the management dynamics behind the decision-making activities of individuals in a business. Finally, characteristics of decisions that are made at different levels in a company were considered. The way management creates a structure for the business and otherwise gears itself to meet its business goals is one of management's major functions.

In this chapter the issue of control, the other main function of management, together with the related topics of information and data will be looked at. Management control consists of management making appropriate responses to disturbances and problem situations in the organisation at all levels of activity. The responses will usually include decision making which, in the context of control, is often corrective in nature. Effective management control is impossible without information about the business activities since without information we would not know whether any response was necessary. It is because of the very close link between control and information that the topics are treated together, although it is clear there is also a strong link with decision making.

The term *information* needs careful attention, because we need to be clear about what it is and what is so critical about it that a comment such as 'Information has become the critical resource of the modern economy' (Reto Braun, President of Unisys, 1992) would be regarded as almost too obvious to be necessary in many major companies today. There are international companies which are now restructuring the way they are organised so as to take the most advantage of the rapid communication of financial information. Other organisations which have a heavy dependence on information are beginning to realise that good management of information is not just desirable – it is essential.

3.2 MANAGEMENT CONTROL

A very simple and straightforward definition of management control could be: *'the establishment and use of defined processes to ensure that the aims of the business are met effectively and efficiently'*. It is one thing to develop an organisational structure and adopt a management approach with a view to achieving business success, but it is quite another to make sure the business is 'staying on the ball'. In Chapter 2 it was suggested these are the two major functions of management; it is a common failing of businesses to stress the first function and only take a casual approach to the second. Experience has taught us that the most successful companies tend to place more emphasis on control and then use the information gained to, perhaps, review their organisational structure when necessary. Changes in demand, competition and the economic climate may require changes in the how the business is structured, run and monitored.

The principles of the control process are:

1 *set* standards or goals;
2 *evaluate* performance related to the standards or goals;
3 *do* something if the performance differs significantly from the desired standards or goals.

Good management control should be one of the main ingredients of continuing business success, and the principles can be applied at every level of the business. Each of the principles will be examined in turn and related to the strategic, tactical and operational levels of management.

3.2.1 Setting standards or goals

The idea is, in order to model or understand what businesses do in order to achieve success, there will be numerous functions and processes that people or machines have to perform that all contribute to the company's aims. Good management should be concerned that all the business functions and processes are achieving what they are meant to achieve. By setting standards or goals for them it is possible to assess whether or not they are performing as expected and it is also possible to see how far they fall short of, or exceed, the goals set.

3.2.1.1 The strategic level

Strategic decision making was examined in detail in Chapter 2, where it was demonstrated that decisions at strategic level tended to be forward looking and usually related to the long term. Strategic decisions were specific decisions which had a wide effect on, or significant implications for, the business as a whole. If progress towards a long-term goal is to be monitored, then the goal should be clearly defined and measurable.

EXAMPLE

> A manufacturer of plumbing parts and materials may take a strategic decision to manufacture the parts from new materials, ultimately to cut costs and remain competitive in new markets. The directors set target completion dates for construction of the new manufacturing plant, testing it and for the beginning of production. These dates are goals against which progress can be measured.

3.2.1.2 The tactical level

Goals or standards at this level often have relevance to the near future. They may be a co-ordinated and interdependent set of short-term goals which, together, will ensure a strategic goal is reached or they may play a significant, yet less tightly constrained, role in the larger structure of the business.

EXAMPLE

> In the manufacturing plant example, electricians agree to install and test the electrical supply for the new production plant by a certain date. The suppliers of the equipment for the plant agree to deliver and install the machines during the period immediately following the completion of the electricians' work, on which they depend. The electricians and the equipment suppliers have tactical roles in the project and each have short-term completion dates for their specific tasks which are discrete, but related parts of the overall strategy to revitalise the plumbing company.

EXAMPLE

> A farmer decides to hire a subcontractor to harvest half of his cereal crops while his own harvester is busy on the other half. His goal is to harvest all his crops before the weather breaks and maximise his yield. If the good weather were to hold long enough for his own harvester to complete the job, he would make the most money. If the weather were to break in that situation the rain would ruin a significant part of the crop and his profit on the crop would be severely slashed. To reduce the risk he has to pay some of his profit to the subcontractor but he at least has some control over the outcome. If he is fortunate and harvesting is completed before the rains, he will reach his goal.
>
> The farmer is using the live monitoring technique. From his monitoring of the environment he receives information which suggests rain may be imminent. From his monitoring of the rate of harvesting with just his own machine, the information suggests the crop may not be gathered before the weather breaks and he, therefore, intervenes while there is still time to achieve his tactical goal.

3.2.1.3 The operational level

Operational goals and standards usually apply on a day-to-day basis.

EXAMPLE

When a customer gives cash to a checkout operator, many systems require the operator to key in the amount given and the correct change is displayed for both the operator and customer to see. The displayed amount is the operational goal for the operator to reach when getting the change from the till.

An airline trains its cabin crew to go through a set briefing for passengers prior to takeoff. This is an operational standard that all cabin crew should meet as part of customer service and safety procedures.

In another situation a new worker in a garment factory is told what the quota for the day is if she is to get a productivity bonus.

In each case, a goal or standard is set, against which actual performance can be measured.

The examples given above demonstrate that it is possible to set different kinds of goals or standards. The type of goal or standard will depend upon the context and what is to be monitored. Some monitoring activities relate to things that are easy to quantify and can be monitored; the information sought usually consists of genuinely hard facts, for example, if a deadline were set for a project for June 15 and it completes on June 12, it is three days ahead of the target date. If a standard set is such that a worker is only allowed to produce up to one defective part in two hundred and he produces on average 1.5, then it is easy to quantify the difference and investigate the problem. On the other hand, activities or other matters on the basis of qualitative assessment can also be monitored.

Criteria by which qualitative standards or goals can be measured can be determined, but sometimes qualitative criteria are assigned quantitative values. The resulting 'facts' will not be absolutely hard, but subjective, for example, a company may have a dress code for its employees and the manager may rate staff on a scale of 1 to 10 for that standard; the numbers represent a mixture of fact and opinion.

A service company may monitor its activities by asking customers to fill in a questionnaire to get feedback on how customers perceived the quality of service. The questions may ask for graded responses but a grade value would represent part opinion and part fact as an indication of quality. Standards based on either quantitative or qualitative criteria are useful and necessary for a business but special care needs to be taken when using qualitative measures.

When standards are set, it is good to ask why a particular quantitative value has been chosen and what it represents. In the case of qualitative goals or standards, what the best criteria are to measure the performance or effectiveness of the service used must be considered.

3.2.2 Evaluating performance against the goal or standard

The business and its activities should be monitored because it is necessary to know how well it is meeting its goals. It might be assumed that if performance falls below the goal that was set, the problem lies with the performance, but monitoring can also show up problems with the goals or standards. As the issue of evaluating performance at each level is examined, so is the time relationship between the monitoring process and the activity or business situation that is being monitored.

Live monitoring provides the information about what is actually happening and *post-monitoring* gives us information about what has actually happened. Evaluation tells us how far the reality differs from the goal or target. Managers have discovered that it is often wise to monitor activities, not only when they have been completed but while they are in process because, for example, in a large building project if one key phase is running late because of worker sickness, it is better to be aware of this early and hire extra help. The alternative may be that a number of other phases cannot start until the key phase is finished; workers might have to be paid to be idle while waiting to start and unmet deadlines may incur additional financial penalties.

It is possible for a type of *pre-monitoring* of activities to take place called *feedforward control*. In this case the aim is to anticipate problems and to take action to reduce the risk of them occurring. The evaluation cannot be of the activity itself – since it has not happened – but it will be applied to the 'tangible resources' used in the activity, or the immediate environment that can influence the activity. For example, many government departments are now being encouraged to give contracts only to private businesses that practise 'quality management'. This pre-monitoring is an attempt to reduce the risk of poor performance by contractors or for the government having to pay excessively for products or services loaded with management inefficiency costs.

3.2.2.1 The strategic level

Pre-monitoring/feedforward control

If a company decides to invest in the development of a major information system, the management may attempt to limit the risks involved in development costs by limiting their invitation to tender to only those contractors who can show evidence of quality management in the computer industry.

EXAMPLE

> A Japanese car manufacturer looked at several locations in Britain to invest millions in a car plant. Knowing that their quality products and quality management depended on not just skilled, but also highly motivated, workers the company considered not only the logistics of the locations and the skills base, but also the history of employer/worker relations in the areas. Otherwise excellent sites were rejected on the last issue alone because the company wanted to reduce the risk to their culture of excellence and, hence, the standards of performance at the plant.

Pre-monitoring, in this case, used knowledge about the reputation of British workers for causing costly strikes and information about the history of employer/worker relations in specific areas to reduce the risk of future disruption.

Live monitoring/concurrent control

EXAMPLE

> A toy company decides to invest in developing a new product line. The initial goals are set against a background of current intelligence about market conditions and competition. The company monitors the current development progress along with conditions in the environment. Information from the environment alerts the company to impending safety regulations that will affect the new toy. Modifications are made to the manufacturing process to ensure that the toy will comply with the new safety code.

Had the development process gone along as originally planned the modification costs could have seriously jeopardised the project. An even worse possibility would have been if the original production process had gone ahead and the resulting toy had to be withdrawn in a blaze of adverse publicity for the company because it failed to meet the new safety standard – *post-monitoring*. Live monitoring of the development progress had to be paralleled by monitoring of the environment because, over the time, changing conditions in the environment could be relevant to the development itself.

Post-monitoring/feedback control

At the strategic level this kind of control may not be the best because goals and standards at the strategic level are usually long-term, and deviation discovered after the fact may have an adverse effect on the whole company, or may have already adversely affected it.

Some retail stores and mail order companies originally made a policy decision to *beat* the price of the competition if a customer could show that an identical item was being sold cheaper elsewhere. As trading conditions became tougher and profit margins dropped, some businesses found that their pricing policy was driving them out of business. Some businesses now claim, more conservatively, to *match* the prices of the competition if the customer can show a competitor's price is better.

3.2.2.2 The tactical level

Pre-monitoring/feedforward control

In the above two scenarios evaluation occurs prior to activities or services being performed. The aim is to reduce the possibility of deviation from the goals or standards which have been set.

EXAMPLE

> Following a recent take-over, the board discovers that senior managers in the newly acquired subsidiary are not fully aware of the problems or potential of their part of the business because they have a reluctance to make full use of the information systems available to them. A new post is created for a senior management trainer with special responsibility for encouraging the full exploitation of IT resources. At the interviews the personnel director and other senior colleagues are particularly interested in the personal qualities of the applicants. They realise that if the trainer is to be successful in the job, the person will need exceptional personal qualities as well as other appropriate competencies to win over employees like the Luddite managers.
>
> In another context, a transport manager has all his vehicles serviced every X thousand miles.

Live monitoring/concurrent control

The building project example given at the beginning of the section would be an example of live monitoring at this level.

EXAMPLE

> Another example could be where a company that develops bespoke business systems, agrees with its clients to respond to a system failure within X period of time and to have the system up and running again within Y period of time. The company monitors the progress of the maintenance engineer assigned to the job and as a result of information he sends back, they may direct additional resources or expertise to the site in order to meet the deadline.

If monitoring only occurred after the event, the information obtained would not help the company keep its reputation for service, nor avoid any cost penalty that might be tied to the contract. Post-monitoring might help, however, if it causes the company to identify why they could not satisfy the standard embodied in the terms of the contract.

Post-monitoring/feedback control

EXAMPLE

> The general manager of a department store decides to try and stimulate the sales of the soft furnishings departments by special displays in prominent windows. Sales in the departments have been poor and very flat; the new window displays will be in for a month. The hope is that the promotion will be sufficient to increase sales by 10 per cent.

Post-monitoring will suggest whether the displays by themselves were sufficient to stimulate sales by the desired amount. The actual sales would be monitored in the departments, giving information based on 'hard' details, but the link between the promotion and any sales increase would be 'soft' because it would be difficult to prove. Therefore, the way in which we use or interpret information is distinct from the substance of it. In this case, other environmental factors, even chance, could be responsible for a sales increase.

EXAMPLE

> A hospital manager decides that consultants should spend a maximum of X minutes with out-patients on each visit. Patients are to be logged in and out of the consultants' rooms for a period of three months to monitor the actual time being spent. Regardless of the ailment, it might be found that the average consulting time is greater than X, but a common factor associated with the majority of those who push the time significantly above X is the factor of age.

Again, in this case, a measurable goal has been set and the reality is measured and 'hard' facts are produced and compared against the goal. The reason(s) for the deviation from the goal should be carefully examined before conclusions are drawn from them. It is in the nature of tactical contexts that 'hard' and 'soft' factors have to be taken into account when making decisions.

EXAMPLE

> The newly appointed manager of a hotel decides to buy in cakes and pastries, but is unsure which of four good local suppliers to choose. She gives a three month contract to each over the course of a year, and is careful to see that each supplier's products are given equal prominence and are kept in optimum condition prior to consumption. The deliveries are recorded on the computer, and any remaining items of the products are recorded also. At the end of the year she looks back over the sales and remaining items for each supplier and compares sales.

The standard or goal in this case was provided by comparison with the competing suppliers. The supplier whose pastries had the most appeal may get the contract for the next year.

3.2.2.3 The operational level

Pre-monitoring/feedforward control

EXAMPLE

> A nurse disinfects a thermometer before she takes a patient's temperature. The actual temperature is compared against 'normal' and some action may be taken if there is a deviation.

Disinfecting the thermometer is the pre-monitoring in this instance and is designed to eliminate the possibility of passing on an infection to the patient which might later cause the temperature to deviate from the normal.

EXAMPLE

> A machine tool operator has to produce 50 units an hour. Before he begins a new batch he uses the pre-monitoring approach and checks that all the settings are correct and that there is no obvious damage to the machine. The target is that he produces 50 units an hour and that the units conform to a certain specification.

In actual fact there are two measurable targets here – one has to do with the numbers of the item and the other has to do with the specification. If, say, the last batch had been for units of another specification, and the settings had not been changed, would the 50 units an hour be classed as incorrectly specified instances of the desired batch or unwanted instances of the previous batch? In practice, it is hard to separate the quantity and specification targets and the pre-monitoring is clearly intended to ensure the job as a whole is completed satisfactorily.

Live monitoring/concurrent control

EXAMPLE

> In a brewery it is found that fermentation of beers takes a certain length of time, provided various factors remain constant. The most important factor seems to be the need for a constant temperature. If the target is to produce a beer of strength XXX then the time and temperature should be reasonably constant. Live monitoring of the temperature and specific gravity ensures that the fermentation process is progressing well.

The interim monitoring could, in theory, be considered as comprising discrete mini-processes in which actual measurements are evaluated against known intermediate targets.

EXAMPLE

> When a borrower takes out a book on loan from, say, a college library, the library system keeps track of where that book is, i.e. who has it on loan. The goal is that the book is returned by the 'due date' but, meanwhile, the state of the book/loan is being monitored.

In both the library and brewing examples it is possible to take some action on the basis of the information provided. In the brewing process the temperature may be adjusted to encourage faster fermentation. In the college library if, say, a student needed a book which was out on long-term loan, the library could identify which academic student had the book and request an early return of it, thus pre-empting the standard target date.

A supermarket checkout person is usually trained to count out the change to a customer. The goal is to give the right change and, by live-monitoring the process of giving change, the customer and the checkout person are in a position to remedy any discrepancy before the transaction is complete and the customer leaves. Post-monitoring by the customer can cause suspicion and ill-feeling if the customer believes the change is incorrect.

Post-monitoring/feedback control

EXAMPLE

> At a local bakery the manager keeps a note of when items have sold out and records, at the close of business, any items which have remained unsold. The manager also records any exceptionally large purchases. The records help the bakery to know whether to try increasing or decreasing the numbers of items to maximise sales and minimise wastage.

The goal is not merely to sell every item but also to sell as many of each item as possible. The information provided by the manager helps to identify what the optimum numbers for each item might be. In a real scenario, a variety of environmental factors would have to be taken into account as well, such as seasonal demand, market days, etc.

EXAMPLE

> A person applies for a loan, but the form is returned with a note because the person entered the bank's sort code number where they should have entered the bank account number. The goal was to fill out the form correctly; it was checked or post-monitored by a bank clerk who then provided feedback to the customer, enabling them to correct the fault and send in the form again.

The role of pre-monitoring, live-monitoring and post-monitoring at different levels of management activity have been considered. The aim of live and post-monitoring is to gain information about processes and activities that will result in the better management and control of the business. Live-monitoring allows us to use information about the ongoing process to influence the outcome but post-monitoring provides information about the outcome, which can be used as a basis for modifications in the next cycle of a process. In the case of pre-monitoring, our knowledge of the business context is used to guide us in choosing what components of a business activity can be evaluated ahead of time. The components could include quality checks on human or other resources, or on aspects of the processes involved. Pre-monitoring can reduce the risk of long-term failure.

3.2.3 When the performance differs from the goal or standard

When the output of a process is monitored or measured and it is found to differ significantly from the goal or standard that was set, something has to be done about it. After all, the reason for monitoring a process or (sub)system is to learn something about it from its performance. The standard process model is not entirely suitable for business because it envisaged simple mechanistic processes in which the only element that could be varied was the input. In business, what we do depends upon what the most appropriate response is once we know that the process in the real world is not performing as expected.

3.2.3.1 The strategic level

Goals at this level are usually set with a strong awareness of the company's competitive position in the business environment. Changes in patterns of demand, services or products offered by the competition and technology that gives competitive advantage are the kinds of circumstances that may weigh heavily in decisions taken at the strategic level. Because strategic goals result from long-term planning, the goals themselves are goals to be achieved over the long term. The special problem of 'doing something' in a strategic context is that just as the initial goals may result from a response to change in the environment, change will continue to happen even while the businesses progress towards the goals. Monitoring of progress towards strategic goals is usually accompanied by monitoring of the environment.

The directors of a freight haulage company might take a strategic decision to site new distribution depots at strategic locations near access points for the channel tunnel. Target dates for the development and completion of the depots may be set, but it would not be appropriate to ensure the plans are implemented in isolation from careful monitoring of developments in the environment, such as progress in tunnel construction, development of rail access points, political and policy decisions regarding rail and roads, etc. 'Doing something' as a result of gaining information about the environment and progress towards meeting the goals, may consist of adjusting the goals in the light of political and policy developments, rather than ensuring the schedule is adhered to.

A strategic goal for a furniture kit company is to create a new range of products and establish a name for quality bolt-together products for the business and office world. The company will have to invest in design and development, new machinery and in new workers. Research suggests a good market should exist – but it is a risk. Target sales are set for the products for the first year of production. If sales of the furniture deviate significantly from the target, something needs to be done. Monitoring on a regular basis throughout the year may provide information which identifies good and poor selling items and the possible modification of the range. Alternatively, the information may suggest the need for advertising and special promotions to stimulate sales. The information received from live monitoring of sales through the target period will help determine what type of action is necessary in order to achieve the desired breakthrough into the new market.

3.2.3.2 The tactical level

At an exclusive residential clinic for the pets of wealthy owners, a holistic approach is taken to patient care programmes. As part of this approach, meals are not considered as just meals but as a vital part of the whole recovery process of the pet. A small team meets to produce individual meal plans for the following days. The nutritionist, chef and veterinary nurse for those patients examine each patient's progress so far, and set progress goals for them. The health indicators include brightness of eyes, wetness of nose, condition of coat, etc. Information received from monitoring is then used as a basis for adjusting diet, medicine, or exercise when appropriate. The 'doing' part of the control cycle is, in effect, the making of a new tactical or shorter term decision about the treatment regime which is part of the overall strategy for the patient's recovery.

3.2.3.3 The operational level

New supermarket stackers are told to sort and restack a row of shelves in X period of time. If they fail to complete the job in the time specified, it could be because the supply of products to restock the shelves did not keep pace with the demand for them. It may be that they have to learn to do the job faster or they may have to assess their technique to see whether there is a better way to do it. There is the possibility that the goal was unrealistic. The information draws attention to a problem, but only by examining the cause can the right thing 'be done' to address it.

A counter manager for a cosmetic house in a department store counts how many of each type, size and colour of the cosmetic products are in stock. The quantities are compared with the quantities held at an earlier date and, once any deliveries or returns have been taken into account, the manager calculates the number of sales. The information indicates how many of each product the manager needs to reorder.

Management control consists of setting measurable goals or standards, monitoring the business or business activities for which the standards are set and then doing something if there is a significant deviation between what actually happens and the goal or standard that was to be achieved. The situation is not quite as straightforward as that because even if monitoring of the business activity shows good progress towards a long-term goal, monitoring of the environment can identify changes that demand the goal should be changed. The essential point to grasp is that good control depends upon good information. Information about what is happening in a business, and information about the environment in which it operates are both crucial to its good control and ultimate success.

3.3 KNOWLEDGE, INFORMATION AND DATA

The issues so far have been of management control, the principles of setting goals or standards, the need to evaluate actual performance against the standards or goals and the necessity of doing something if the evaluation shows up a significant difference between what is desired and what really happens. The information that is produced by monitoring the business, business activities and the environment is the essential ingredient of the evaluation phase. Information is the output of the monitoring process and it is input for decision making because good decisions need to be based on information. Knowing what to monitor, and what to do with the information that results from it, requires knowledge of the business: the knowledge of what is important for decision making.

Knowledge, information and data are related terms but have distinct meanings in the context of information systems and databases. The relationship between these basic concepts is shown and defined below.

Knowledge is the understanding of the world or context in which information has meaning. It is knowledge that determines what is significant about a business activity, what information should be sought when monitoring it, and what should be done when the information flags a problem situation.

Information consists of meaningful facts. They are meaningful in the sense that they:

1 are significant and relevant to the person who needs them;
2 are relevant to the person's position or role within the business;
3 are relevant to the decision or action that might depend on them;
4 have the power to precipitate change.

Knowledge of a situation or world of activity will tend to determine what things are seen as having special significance or meaning; information gives knowledge about those things.

Data consist of facts or details about things, activities, transactions, etc. Data are stored as a resource that can be drawn upon to produce information for the people and activities that need it.

3.3.1 A closer look at 'information'

3.3.1.1 Information and its relevance to the individual employee

People in business, and many other professions, tend to be bombarded with all kinds of documents and messages, all of them competing for the attention of the individual. For any particular person only some of the documents and messages will qualify as being significant or relevant enough to count as real information. An important memo directed to the wrong person, in this sense, does not count as information since it is not relevant to that person, even if it is interesting!

3.3.1.2 Information and its relevance to the position of the employee

Managers or decision makers need enough information to be able to do their job effectively. The information may be about the context or about the activities the managers oversee. Organisations sometimes use the scatter gun approach and send memos to all managers of a certain level, hoping that some will find the memo useful. Unfortunately, if such messages are often found to be irrelevant, a busy manager may consign *all* memos from that source to the round pending tray.

A technical director may be ultimately responsible for all production, research and development, as well as other technical activities in the company. The director may want to know about the efficiency or trends in production output at factory X, but it is unlikely that details will be needed about overtime schedules. Only exceptional circumstances at the plant would cause the director to view such details as information.

The production manager at factory X, on the other hand, may be particularly interested in the overtime schedules if they featured in difficult negotiations with a union. The manager may be concerned that unless enough overtime is worked, production targets will not be met. The manager may not even be interested in the names of the individuals working the overtime; such facts may be too detailed to be relevant to someone in that position because there is nothing the manager can do with them to improve the running of the job.

3.3.1.3 Information and its relevance to decision making

The business should be organised so that appropriate information reaches those who have to make decisions and take actions, whether the information comes down, across or up the organisation. The quality of information may be judged by how well it supports the decisions or actions which require it. It should always be borne in mind that since it is people who are making the decisions, the information should be packaged so that it can be communicated well. To some extent, the background and knowledge of the manager will influence what information he or she looks for to support decisions. A technically oriented or insecure manager may take little account of the human dimension in actions to be taken and may, therefore, not look for information that would invite staff or client input. A less technically oriented manager may fail to see the correct significance of some technical information. Decision makers may have the power to control what information is sought and the freedom to apply it as they see fit; the responsibility is theirs.

3.3.1.4 Information and its power to precipitate change

Some would say that any facts which do not have the power to precipitate change in an action or a decision do not constitute real information. This characteristic of information is sometimes referred to as its 'surprise value'. If there were no surprise value, then whatever the content of the report, document or other message, it would be irrelevant if it could not make any difference to the decision which is made, or the action which is taken. Information for decision-makers is usually the product of monitoring the business environment, or the activities in the business itself, reflecting the dynamics of change and the relationship of the business to its environment. If information is to have the power which it ought to have, then great care needs to be taken to ensure that decision-makers are neither swamped with details nor starved of crucial facts when they need them.

3.3.2 The dependence of information upon knowledge

Perhaps the difference between good and great managers is the ability of the latter to see significance in facts that would be missed by others. Knowledge is related to the way we believe the world works. This is also true in the world of business. Bank managers are sometimes accused of taking a cynical and all too narrow view of a struggling business when they appear to focus solely on the financial aspects, but their knowledge of the financial structures of businesses predisposes them to regard certain financial details as more significant than perhaps the value of the products, services or even the value of the employees in the business; that is the way bank managers tend to see the world. An exceptional entrepreneur may defy all the financial indicators and turn an ailing business into a roaring success but, in a world where the decisions of a bank manager have to be justified on the basis of hard facts, the bank manager has to act as if the figures tell all.

Medical knowledge today is incomplete but research into almost every area of medicine gives us more knowledge of the human organism. Not so many years ago medical knowledge was more rudimentary and medical diagnoses of diseases, together with their cures, were very bizarre. Large strides in medical knowledge, especially since the latter part of the 18th century, now make medical diagnosis safer. Poor explanations for human reactions to disease and injury have been replaced with better ones, but even now we still know little about some illnesses and we cannot predict with certainty the effects of drugs on individuals. Scientists and doctors have learned that certain kinds of organisms tend to affect humans (and other animals) in certain ways. It is now possible to associate specific sets of signs and symptoms with certain diseases. We know there are patterns to the development of certain diseases and both the symptoms and patterns of development enable doctors to make a reasonably accurate diagnosis much of the time. A physician, therefore, recognises some signs and looks for other specific ones to confirm his hypothesis and/or to eliminate alternatives; knowledge tells the physician what signs, symptoms or patterns are significant and they constitute the information that tells the doctor what the disease is, how bad it is and it implies an appropriate response.

Some physicians are better than others at diagnosing conditions or they may get to the root of problems more quickly. The reason for this may be that their practical and theoretical knowledge base allows them to associate a greater range of possible explanations for what they see. Thus it is suggested the principle that knowledge tells us what factors are significant enough to be considered as information; information is important only because we know that it matters in the context – and what tells us it matters is knowledge.

Information tells the catering manager in a large hotel that his wine cellars are fully stocked and that he need not place any large orders to suppliers. His world of catering means that he maintains certain optimum levels of wines and spirits in the cellars. In a different but related world, the hotel owner, in conversation with one of his wealthy clients, becomes aware of an opportunity to buy a large quantity of a very good wine at a very low price. Discussion between the owner and the catering manager changes the manager's knowledge base and on reflection he may put in an order for the wine.

People who believe their future is determined by the stars may look for information in their favourite horoscope column. Their knowledge or understanding of the world causes them to feel the comments in the column are meaningful.

An investor who makes a living on the stock market consults papers like the *Financial Times* for relevant trading information. The investor's knowledge of how the market works and of past performance causes the investor to identify meaningful patterns of activity. An active search for information relevant to those patterns will probably influence the next round of dealing.

3.4 INFORMATION AND INFORMATION SYSTEMS

It would be hard to dispute the need for information, or its value to decision-makers. Information, however, does not just suddenly become available; a business has to be planned and organised to ensure the right information is available to the right people. The formal, or planned, means for gaining, communicating and producing the information is the information system. The system may or may not be computerised and, in either case, its effectiveness and efficiency will depend a lot on how the system has been designed. In practice, formal, computerised information systems tend to provide only some of the total requirements for information while other requirements are met through means such as reading financial newspapers and journals, seeing new advertising campaigns, talking with people, sending and receiving memos, etc. Informal, or unplanned, systems usually complement the formal. There may be a need for action or a decision to be taken but the necessary information will not be received if no information system has been set up, to ensure that details were collated and organised as significant information, and that it reached the right people.

Traditionally, computers were successfully used to perform high volume repetitive tasks which were relatively straightforward to design and program. Typical early uses were in payroll systems and, later, such functions as stock control systems. Most early systems probably owed their success to their quite specialised and restricted scope. Most applications were applied to contexts in which calculations were involved, a particular strength of computers. The aims of these systems were clear and managers knew precisely what was required of them. Management tended to value these systems as means of cutting costs and improving accuracy compared to the manual equivalent. Apart from their ability to produce summary reports about the activities which had been carried out, most early systems were not primarily information systems but, essentially, data processing systems.

As information systems are being used more extensively to monitor business activities and provide information for a greater range of decisions, the types of information required are consequently more extensive. Accepting that information technology is assuming a greater range of functionality in the business it is possible to conclude that greater complexity is involved. Perhaps the issue of complexity has been underestimated in many of the systems which have failed. The characteristics of organisational complexity mentioned in Chapter 2 suggest there are significant implications for the provision of information and for information systems. Complex organisational design implies at least as much complexity will be required of the information system which monitors the activities within the business.

Efficiency and cost effectiveness, primary motivations for earlier systems, are still important considerations for management when they plan to install or update an information system. However, the importance of information as a resource in its own right and the rapid communication and control of information are considered by many larger businesses to be vital to improving performance and competitive advantage. The simple cost comparison between human and computer-based systems no longer tells the whole story. Ignoring some of the advantages of computer-based systems could lead to a business being consigned to history. For example, the introduction by banks and building societies of cash point machines achieved a number of objectives. It meant that some bank teller positions could effectively be automated. It also meant a reduction in the amount of cheque handling. In both cases we can see that this is cost effective for the bank. It also meant an added service which allowed round-the-clock banking for the customer, thus going beyond what the traditional service could have offered. Automatic cash point machines allow customers to withdraw and deposit cash; customers can monitor their accounts via mini statements and ask for their latest balance. Would you consider having an account at a bank that did not offer cash point machine facilities?

Another related use of information systems is the facility to use major credit cards at so many locations around the world. In fact, it is hard to imagine financial institutions without these services now. The information available from these systems include: a record of individual transactions for the customers' and the institutions' benefit, monthly accounts, buying patterns or account activity patterns for marketing and other purposes.

Information systems can tell us about those things that the business or organisation processes, produces, uses or sells. They can also tell us how the business is functioning, whether targets are being met, etc. Information systems are available which contain details about competitors, economic activities and other factors in the business environment that might affect the business. Information is not only a valuable resource but, for some companies, information is at the heart of their activities. Accurate, rapid and relevant information can be absolutely crucial to business survival. It is the responsibility of management to ensure that information systems are designed to deliver real information as required by the business. The following section takes this theme further.

3.4.1 Information systems provide specific answers to specific questions

Information systems are as valuable as the information they produce. In the definition of information, in order to satisfy all the criteria, specific questions about the context in which it is required needed to be asked. Is the information relevant to the person *who* needs it? *What* information is required by someone in that position in the company? *Why* does the person need it and *what* decisions or actions might depend on it? Given that the goal of information systems is to produce information, then to get full value from the system, specific questions need to be asked to ensure that the service provided is appropriate.

In Chapter 2 some of the characteristics of management decision making were explored and in the previous section the relevance of information to decisions was expanded. It is clear that different sorts of decisions will require the support of different sorts of information. Not only that, but some of the questions mentioned above concerning the context in which information is required, can only be answered with respect to the individuals who need it. By now, it should be obvious that when talking of information it is important to bear in mind the context in which it is used or needed. There is no simple definition of it but, to those who need it, it is quite easy to tell when what is given does not communicate as it ought or does not contain what is really relevant.

It follows that if it is hard to define what individual users of the information really need, because each context and person is different, then the challenge of providing a computer-based information system to satisfy managers and other decision-makers in a business, is a substantial challenge indeed. One of the greatest difficulties is that it is in the nature of information systems (and the database management systems that support them) that almost all information that is required of them has to be precisely specified. This is a problem because it is not in the nature of most people (for example, the people who would use an information system) to specify, as precisely as a computer requires, what they want or need. Some further considerations or factors that can be brought into the debate about information and information systems include:

- Who really wants the information?
- What kind of decision is it really for?
- What sort of information does the manager really need?
- Will the information change the world?
- Will the information exceed its 'sell by' date?
- Are there other, or better, ways of obtaining the information?
- Are there any obvious challenges to the system resources?

3.4.1.1 Who really wants the information?

Earlier, the principle that information is only information if it is relevant to the individual who needs it was stated. The information may need to be tailored to the background of the person, his or her role within the organisation and the decision-making context implied by the management approach. However, it is also necessary to consider that decisions are often made by groups such as in a board meeting or a multidisciplinary team. Quite clearly, the members of a group are likely to have different backgrounds; most will probably be able to appreciate issues but not all will feel comfortable trying to find information hidden in the details on pages of figures. The goal of the information systems specialists should be to package the information in such a way that *all* members of a decision-making group are able to appreciate the significance of the content. The analyst would need to know in this type of context who *really* needs the information – who would tell the analyst?

From a technological point of view, ensuring that information is really communicated to the people who need it could take a considerable amount of time when developing the system. If managers put more emphasis on visual representation, such as charts and graphs, as they very well might, then extra attention may also have to be given to printing resources; documents containing graphs or pictures can take a long time to produce, creating potential bottlenecks if the printing resources are limited. Audio and video media now provide additional ways of storing data and of presenting information but, as yet, they are not part of commercial information systems, although more systems now incorporate colour images. In an ideal world, the information system would produce information perfectly suited to the person, or persons, who need it but practical considerations of development time and costs force most businesses to make some compromises.

3.4.1.2 What kind of decision is it really for?

Strategic, tactical and operational decisions tend to depend on different kinds of information. Decision making at the strategic level would be expected to be supported by external information about the environment of the business and internal information about trends and facts related to overall business performance, not operational details, etc. From a technical perspective, some of the characteristics of decision-types have implications for what level of information the information system should provide in specific contexts, for example, operational information may provide immediate feedback about live business activities such as a hotel receptionist who handles a request for a room and needs immediate information about room availability. The technology has to be designed to provide an immediate response to such relatively simple queries.

A tactical-level manager may need information about suppliers who have failed to deliver raw materials on time. The company may have a policy of warning suppliers who have greater than X per cent late deliveries over a three-month period. The system would have to comb through delivery details over the time period to find the result. If the system has to search through very many details, it may be better to run such an application at night when the computer does not have to handle so many requests for immediate responses.

The directors of a major hotel complex want month-by-month operating figures for their major conference suites for the current and previous financial year, with a view to, perhaps, finding more profitable uses for the resources. The information needs to be presented so as to highlight patterns of use, and major areas of loss and/or profitability. These tasks are typically more complex than the tactical and operational ones. The period of interest covers a greater span and, while the information could be presented as lists of details, all the details are not significant, but rather the relationships that can be found in them. To produce information of this sort requires appropriate knowledge, processing of the details and, perhaps, various charts and graphs. This strategic information may support a decision to convert the suites to a more profitable use.

The different levels of decision making in management were discussed earlier, but what about a middle-level manager who regularly prepares vital reports for a director who makes strategic decisions based on the reports? Many managers actually attempt, or are required, to provide information in some form for their superiors to act on. In practice, a manager at one level in an organisation may have roles to play at higher or lower levels within a hierarchy, or elsewhere in the business. While a rigid view of who needs what information may not benefit the organisation, not everyone can have access to all the information they might say they want.

3.4.1.3 What sort of information does the manager really need?

It is possible that different decision-makers may set different objectives for decisions. It is also possible to argue that each problem or situation requires action, or that a decision has a correct or best solution. The correct solution would be the most rational one, provided sufficient information has been given to lead to that decision and no other. Some managers aim, in appropriate circumstances quite rightly, to make rational decisions. The assumption would be that information would supply 'hard' evidence to support such decisions. If, by their nature, problems with clearly optimal solutions tend to be at the operational end of the decision-making spectrum, then the burden on the information system may not be too great. If 'soft' (qualitative) facts have to be given (quantitative) weightings and the range of relevant factors is large, the burden on the system could be quite large. The 'burden' would include the degree of design complexity and possible demands on processing.

It is known, however, that some kinds of decision are difficult to make on purely rational grounds. Others have argued that some managers do not seriously attempt to make purely rational decisions but seek to make satisfactory or simply good decisions. A solution or decision that is good enough could be explained by pragmatism, laziness or by a limiting view of human problem-solving ability. Perhaps all three explanations are close to the truth in individual cases. Where decisions depend on a complex range of factors, including perhaps soft facts, a 'good enough' decision may seem like a very good solution. There are some cases where a best solution is possible but the time, effort or cost involved in finding all the required information may make a satisfactory solution a better solution in that context. The implication here is that the information required should support the minimum criteria for a satisfactory decision. The burden on the information system is, therefore, probably less for the pragmatic solution than for a best solution.

A compromise view says that while many managers may not be convinced of a single best solution they may still aim to make the best decision they can by narrowing down the range of alternative solutions. The final decision may lie somewhere between the optimal solution and ones which might have been just good enough. In order to practise this form of decision making, the implication is that a good information system would provide sufficient information to allow different solutions to be evaluated by the decision-maker. The burden on the system designers and on the information system could be quite heavy since, to arrive at one good decision, the system needs to provide enough information to reject the other possibilities as well.

3.4.1.4　Will the information change the world?

Information is always wanted for a reason but the reasons given by people who may use the information system are not always closely related to the decisions they have to make. Some have suggested that there is a priority wish list for information: there is information that we *must* have, there is some it would be *useful* to have and then there is some we would *like* to have. In the real world, every extra request for information can add to the costs of developing the information system. Large information systems can cost many millions of pounds and, therefore, there is good reason to prioritise the demands that users would like to make on them. Legitimate requests should relate to providing information that directly supports the decision making individuals have to perform and, possibly, useful contextual information that may influence decision making. One way to look at this is to say that if information, by definition, should have a surprise value, that is to say it has the potential to influence decisions that are made, then real information is, by definition, only that which a user must have to support decisions for which they are responsible or which they can directly influence.

3.4.1.5   Will the information exceed its 'sell by' date?

Time can be related to *how long* a period the information covers or it can be related to *how quickly* it needs to be made available.

EXAMPLE

A national retail company may be interested in how one month's sales compare with the same month the year before. The time span of interest covers one year or so. In a different instance, if interest is in some highly seasonal lines and for some food items, it is imperative that information about sales is communicated very rapidly otherwise the information is old and has lost its value. Summer dresses come in a range of sizes and colours, some of which sell better than others. The stores do not want to get caught with stock when the short window of demand is closed, but they do want to maximise sales. Rapid sales information allows the company to order the more popular colours, styles and sizes from their suppliers. Popular food items can be produced and distributed overnight to replenish the shelves for the next day.

Time implications for the system include how long details of sales, etc. are kept readily available on the computer and what the most efficient ways of using the computer resources to get the information are. When no rapid response is needed, a larger company may decide to process regular reports, etc. automatically through the night, but time critical reports might have to be available on demand.

3.4.1.6   Are there other or better ways of obtaining the information?

Although there might be several ways to obtain information about something, it is also true that an information system may not be the best means of obtaining some kinds of information. In some organisations it is not unusual to find the same or similar information being required on different forms by the same department: a remnant of how old systems worked, but no longer sensible. In other situations where human contact is involved in communicating information, that contact in itself may be valuable, providing additional insight which a computerised system is unable to do. It is important to remember that, while an information system can be used to provide quantitative and qualitative information, its strengths tend to lie much more in the quantitative area. The monitoring of activities involving qualitative judgements are usually undertaken on a human level first – even if the results later become available through the information system.

The technological interest here may be that if the technology is used to monitor some work activities rather than monitoring through human contact, while a management case might be made for efficiency, work effectiveness may suffer if it is felt inappropriate by those being monitored in that way, or if the human contact itself played a part in work motivation.

3.4.1.7   Are there any obvious challenges to the system resources?

All computer-based systems have limitations. It is not necessary to have a good technical knowledge to appreciate the points made here, any more than you would need great knowledge to realise that the effect on your 1300cc mini is going to be somewhat different if you take four ten year olds for a trip in the hills, compared with taking four 16 stone rugby players on a similar trip. Just as cars have limitations on their performance and space for passengers, etc., so do computer systems. In neither case do we need great technical expertise to recognise there is a relationship between the things we ask technology to do and the characteristics of the technology itself. We suggest there are five common contexts in which we become aware of the limitations of our technical resources:

1 getting details into the system;
2 getting information out of the system;
3 keeping details in the system;
4 processing;
5 moving details from one place to another.

Sometimes, the system will roll over and die if it cannot cope but, usually, awareness of the limitations through a common experience of waiting arises. When one or more of the resources are limiting the performance of the information system, it slows down; then all that can be done is to wait.

Getting details into the system

A simple warning of a possible challenge comes when there is a need to get a lot of details into the system within a given period of time. A number of people entering details into a system at the same time at different points of access could cause the system to slow down – otherwise there could be a problem if a large amount of detail needs to be entered by too few staff, or too few staff with experience have been allocated to the job.

At supermarket checkouts, it is important to process each customer as quickly as possible and, therefore, the means of getting details of the items sold and into the information system have to be consistent with the goal of rapid service. Bar codes and bar code readers are the most commonly favoured technology for speedy data entry.

Specially coded tearoff tags are attached to merchandise in certain retail stores; when an item is sold, the tag is torn off and put in a box for later collection. Tags are collected at regular intervals with the idea that rapid information about sales of seasonal merchandise will allow immediate reorders of popular lines. Unfortunately, experience has shown that sometimes boxes are moved or covered with products or wrappings during busy periods and the tags, when detached, are put in a 'safe place'. Lost tags and late discovery of bundles of tags can be significant enough to make the results an unreliable indicator of sales. The idea is good, but may not be quite good enough to make effective use of the technology because the human work environment may not be fully appreciated.

Getting information out of the system

There are various ways in which information can be got out of the system. The video monitor is one way – this provides few problems as long as the people who need the information have access to a monitor and the monitor is capable of representing the information appropriately.

A common way to get information from the system is for it to be printed. Printers can cause bottlenecks because they can only print one document at a time. If many copies of a document are needed or, if a document has a lot of pages or even if there are a number of people who are sharing the use of one printer, printing can take a long time.

Printers have different capabilities: e.g. some can print charts and graphical images, but a number cannot. Some printers are a lot faster than others and some printers change speed if they are printing in draft or letter quality mode; they tend to slow right down when printing pictures or graphs. Too much work for too few printers can lead to serious delays in getting information out of the system. Supplies like paper and ribbons or toner need to be on hand – as do some people who know how to perform basic routine tasks on printers, like putting in a new toner cartridge, replenishing paper, or using the basic controls to adjust the paper, etc.

Keeping details in the system

Just as paper files might be stored in a filing cabinet or books in a bookcase, computers usually store details (data files) on disks. Actually, they store other vital things like programs on disks too, but for now it is enough to know that when details are put into the system, they are stored on disk(s), and when information is wanted from the system, it has to hunt through the details on the disk(s) to find what has been asked for. Some disks can hold relatively small amounts of data, while some can hold very large amounts but, even the largest disks are finite in capacity, and are, therefore, limited resources. The storage space on disks has to be managed carefully; the computer itself will decide where to put the details and remembers where to find them, but it does not decide what details should be held and for how long. In our experience, bookcases are rarely big enough and many feel computer storage suffers from the same problem.

It should be recognised that quantities of details being added to the system regularly poses a potential challenge to the storage resource. Decisions about what details need to be kept and for how long may need to be made. Some kinds of details, like pictures, can take up quite a lot of space compared to standard text, if a screen worth of information of each is compared. With very full disks it can take a relatively long time to search for data and storing more details may become difficult or unreliable.

Processing

If this heading includes both the raw power of the processor and the amount of space the machine has in its active memory to do the processing, then it can be said that, here too is a limited resource. These factors significantly affect the ability of a machine to use some kinds of software and/or the speed with which it can process some applications. Although some technical knowledge is useful to address this topic, nevertheless it is still possible to recognise some of the potential challenges to this resource.

For a small business, where there is just a single PC, the main concern for the business is whether the processing capability of the machine is adequate for the software packages it wants to run on it. Larger businesses have to address the same concern but, in addition, it is important to find out whether the performance of the system might degrade if a number of people use it at the same time for moderately demanding work. Whenever a number of people *can* use the same resource at the same time, it is necessary to know what really happens to the performance of the system if everyone *does* access it at the same time. It is also worth knowing what would happen to its performance if more access points were to be arranged or if more work were to be found for the system than was originally anticipated. The reason for the last is that salesmen may sell a system based on possible expansion but may forget to say how the performance would be affected.

Moving details from one place to another

It may be necessary to access an information system through a network of computers. When computers are linked into a network through which they can communicate, the cables which link them become a communication highway. If access to some information is needed from a database held on a disk by one machine, then the information has to be sent to another machine through the cable. A network, or communications component of the system, is a resource with limitations. The more data or information travelling through the cable at the same time, the more competition there is for the communications space. There are different kinds of cable and different kinds of network that offer different levels of performance but, as before, if there is an awareness that many people are likely to be using the network quite heavily for accessing, for example, a common database, then the effect on the performance of the network needs to be known. These are not technical questions, but questions of the technology.

It is hoped that the importance of asking specific questions involved in the development of an information system, for instance by managing the development team, has been demonstrated. The questions assume that the development will be costly and that the technological resources are limited. There will always be a tension between what is desirable and what is possible, given finite financial and technological resources. Some suggest that the value of an information system should be measured in terms of the value of the information it can provide for the business. It is doubtful whether an absolute value can ever be assigned to information, or the resources that provide it.

3.5 DATA AND INFORMATION

The terms 'data' and 'information' are often used as if they mean the same thing in ordinary everyday language but, in the context of information systems, care has been taken to distinguish between the two. Earlier 'data' was defined by saying that it (or strictly speaking 'they' because a *datum* is singular and *data* plural, however most people now use data in a singular and plural sense) consists of 'facts or details about things, activities, transactions, etc.'

Data are the details that are worth storing about the products a business sells, produces or the services it offers. Details are also stored about the resources controlled by a company, such as its factories, outlets, and staff, etc. It is usual for a business to keep details about the people or other businesses it deals with, such as its customers and suppliers. More companies now are beginning to keep details about competitors and other factors in their business environment, such as demographic details. All these data refer to what we not very imaginatively called 'things' in Chapter 1.

In this chapter there have been discussions, at some length, on the issue of management control and the consequent need to monitor business activities. Data are also kept as a result of monitoring the activities and processes in business. Many of these details are kept only for as long as they are useful which could be, perhaps, not much longer than the control cycle takes to complete. Sometimes, only exceptions or deviations are stored for, after all, if every detail about every activity in a business were recorded and stored it would pose severe problems for the system, probably overloading it.

The data that is stored is determined by the information that is needed, in fact, the business does not want to store any more nor any less than is needed to run it effectively. It might be thought that if only the data required for information was going to be stored then, in fact the business is storing information; however different parts and activities in a business require different kinds of information about the same things.

3.5.1 Information consists of only the data we need

When a marketing department for a men's retail and mail order business publishes a new catalogue of products, it needs the product code, description and selling price for each item to go with each photo.

The merchandising manager for men's outerwear may want to put some items in a seasonal sale and may use the opportunity to reduce the remainder of a previous season's stock, possibly reducing slow selling items to stimulate sales. The manager will need the product code for each item so that the information system can find the rest of the details, such as the number in stock, the sizes and colours, the price they were bought at, the selling price, etc. The manager will then know by how much the items can be reduced and what the sale might cost the business in lost profit.

The marketing department would not need as much information about the products as the merchandising manager. If marketing had been given the same details as the manager, it would have had to pick out the informational details and ignore the rest. Information systems should be designed to discriminate between details so that, having requested information, a manager does not get unwanted details as well.

3.5.2 Information can come from relating different data together

A typical business activity occurs when, say, an electrical wholesaler orders some products from a manufacturer. From the manufacturer's point of view, the business makes money when it sells its products for more than it costs to make them. The cost of making them needs to be known and will include the cost of raw materials, running the plant, wages and other overheads. The manufacturer also needs to keep track of how many items it sells, to whom, etc. The order, which comes from the wholesaler, contains details about different things; an important document in its own right, it documents a business transaction and will normally have its own number by which it can be identified. It will also contain some details about the wholesaler so that, as the purchaser, it can be identified and the products sent to the right place. Of course, it also records which products and how many of them are required.

The manufacturer's information system may store details of the company's customers as one kind of 'thing', details of its products as another kind of 'thing', details of orders that it has received as yet another kind of 'thing', because each of these 'things' has its own characteristics and relationship to the company's operation. The things are clearly different: one is a wholesale business, one consists of the manufacturer's products and the other is a document that records transactions – they are also related as the order shows. An information system can ensure that the relevant details or data about each of the things can be related together. If a manager in the manufacturing company wanted to find out how much business they had done with the wholesaler and what kinds of products had been ordered, the information system would link the different things together and produce a report listing all the relevant details which together would be the information required.

3.6 SUMMARY

This chapter began with the premise that one of the key responsibilities of management is to exercise effective control over the business functions or processes that come within their remit. We said that control is effective when management set long and short-term goals in line with the mission and purpose of the company, they choose relevant criteria by which they can judge how the business is performing with respect to the goals and, when the performance differs significantly from what was expected or desired, then management determine an appropriate response. This, in a nutshell, is the essence of management control; the special interest in this process is that in order for this sort of control to happen at all, managers need to be using the right criteria to evaluate performance and they need information to be returned from the monitoring of the functions or activities.

A government-sponsored report on police practice and performance made recommendations that angered many, if not most, of the senior police officers because the report, in their opinion, selected a number of performance criteria that were incompatible with the mission and purpose that they feel the police have. This sort of problem would stem from the author(s) of the report not having enough knowledge or understanding of the role of the police force in society. Knowledge will often determine what is identified as information that is critical to effective management control and, by implication, a lack of knowledge or understanding may lead to using less important criteria to monitor business processes.

Following the discussion of monitoring business functions or processes it was noted that knowledge of the context, and of the kinds of information that can reasonably be expected of an information system, are important ingredients for it to be effective. If information is the currency of business communication then, for it to be valuable to its users, there are a number of factors about them and it that need to be addressed before any claims that an information system actually delivers it.

In the following chapters some of the more analytical thinking and principles will be introduced. These are helpful to both managers and information systems developers in that the ideas and techniques that are used, can give insight into management issues that may need addressing and that need to be considered by developers. The approach followed is very much business information driven.

QUESTIONS

1 The principles of control are relatively simple but surprisingly, perhaps, management does not always exercise good control and, sometimes, when control principles are used they are not necessarily used appropriately. Take the case of a sub-Post Office in a small Scottish town. If you were responsible for setting up some monitoring criteria for your Post Office bosses, what criteria would you use and why? Also consider whether it might make a difference if you viewed the sub-Post Office as a public service or purely as a business.

2 Setting standards or goals for management control may occur at a strategic or a tactical level and one of the ways in which we differentiate the levels is to say that strategic goals are set with a long-term perspective and the tactical ones with a shorter time frame. Explain why this is likely to be the case and comment on whether the time periods could differ according to the type of business being considered.

3 Information systems should produce information and we gain information as a result of monitoring. Given that computer-based information systems have to operate on the basis of logic, mathematical calculations and precise details, discuss what you see as the limitations and possibilities of using computer-based technology in management control in business.

4 Explain the purposes and roles of pre-, live and post-monitoring in management control.

5 Discuss the relationship between knowledge and the information that is needed for management control.

6 Some writers say that we are in the 'information age', others claim that information is a business's 'most significant resource' and there are those who refer to information as the 'most valuable commodity'. If this is so, then comment on why there also seems to be such a problem in recognising what it is, or in specifying exactly what information products are needed for management control.

7 One of the characteristics of 'real information' is said to be its surprise value and this is a quality that data does not have. What is meant by 'surprise value' and why can we say that data does not have this quality?

8 Comment on the essential differences between the concepts of data and information.

BIBLIOGRAPHY   Cooke, S. and Slack, N., *Making Management Decisions* (2nd Edn), Prentice Hall, 1991.

CHAPTER 4

Asking the right management questions: a systems perspective

4.1 INTRODUCTION

In Chapter 2 'systems' in the guise of one of the 'modern' approaches to management were introduced. It was noted at the time that the value of systems ideas to business management is that they are very useful as an aid to explaining and understanding complex organisations. It was also recognised that 'system' is a term that can have a number of different meanings and it is only the context in which it is used that helps to clarify what precisely is meant by it. This chapter will expand on the discussion of *systems principles* which began earlier in Chapter 2. Systems principles or ideas can be very helpful in two major ways that are relevant to the development of information systems in business. Systems ideas provide:

- a valuable set of diagnostic criteria that help to pose sensible questions about how effectively a business is functioning
- a very useful means of relating business activities to information systems design and development.

As the systems ideas are explained in more detail the view is taken that they are *generic* principles that enable the evaluation or the testing of any management approach or practice, in so far as management should have a means of answering the questions posed, and addressing the issues raised, by systems theory.

4.2 A CLOSER INSPECTION OF SYSTEMS PRINCIPLES

In Chapter 2 a number of basic characteristics were identified with the idea of a system. The focus of the characteristics was on a system as a sort of coherent dynamic entity and each of these characteristics is illustrated more fully below. The usefulness of systems thinking cannot really be appreciated without considering other key concepts that also belong to systems theory; these concepts focus more on the notion of a system as it functions in the context of the patterns of relationships of which it is an integral part.

4.2.1 Basic systems characteristics

Systems are assemblies of parts that are organised in a pattern, or in a particular way. The parts consist of sub-systems and resources used by the system to achieve its purpose. For example, a production system may convert raw materials into a desired product. An information system may take data from the production system and give us the information we need to exercise control over, or manage, the process. Each of these (sub)systems include components we can identify as sub-systems or resources. A production system may need people to provide the system with raw materials, manage the processes that are involved in transforming the raw materials into the finished product, and deal with the products once they are made; people are resources. Other resources are the raw materials and the products themselves become resources in a larger context. Yet another category of resource must be the technology or the machines that are used to produce the products.

The related information system has sub-systems that pick up and process the data gained from the production activities. It may not need human resources if all the data collection and processing are automatic. When people monitor the information that it provides and use that information to intervene in the production system's sub-systems when necessary, then the people are acting as a resource in a production (sub)system process of control. Technological resources may include the devices that pick up the data, the computers that process it, the communications network that sends data or information from one place to another and the devices used to display or print the information. A partially manual information system could use documents as resources if they contain some of the details used in the system.

The assembly of parts has an identifiable purpose, and there is a reason for them being assembled in the way they are. For example, the purpose of a production system is to produce a specific product. Information systems are set up so that specific information about the activities of a business such as quantifiable information about the effectiveness or efficiency of a production system can be accessed.

Each part is affected in a particular way, or ways, by being in the system, and if a part is removed its role or function is changed. For example, if a bank's Automatic Teller Machines(ATMs) are really successful, the management may decide to eliminate the part played by their tellers in accessing customers' accounts and amending them. The result may be that access privileges to customers' accounts enjoyed by most tellers become restricted to a few specialists: the role of tellers becomes more directed to developing better rapport with customers, identifying customers' financial needs and selling the bank's financial packages as appropriate solutions, generating more business. The tellers would have been a *part* (resource) in the bank's traditional system of handling 'high street' customer banking but, under a new arrangement, would become resources within the local sales and marketing system.

Systems normally produce something, or at least have an effect. For example, a system set up to deal with customer complaints should, at least, ensure that customers feel that they have been heard and understood and that the business values its customers. An information system attached to such a system could enable management to test the results or outcomes of the system against a sensible set of criteria, such as testing to see that all customer complaints are responded to within a set time limit. In each case, the (sub)systems have clear purposes and must be assessed on their tangible results.

Systems have boundaries. Inside the boundary should be under the system's control, but outside is beyond the scope of its control. For example, system boundaries help us to focus on the purpose or object of the system in question and to differentiate one system or sub-system from another. A system which is set up for the purpose of turning raw materials into a finished product is different from a system which is attached to it in order to produce the business (i.e. non-technical) information to manage it. Even though the two are linked, the purpose of each is distinct. The boundary of each system is determined by its purpose.

Systems exist within an immediate environment which consists of a set of external influences or factors which can impact on the system, but over which the system has limited or no influence. For example, a system to handle customer complaints may be affected by poor advertising by the company which leads to unrealistic expectations of a product by customers. A resulting high volume of complaints by customers could seriously impact on the system, but it is unlikely the customer complaints system would seriously be able to impact on the company as a whole. Thus the boundary of the customer complaints system includes within it only those sub-systems whose purposes come within its remit and responsibility, and over which it has the authority to effect change. Any factors which affect the system but which arise from systems over which the customer complaints system has no control, are factors within its environment.

4.2.2 Key systems concepts

4.2.2.1 Hierarchy

There is an assumption within systems theory that complex organisations such as a business can be analysed as a system that contains systems and that typical components of systems are also systems or, more properly, sub-systems. 'Sub-system' is for our purposes simply a term which recognises the subordination of a system within a larger system, thus it is a relative term and does not imply any major distinction in kind between a system and sub-system. The theory, therefore, recognises that there may be a hierarchy of systems within systems, etc. When it is impossible to decompose a system into any further meaningful parts, the extremity of the system has been found and probably no further sub-systems can be identified.

A point which should be made here is that we feel it would be a big mistake to imagine that we can analyse or model a business as if there were only one hierarchy to be discovered or represented. At the very least, it is wiser to think in terms of a 3-D model. For example, it was suggested in Chapter 2 that there are two main functions of business:

1 to set up ways of achieving the goals of the business;
2 to set up ways of gaining the information necessary to monitor the performance of the processes designed to achieve the goals.

While there must be a close relationship between these major functions, it should be clear that, say, in an engineering firm the ways of achieving its trading goals are probably going to be strongly influenced by engineering concerns. An information system related to the management and control of engineering processes would be strongly influenced by what engineering knowledge tells us we need to know.

It is also true however that, because the engineering firm is trading as a business, there needs to be an information system which reflects a different sort of interest in the activities of the firm, i.e. a business information system. Each of these major activities has its own hierarchies dominated by its own main purposes and interests. Each is informed by a different body of knowledge with its own hierarchy of meaningful parts, yet there are relationships between the hierarchies. It is suggested there are many different systems hierarchies in businesses and other organisations; some of the systems are formal and may be specified in a company manual, while many originate spontaneously and then simply become accepted ways of getting things done.

Systems theory recognises that a complex system can be analysed into smaller meaningful parts, which themselves can often be reduced into even smaller meaningful parts, etc.; these meaningful parts usually consist of sub-systems and resources. This is called a hierarchical perspective, where a complex whole can be reduced into meaningful divisions and subdivisions until no more meaningful subdivisions can be made (*see* Fig. 4.1). The system in question is one which has been set up with the purpose of gaining better management control of the estimating process in a curtain-making business. In Fig. 4.1 there are three meaningful parts:

1 recording job details on the job card;
2 checking the details to ensure they are all correct; and
3 filing the job card when it is returned to the office. Each of these processes can be viewed as sub-systems and are thus parts of the

estimating information system, but other parts of the system should include the resources that the system relies on to achieve its purpose such as the job card itself, the person who does the estimating, and the person (if different) who files the card.

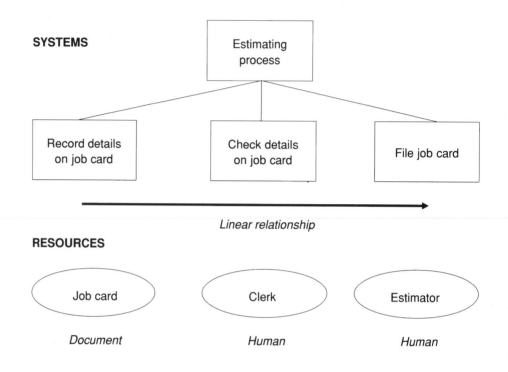

Fig. 4.1   A system and its parts

Some critics think that the systems concept of 'hierarchy' implies a similar motivation to that in the scientific notion of 'reductionism', in which people try to reduce the amount of complexity by simplifying or reducing a structure into simpler parts. However, in systems theory, it is emphasised that reductionism by itself can also reduce our ability to understand the relationship between the parts and the whole or between parts and other parts, thus systems is also concerned with 'holism' (*see* section 4.2.2.2).

The stress on the word 'meaningful' is important for an analyst or manager to preserve a sense of meaning throughout the analysis or the development of a system. Three elements of meaning have already been mentioned:

1   the idea that a system or sub-system should have a purpose;
2   that a part may be a sub-system, which in its turn has a purpose; and
3   that a part may be a resource which of course must have meaning for and within the system.

Strictly speaking, a systems hierarchy implies that every sub-system has a defined place within the structure, but it is worth remembering that when a (sub)system is decomposed into lower level (sub)systems, the relationship between the (sub)systems may represent a tight linear sequence of processes, or it may comprise a looser set of processes that 'belong' together. The idea of a hierarchy is, in practice, more usefully thought of as showing that (sub)systems function within structures of this sort, rather than as structures that represent perfect logical realities in the business world.

The word 'meaningful' in the above paragraph carries with it the advantage that an individual manager or analyst can recognise an activity or pattern of activities in terms of their experience or knowledge of the activity or activities that warrant the definition of a system. The disadvantage is that someone with different experience or knowledge may not immediately be convinced that the activity or pattern of activities is actually meaningful. This is one reason why it is always wise for analysts or managers to check out their perceptions of 'systems' with relevant and knowledgeable observers of and participants in the business context.

EXAMPLE

Suppose there is a small, but up-market, curtain-making business in a London suburb. It may be decided to take a careful look at how the business operates so that it can move towards greater efficiency and effectiveness. In this case, this is crucial since it has limited resources and must use them well. It has one van (a resource) which senior employees use for going out to measure for estimates; the curtain fitter uses it also for delivering fabrics and fittings when the product is finished and sometimes it is used for collecting fabrics, etc. for urgent work (employees are human resources).

If a system were set up to help manage the employee time better, for example, preparing estimates (purpose), it may be possible to start monitoring the estimating process and thus record exactly what is done and what the job entails. For instance, estimating cards (document resource) may be made that enable records (sub-system) of the client's details, the type of job, type of windows (data resources) and who (human resource) actually measured (sub-system) for the job, etc. Once the idea of monitoring the estimating process has been thought of, a start has to be made somewhere and the real interest is in the information (output of the system) that is going to be gained from it, such as whether jobs can be classified into types and sizes and, on average, how long the various ,kinds of jobs take to do. The information gained about how long what sorts of jobs take, etc., will be used to help plan with clients when visits should be made to measure

▶
up because it will be clearer how much time to allocate and when to book the van. Perhaps it will also show just how much this 'free' service is actually costing the business.

This system, not yet computerised, is only designed to monitor a part of the business; it is only one of its activities (i.e. relatively speaking, one of its sub-systems). It therefore fits into a larger whole (relatively speaking, a system). On the other hand, there are meaningful activities which are parts of this sub-system. For instance, the address on the card has to be written (sub-system), and checked for accuracy (sub-system), perhaps there is a line on the card for the agreed time of arrival for the estimate and another line for the actual time of arrival, etc. There is a hierarchy of systems within systems, or of sub-systems within sub-systems, each one with a lower or higher level purpose and a place within a whole.

Note that this is not an estimating system that is concerned about the actual estimating techniques or procedures; it is not designed to produce an estimate. This system is only concerned about helping to manage the process better by providing information about it, as part of the overall management of the business.

A general principle in the theory is that the purpose of a sub-system is to contribute to the goal of the next higher system/sub-system and, thus, has a specific role within it.

4.2.2.2 Holism

This idea can be summed up by the expression, 'the whole is greater than the sum of the parts'. The idea of holism is an antidote to the notion that greater understanding can be gained by simply reducing complex structures into simpler parts; instead, it asserts that only by recognising the whole can the purpose and relationships that a part will have with the whole and with the other parts be seen and understood. If the whole is thought of as representing a 3-D structure as discussed above, then valuable insight into a (sub)system by looking into the holistic relationships of which it is a part can be gained.

Holism means a consciousness that any system or sub-system which is identified within an organisation will almost certainly only be fully understood (i.e. fully analysed) as long as the vertical, horizontal and depth relationships of which it is a part are recognised. *Vertical relationships* are those where a system or sub-system exists in a hierarchy of relationships, with itself being clearly part of a larger hierarchy and where it may also have its own sub-systems and resources as components (as discussed in section 4.2.2.1).

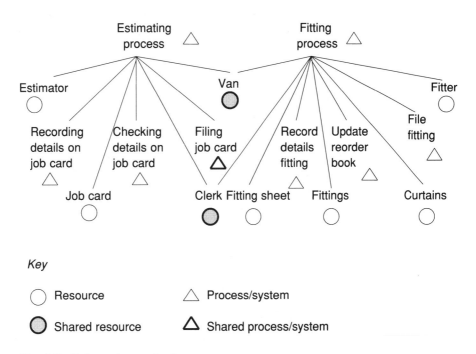

Key

○ Resource   △ Process/system

◉ Shared resource   ▲ Shared process/system

Fig. 4.2 Sub-systems sharing resources

Horizontal relationships are those where a system can be seen as one of a number of components or sub-systems on the same level of a larger system within the same hierarchy. There may be a linear relationship between the sub-system and other sub-systems at its level in the hierarchy where, say it receives an output from one sub-system and provides the input for another; the degree of dependence is usually spoken of in terms of 'coupling'.

A *depth relationship* is where, for example, a system shares one or more of its resources with another system in a parallel/different hierarchy. Systems in depth relationships thus compete with each other for the use (or time) of the resource(s).

For instance, taking the example immediately above, the concept of holism is a reminder that only a part of a whole is being looked at and that some of the resources that are being used in the estimating system may be shared resources. The person doing the estimating, the clerk and the van are all resources that have to be shared with competing systems or activities in the business. The estimator might well have to put down one important job to do a promised estimate because it is important to the business to maintain a flow of work which is initiated by estimates. The clerk has to find extra time in his or her day in order to play a role in the new estimating system. It will be easier to manage the van as a shared resource if the new information on estimating allows better planning and time management.

Note that a particular job may be modelled as a system in which the goal is to provide a complete custom curtain-making service for clients. If so, the estimating and fitting processes would be two of a set of sub-systems that are in a linear relationship to each other. However, because more than one instance of the curtain-making service or system can be in process at the same time, it would be foolish to ignore the fact that a job for one client may be in competition with the job for another. The depth dimension gives a warning that the estimating and fitting sub-systems are only in a linear and non-competitive relationship within the context of one instance or implementation of the system, but when two implementations are running concurrently potential competition has to be managed. Depth relationships not only denote competition between different hierarchies for the same resource(s), but also by different implementations of the same sub-system within a hierarchy.

4.2.2.3 Emergent property

Closely associated with the concept of holism, the 'emergent' property or properties of a system are those properties that can result from the combination of sub-systems and resources to form a system. One of the emergent properties of a system should be the gain(s) expected from it, in other words, the gain would be the desired emergent property. Not all emergent properties, however, are expected or desired. The emergent nature of the properties comes from the realisation that when a number of parts are combined together, so as to produce a desired outcome, it is not always certain what other outcomes might result, or emerge. This is a problem with building complexity and not fully understanding the consequences.

For example, suppose an introduction to 'good management practice' was desired for an organisation that is regarded as having a specialist orientation. The good management practice may be intended to prove to an outside funding body that good accountability is expected of the experts' use of time and it consists of getting the experts to submit a report of their week's activities to the director of the institute. This may seem like a reasonable procedure and, furthermore, it might be thought to encourage greater productivity in the future. However, if the previous work climate had been built on trust and a mutually supportive, collegiate culture, the new approach might be considered in a very negative or competitive light by the experts, leading to mistrust of the management or colleagues, loss of good will and, perhaps, a 'brain drain'.

At a more practical level it can, perhaps, be appreciated that while a report might take a small time to actually type, thinking about what should be in it might take a lot longer. The depth dimension of the holism concept should provide a warning that, in fact, the *reporting system* and the *research system* in which the specialists are now shared resources may be competing for the valuable time of these individuals;

the new reporting system introduces a stress element that was not there before. Competition for resources is a challenge for management but is one which is not always recognised. Both the potentially beneficial and negative aspects of setting up the system might be considered its emergent properties.

Systems thinkers are aware that systems cannot be viewed in isolation and that new systems may produce results not originally envisaged by the designers. The addition of a new (sub)system creates a new set of relationships within a larger context or system and a new set of relationships with (sub)systems in other hierarchies. The consequences of these new sets of relationships may not be known until they *emerge* later.

4.2.2.4 Sub-optimisation

Sub-optimisation can occur when a sub-system is *optimised* without regard to its place and purpose within the larger whole. This would mean that related sub-systems and the greater system of which they are components, would not benefit, or might be harmed by the advantages gained by an optimised sub-system alone. For example, returning to the case of the small curtain-making business, it can be seen (hierarchy and holism) that if the estimating system was optimised to the point where it ignored the competition for human and physical resources by other business demands, it could have a negative impact on the business as a whole. Only higher-level management is able to determine whether an estimate should take priority over a rush production job or whether an estimate should have the use of the van rather than the fitting of an important order. A higher-level view should enable the most effective and efficient use of the vehicle and people for whose time there is competition. Care has to be taken to evaluate what impact the optimisation of one sub-system might have on its vertical, horizontal and depth relationships.

4.2.2.5 Stability and control

Stability, otherwise known as 'homeostasis', is usually achieved by means of control. This word 'homeostasis', which is more common in biology than in the ordinary conversation of business, draws attention to the challenge that living organisms have in responding to constantly changing or hostile environments. There have to be mechanisms that enable an organism to maintain a relatively steady and healthy state when changes in the environment occur. Businesses and other organisations also have to be able to survive and even thrive in competitive and changing environments.

In order to thrive, it is essential for a business to be able to respond to changes which affect it. The changes are detected, and responded to, by the systems over which they have control, and the systems approach assumes that management control (*see* Chapter 3) will actively seek the information that will enable best control of the systems which sustain the business to be maintained. The role or purpose of 'information systems' is to monitor business activities and, perhaps, the environment – through on-line information systems – in which business operates so that managers can make suitable decisions and take appropriate actions to help maintain a steady, healthy and thriving business.

For example, a simple case would be for a toy manufacturing company to monitor the demand for its products by ensuring that an information system provides regular information about the level of orders from customers. Too high a level of production would mean money tied up in dead stock, while too low a level of production would result in lost sales and customers. Monitoring of trends in technology, children's films that are box office hits, competitors' products, lending rates and other environmental factors relevant to the toys sector and business in general is also an important part of management's responsibility in maintaining a viable business (*see* Chapter 3, section 3.2). Homeostasis for that company would mean monitoring current demand, anticipating future demand and fighting to keep healthy order books.

Businesses must avoid being simply reactive to its business environment, otherwise the scope for maintaining stability is reduced to an almost crisis level. Instead it is preferable, as far as possible, to monitor the environment and sales trends, etc., in order to take action at the first signs of change.

4.2.2.6 Law of requisite variety

This phrase means that if a business is to survive or thrive in a competitive or hostile environment then it is necessary for it to ensure that it responds to any forces or factors that have the power to destabilise it. If the role of information systems is primarily to provide information, then clearly they should be designed to monitor all the activities and dimensions of a business that are necessary for full and effective management of it. It is still true, however, that formal information systems, of which computerised systems are a part, tend only to provide management with quantifiable information. Managers should supplement this through good formal and informal communication networks.

For example, in the case of the toy company above, it would not be adequate to solely monitor current sales activity – there is clearly a need to be able to respond to changing trends in toy buying. This might necessitate close monitoring of developments in microchip technology, safety regulations to create new hi-tech toys and to ensure that new creations do not infringe existing safety laws. Up-to-date information about progress of development and production, especially for toys manufactured in the Far East, would be an essential element in the bank of information to do with the quality of the product, etc., in a time-critical business domain such as the toy trade. The requisite variety should include every aspect of information necessary for good management and success of the company.

4.3 USING THE SYSTEMS IDEAS TO GENERATE MANAGEMENT QUESTIONS

At first glance, the systems ideas can seem rather removed from the real world of business, but they have a valuable role in helping promote clear thinking about business activities in their inevitably complex contexts, and in particular, about the management issues of monitoring and control. Since this is a book about the principles of business information systems, emphasis is on the issues of control and the production of information needed for good management. There are three basic assumptions which explain why this approach is useful. It is assumed that all of the systems principles discussed above either have, or should have, validity and real counterparts in an effective and well-run business. It is also assumed that the size and complexity of most businesses make it impractical to start analysing a business by taking a very high-level view and then breaking down this view into more and more levels of detail until the point is reached where all the lower-level activities have been identified.

1 Even though businesses have different purposes, different organisational structures and different styles of management, nevertheless it should be possible to identify all of the systems principles and see their relevance at any/every level and part of a business or organisation.

2 Modelling problems quickly become apparent when attempting to model or analyse complexity beyond understanding. Even the approach adopted here will reveal considerable complexity despite attempts to constrain the process of analysis and modelling to what can be comprehended.

3 By using systems principles it is possible to formulate a set of questions that are applicable at any level of an organisation and that allow a picture to be built of how the organisation functions and how well it can be managed. The important consideration here is that the analysis begins with business-motivated diagnostic questions that are understandable, rather than starting with a complex whole that is manifestly too big and complex to be comprehended. This approach could be compared with constructing a jigsaw puzzle piece by piece, but without the benefit of the final picture as a guide, since at the beginning of the investigation it was not known what the whole picture would look like.

4.3.1 The systems concepts: validity and real counterparts in an effective and well-run business

What does this first assumption mean when the processes of *analysis* and *modelling* are involved? The process of analysis implies the use of some specific criteria in order to get some specific answers; to look for specific things it is necessary to ask specific questions. Important criteria are provided by the systems principles above, and when analysing a business or other organisation, the criteria can be thought of as a set of questions for which answers are sought.

In the process of modelling, either a model can be built to represent the way a business currently attempts to achieve the goals that management sets or, in the case of information systems, how the business is organised to produce the information needed to manage and control the systems within it. Alternatively, a model can be built to represent the way a business *ought to* go about these things. In practice, these two modelling processes tend to be linked and the business practices or systems may have to be modified or changed in order to achieve their goals more effectively and/or efficiently (however *see* Chapter 6, section 6.6). When developing a new computerised system to provide information, it is not desirable to provide a computerised version of the way things are currently done if current practices are shown to be ineffective and/or inefficient.

A new computerised information system could profoundly affect how the business is organised to meet its goals. A model for this purpose although, perhaps, related to current practices should take into account the probable need for:

- new ways of collecting data that will be used for management and control
- a fresh assessment of the information needed for effective management
- a fresh appraisal of the types of information that could be provided for management by a new system
- a realistic assessment of the impact of introducing a new system on the resources that are required by it, for example, where human resources are shared with (or are competed for by) other systems
- dialogue with those who might feel uncertain or negative about the introduction of a new 'system' whether for apparently valid or invalid reasons – the goodwill of staff is an important factor in helping a business achieve the success it desires.

The modelling process in an information system's development can, therefore, have a profound impact on how the business operates and responds to its environment. It should be clear that when talking about information systems a lot more is intended than just computing technology; a number of choices as to how the information should be provided and a search for the best ways are involved, rather than the assumption that computing technology always provides the key.

At this point it is appropriate to introduce the terms 'soft systems' and 'hard systems'. These expressions represent a commonly understood way of making a distinction between a human-biased view of systems in which there is a strong emphasis on the identification of problem issues through consultation with those who might be affected by a proposed system and a technology-biased view which is usually dominated by those who have technical or management influence. The 'soft systems' approach is intended to be suitable for problem situations in which the issues may be fuzzy, or the problem(s) not well defined. Unfortunately, it is not uncommon for managers or computer systems professionals to assume too readily that because a computerised solution *can* be found for a problem, that it *should* be the solution to the problem. Soft systems attempt to clarify the real nature of the problem or problems that are significant in the problem situation and then, through sharpening up our understanding of the problems, appropriate solutions can then be investigated.

Strictly speaking, the soft approach claims to be a 'learning' approach in which the analyst aims to learn about how those who might be affected see the potential problems that might exist in a problem situation. The 'hard approach', by contrast, is said to assume that all that needs to be learnt is how to solve the problem, not what the problem is. These are very simplified statements about the fundamental assumptions made by the hard and soft approaches.

A systems view of any problem situation does not presuppose a hard or soft approach as such. Analysis based on systems principles should help to identify problems, for example, like specific resources being members of more than one system; it is wise to recognise that there are a number of types of institutional forces which have systemic characteristics that influence the behaviour of humans in organisations. Systems in which a human resource, i.e. a person, could be a member at the same time might include:

1 *a power system* in which the purpose is maintenance or advancement of individual power and using the set of power relationships which affect the individual or over which they have some influence;
2 *a social system* in which the responsibilities and advantages of mutually supportive roles are important goals for the individual to maintain or in which the individual has an important part or parts;
3 *one or more functional systems or sub-systems* (within one or more hierarchies) for which the business might have specific goals and objective measures of success and in which the individual has a role or roles;
4 *an information system* (or the proposed development of one) which requires the person to input details, to use the technology in some way or to perform some role(s) in the process of producing the information.

Systems principles, therefore, clearly prompt far wider thinking than just computing or computer-based information systems. The assumption is that businesses and other organisations are, by their nature, characterised not by a single, simple purpose but by a complexity of higher and lower-level purposes and a number of interacting systems hierarchies.

Since systems hierarchies can be assumed to contain a number of levels of sub-systems, it is also assumed that each of the sub-systems too has a role and a purpose within its larger system. It is reasonable to ask, therefore, what their purposes are, how they are achieved and how they are managed for success. The identification of competition for the use of resources through a holistic systems analysis helps to better predict, understand and think through some of the problem issues that might be discovered through the somewhat *ad hoc* methods adopted by the soft systems approach.

If, in analysis, good answers that tell how a business is functioning are required, then good questions are required to obtain the necessary answers. Systems principles help us to know what sorts of questions to ask and what to look for.

4.3.2 The impracticality of analysing a business from a high-level view

While it is true that systems thinking takes a holistic view which means that there should always be an awareness of the larger picture, this does not mean analysis must begin at the highest level of a company or organisation. There are two good reasons to resist such an approach: first, most medium-sized to large businesses are so complex that it would defy the ability of anyone to comprehend or know whether a comprehensive analysis represented all the necessary processes and relationships that exist to achieve all the organisation's goals. It is contended, therefore, that it must pose serious problems if the intention is to build a correspondingly comprehensive model of the information required to manage something that is not fully understood.

Second, it would be a mistake if a business were represented as if it were a single hierarchy of sub-systems, when it is evident that, if seeing an organisation from a holistic systems perspective, the multi-dimensional nature of such human institutions is discovered. The recognition of these dimensions as being pertinent to the understanding of the role and context of sub-systems in an organisation, is the recognition of the systems concept of *holism*. Information systems not only monitor the activities of complex functional hierarchies or systems, they have their own systemic structures as well and have to be considered in terms of their own vertical and horizontal relationships as well as in terms of their depth relationships. The significance of the holistic concept to this approach to business analysis is that it challenges any idea that a business can be analysed in a coherent and comprehensible manner by beginning with a very high-level view. A systemic analysis does not allow a complex entity to be broken down into smaller units of analysis – it requires the understanding of the systems that cause the entity to act or perform the way it does and how these systems interact and affect the parts.

4.3.2.1 Possible steps in analysis

In principle, the analysis of a business or organisation can begin at any point in a hierarchy, as long as some key questions are asked that facilitate:

1 the identification of a system or sub-system;
2 the location of it along its 3-D axes, i.e:
  (a) vertically;
  (b) horizontally; and
  (c) according to its relevant depth relations.

Step one: analysis could begin with a sub-system within whatever type of systems hierarchy is the subject of interest; the important thing is to be able to identify a system or sub-system in the first place. If the systems principles suggest that a system has a purpose and a way of achieving it then we should be able to identify a system/sub-system based on those characteristics, as well as others mentioned above.

Step two: locating the (sub)system in the type of systems hierarchy in which it belongs – it seems possible that a sub-system may belong in/ have a function in more than one hierarchy. Having located the (sub)system in the relevant hierarchy, an attempt should be made to identify it as part of a larger hierarchy, and a sub-system within it and, if so, what other systems may exist at the same level (tightly or loosely coupled).

Step three: careful examination should reveal whether any of the resources (human, document or physical), or sub-systems used by the (sub)system are also used by other (sub)systems.

The holistic principle indicates the ability to correctly identify a (sub)system and its location within the organisation together with the relationships of which it is part. Holism does not seem to require 'getting the whole picture' which is what is implied when systems analysis is approached by starting with a very high-level view of a business, especially if such an approach prevents gaining sufficient clarity and insight into the problem being addressed.

4.3.3 Analysis begins with business-motivated diagnostic questions

If the interpretation of the systems principles are correct then there are clear implications for how the tasks of analysis and design for information systems development might be approached. One of the major implications is that the decision to work within boundaries that are meaningful and that are restricted enough in scope to clearly identify what information is needed to manage the (sub)system and what the vertical, horizontal and depth relationships are for the (sub)system prescribed by the boundary.

The boundaries can be defined in terms of what quantifiable information might be needed to support management decision making or action within specific business contexts; the boundaries represent the purpose which is to provide the required information and the way in which it is currently provided or would be provided. The boundary is of course the (sub)system boundary. This approach to analysis presupposes that good knowledge (*see* section 3.3) will ensure the right or best diagnostic questions are asked. The questions should identify precisely what information is required.

The *diagnostic* element in this approach can be used in the analysis of a current information system (computerised or otherwise) in terms of what (sub)systems and resources are used to produce the information (if indeed the current system can produce it), and what the implications of doing so are in terms of the 3-D holistic model. In the context of design, the diagnostic element can be understood in terms of asking the appropriate questions sufficient to satísfy the requirements of the business for the information necessary to manage it (however *see* sections 8.5–6). Also the systems principles cause questions to be asked about how a proposed information systems development might impact other systems in the depth dimension, for example, in terms of creating new demands on resources, or even making some others redundant (*see holism* and *emergent properties*).

By approaching the analysis through the use of individual questions based on specific needs for management information, it is possible to look at how the 'system' that would produce that information is located within the 'whole'. In this way it is possible to build up a composite picture of a larger, meaningful part of a business through asking a range of diagnostic questions about it. It should also be possible to identify, as a result of such analysis, patterns of organisation and such like that need to be considered in the analysis and design of the information system (*see* Chapter 8).

Because the quality of analysis is, at least in part, determined by the knowledge of the specific business context and of business management in general, this is the main reason that good analysts consult well with those who know the business and with those who work in, or are affected by, the area of the business being analysed.

4.4 A CHECKLIST OF SYSTEMS-MOTIVATED QUESTIONS

4.4.1 Asking what sub-systems are used and how they are organised

Systems are assemblies of parts that are organised in a pattern, that is to say, in a particular way. The parts are usually sub-systems and resources used by the system to achieve its purpose.

In order to produce information there almost always has to be some organised means of getting or producing it. Systems or sub-systems have to be responsible for picking up the details that are needed for the information: sub-system(s) will be needed to process the details and may be needed to present the information in the form that the manager requires. Human, physical and document resources may be required for one or more of these sub-systems.

Identification of (sub)systems means recognising that there is some patterned or organised activity that occurs when some information is required; some of the activities will be contributing as sub-processes (or sub-systems) to deliver the required information. The analysis assumes that by asking diagnostic questions the business is not going to come up with some unique way of delivering the information each time, but that it would just discover what the business would typically do to deliver it.

4.4.2 Asking for information: the purpose of the sub-system

The assembly of parts has an identifiable purpose, and there is a reason for them being assembled in the way they are.

Starting with the idea that a manager needs specific information to assist in making a decision or taking action, then it can be said that the request for information constitutes the purpose of the sub-system that delivers it. This approach allows a diagnosis of the ability of a business to deliver information and to model the activities and resources that are required to provide the information as a complex sub-system. It should be noted that a set of good diagnostic requests for information helps to build a more complete model of how the business provides management information.

4.4.3 The best way of delivering specific information

Each part is affected in a particular way, or ways, by being in the system and if a part is removed its role or function is changed.

A part or component of a system will probably be a resource or a sub-system. In a system that is intended to produce information, resources could include people who are involved in getting details, processing them or producing the information which uses them. Technological resources such as the components of a computer-based system, or document resources such as sales returns sent by a local store to the head office all play a role in information provision. Sub-systems or, more likely, resources may be shared by other systems; if one (sub)system releases a resource that it shares with other (sub)systems, then this would probably affect its use in the context of the other systems.

Sub-systems could also be removed but, if as a result, the purpose of the sub-system changes one might argue that one system has gone and another has been created if the definition of a system or sub-system is primarily in terms of its purpose. The implication of this factor for analysis is not as significant for an initial analysis as it would be for a more detailed study. If an analysis considered alternative possibilities for delivering information, then it might be that the difference between the alternatives exists in choosing between just some relevant sub-systems. An holistic analysis could provide a valuable insight into the impact on the system and the business of the consequences of each choice.

4.4.4 Asking whether a (sub)system has been defined clearly enough

Systems normally produce something, or at least have an effect.

An advantage of the diagnostic approach is that specific information products can be identified so that, on the basis of this criterion, a (sub)system may be identified. If an analysis cannot be thought through, one of the difficulties may be that a (sub)system is being generalised too much by associating its structure and activity with more than one product – or (sub)systems may be identified with parts of a business that are not actually systems at all. To produce information, a system has to have some dynamic qualities.

4.4.5 The scope of analysis and recognition of significant interactions with the (sub)system's environment

Systems have boundaries: inside the boundary should be under the system's control, but outside is beyond the scope of its control.

One of the most difficult aspects of analysis concerns the matter of boundaries. It is assumed that the immediate inquiry is limited in scope by determining the boundary of a system in terms of its purpose. This definition of the systems principle is useful and meaningful and should be seen in the context of the definition of *holism*. An information (sub)system, in these terms, is concerned with returning information (or playing some definable part in it) about some business function or process. The analysis is bound from a depth perspective by ensuring the consideration of processes that belong within one business hierarchy. Within the vertical and horizontal axes a coherent purpose and an information product is sought, and the inquiry is constrained to only those activities that are part of what it takes to deliver the product. A bonus of having a well-defined boundary is that it is possible to examine more carefully the relationships that the (sub)system has with the (sub)systems on its boundary.

Each requirement for information becomes an additional part of the jigsaw as an attempt is made to build a more complete picture of the whole. In other words, the analysis begins with questions or management decisions that can be understood and that result from a knowledge of business – from these single questions models of how the business provides, or could provide, the information it needs in order to monitor its activities will be constructed.

In this approach, the systems concept of a boundary to focus the analysis and give a principled way of tackling the analysis of a complex entity such as a business or organisation is used. It is, of course, possible to use the principle at any level of an organisation but the usefulness of applying this and other systems concepts at different levels should best be determined by what the analyst or manager wants to know.

4.4.6 Whether any known environmental influences affect the performance of the (sub)system

Systems exist within an immediate environment which consists of a set of external influences or factors which can impact on the system, but over which the system has limited or no influence.

The environment, in the case of a system whose purpose is to provide information for management, consists only of those things which are relevant to the system but are not part of it. If a resource used by the information system has to be shared by another (sub)system, the availability of the resource could become a serious management issue since competition for the resource could indicate a problem to be resolved.

The environment of a (sub)system will often consist of the immediate influence of adjacent (sub)systems in the holistic context of the business structure. Less immediate, but a powerful internal environmental factor, can be company policy, written or unwritten which can affect the behaviour of a (sub)system. The environmental influences are outside the immediate control of the (sub)system, even though its performance may affect it to some degree.

The influence of factors outside of the business, that is to say, the external business environmental factors tend to be more directly significant to (sub)systems identified at the higher levels of a hierarchy. Obviously it would be short-sighted to analyse or design an information system without regard to the environmental factors that are relevant to its performance at its different levels of operation.

4.4.7 How the (sub)system relates to the (sub)system of which it is a part

Hierarchy is the 2-D vertical and horizontal structure of a single system and its sub-systems. The vertical dimension makes us conscious that a particular (sub)system within the hierarchy may serve and be dominated by the purpose of its next higher system. It is recognised too, that the (sub)system may have its own sub-systems that it dominates. The horizontal dimension, which refers to how sub-systems at the same level relate to each other, alerts us to the possibility of there being sub-systems which directly or indirectly influence each other. It seems that the only means we have of identifying a particular systems or systemic hierarchy and the sub-systems within it is by recognising its purpose and the purposes of its component parts. It means that it is necessary to classify different sorts and levels of (sub)systems according to meaningful and logical criteria which, unfortunately, in the 'real world' is not always an easy task.

4.4.8 How the performance of the sub-system is influenced by sub-systems that interact in the depth dimension

Holism takes us further than the principle of hierarchy in appreciating that (sub)systems are located within a 3-D business context. If one of the main aims in analysis is to understand a (sub)system better, such as how effectively and efficiently it performs or could perform in the business, then it is necessary to take a holistic view which means that we should actively examine the vertical, horizontal and depth relations for the (sub)system we have identified because these relations can affect the performance of the system (*see* Chapter 8).

4.4.9 How the (sub)system might impact on the business or other (sub)systems in unanticipated/unplanned ways

Some emergent, or resulting, properties of a (sub)system may be predictable if the holistic context of a system is well understood, however there should always be an awareness that when systems are introduced into an organisation extra complexity results. New and changing patterns of organisational relationships can cause unexpected results, some good and some bad. Good analysis should explicitly consider any direct or indirect spin-offs or changes that are not planned for but could result from the introduction of the (sub)system.

4.4.10 Information (sub)systems that assist business stability

The only way to ensure that the business maintains its healthy state is for it to monitor its position and activities and thus exercise good management control. When undertaking a business analysis we should ask how the business does this: how is it organised so that appropriate management information is produced in order to ensure the business remains relatively stable(homeostasis) in changing trading conditions and that management control is maintained? Business knowledge will often help to recognise that a business must have some means of attracting and monitoring demand for its products or services, unless the company has a 'captive market'. Business training or experience stresses that certain kinds of (sub)systems *must* exist if a business plans to be successful; a successful business usually exercises a managed stability which includes information systems to support management in the task.

4.4.11 Information (sub)systems sufficient to deliver the required range of information

The law of requisite variety is a reminder of the need to check and see whether an information system produces the range of information that would be sufficient for the managers to effectively manage the business. Consideration should be given to the existence of a variety of information sources, formal or informal, that may supplement information produced by a computerised information system. Not all information required by business managers will best be provided by such a system. This criterion thus prompts a look for a minimum range of information that should be available for good management.

4.5 SUMMARY

This chapter has illustrated more fully the basic systems characteristics first discussed in Chapter 2 and it has complemented those ideas with other key concepts that are considered part of *systems thinking*. There is a slight revision of some of the fundamental principles with the aim of increasing their usefulness, particularly in their application to analysis and modelling of information systems (manual or computer-based) in complex business institutions.

The use of systems principles, as a set of ideas which permits talk of business activities (or processes) in a way which makes sense from an information systems point of view, has been discussed. Systems thinking seems to allow the use of a diagnostic approach to business processes and business management, which constrains the scope of analysis to what an intelligent manager or analyst can understand, and it promises significant insight into how effectively or efficiently business or information processes are, or can be performed. The diagnostic approach is particularly valuable as a management technique and gives a strong management bias to business systems analysis. Taking this approach avoids the excesses of reductionism in which the principle is to break complex entities down by analysis into simpler parts; rather the onus on the analyst is to build an understanding of complex business situations through synthesising the results of diagnostic analyses.

Chapter 8 focuses on business process analysis and modelling and takes further some of the ideas contained in this chapter. The ideas expressed here are also the guiding principles of our approach in the chapters on business data and process modelling (*see* Chapters 6 and 7).

QUESTIONS 1 The word 'system' is used in many contexts and according to the context it has different senses. In this chapter we have taken a definition of system that we believe to be relevant to both management control and information systems because both have to be goal-orientated. Describe the essential characteristics of a system (as understood in this chapter) and consider how you could apply them to:

(a) Checking out a book in a library (from the borrower's point of view)
(b) Monitoring loans in a library, and
(c) The role of 'mother' in a given cultural context.

2 The ideas of 'holism' and 'hierarchy' are key systems concepts because they are important correctives to the scientific idea that we can gain better understanding of complex things by breaking them down into smaller and smaller parts until we reach a level of simplicity that we can explain or understand. What sorts of things would holism and hierarchy suggest that we could miss by solely taking a scientific (i.e. reductionist) approach?

3 Explain what is meant by 'emergent properties' and why this idea is an important one for managers to be aware of.

4 The concept of sub-optimisation is one which could give the impression that a sub-system is not performing well. How could it be that if a sub-system does perform well we can speak of sub-optimisation? Explain.

5 The law of requisite variety could be applied for example, if you were to design a performance car for a discerning driver. Assuming the driver is effectively managing a technological resource, describe how the law could be applied to enable him or her to manage the resource well.

6 An important idea in systems thinking and one which is crucial for analysis and modelling is the concept of a boundary. Recognising and defining the scope of the analysis is crucial for us if we are to control and understand the focus of our inquiry. Consider for example a natural system such as the human circulatory system. Suppose a patient came to you with what appeared to be symptoms of high blood pressure you could ask a number of diagnostic questions to perhaps determine some possible causes and eliminate others. What questions might you ask if you assume that the following factors affect the performance of the heart:

(a) heart rate is regulated by electrochemical messages sent from the brain;
(b) heart rate can be affected by the chemical composition of the blood (e.g. high concentrations of sugar, salt, etc. from food processing have to be extracted if they are not being dealt with properly by other organs);
(c) heart rate can be affected by how much resistance has to be overcome in pumping blood through the arterial system;
(d) heart rate can be affected by the performance of the heart muscle?

Each question asked would need to tease out information relevant to different systemic aspects of relevance to the heart's performance. By restricting the scope of each question we can focus on, say, whether the cause may be more stress related (i.e. which might affect brain activity) than physical health related (i.e. which might affect heart muscles).

7 A lecturer, therapist, detective, indeed almost any worker with professional skills seems to 'suffer' from what seems to be an increasing requirement to spend valuable time on 'admin'. Administration often includes monitoring of activities and the sending of the 'reports' to interested parties. If you were a hospital administrator trying to understand the working environment of, for example, the physiotherapy department, how would you represent a physiotherapist's work performance in terms of the concept of 'depth' as a dimension of *holism*?

8 Homeostasis and stability have been discussed as desirable qualities for the survival of a (sub)system. How does the idea of 'stability' in a business-related system square with the need of businesses to change and evolve in a dynamic trading environment?

BIBLIOGRAPHY   Checkland, P., *Systems Thinking, Systems Practice*, John Wiley and Sons, 1981.

Clarke, D.D., and Crossland, J., *Action Systems*, Methuen and Co, 1985.

Harry, M., *Information Systems in Business*, Pitman Publishing, 1994.

Jackson, M.C., *Systems Methodology for the Management Sciences*, Plenum, 1991.

Strategic Managment in the Social Economy, ICOM Ltd and CAG Management Consultants Ltd and the Co-operatives Research Unit of the Open University.

Systems Behaviour, (3rd Edn) Open University and Paul Chapman Publishing, 1981.

CHAPTER 5

An introduction to the relational database management system

5.1 INTRODUCTION

In Chapter 1 it was pointed out that if a business person wants to undertake a business review in which he or she takes a thorough look at how the business has been performing, they will need information about the performance of major functional areas in business – marketing, production, people and finance. If a business is to operate effectively it clearly needs to monitor the states or success of its activities. It must keep checks on things like the levels of resources such as raw materials and products and keep up-to-date information on all financial income and outgoings, etc.

Information about all these things has to be gathered from data found in documents and reports which can either be paper-based, computer-based or a combination of both. Probably most of the information that is regularly used and maintained by business is generated from their databases. Businesses and other organisations have for years stored important business data in databases but, despite their importance, non-specialists have tended to see them as something of a mystery. Successful design of information systems needs considerable business knowledge and input – much of it can only be given by managers and other decision makers. Their intelligent involvement, especially at the conceptual and higher levels of business analysis and design, can therefore have significant benefits for the process.

In the following chapters an introduction will be given to some of the techniques that are used to analyse a business in order to discover *what* data needs to be stored and *how* it should be stored and organised to support decision-making activity – in other words, to support a company's need for accurate and trustworthy information. The technology that underlies most information systems is a database management system: the basic principles of the relational model on which the relational database management system is based will be explained, as will why it is called a *management* system. Finally, some of the practical implications of using computer-based systems will be discussed.

5.2 THE RELATIONAL DATABASE MANAGEMENT SYSTEM (RDBMS)

The RDBMS is probably the most common type of database management system used in the business world today. Other models of database management systems, for example, hierarchical and network, have been more common in the past, and there are newer approaches – such as the object-oriented model – currently being tried but, for now, the RDBMS is a proven, effective standard for general purpose use. A serious problem with the hierarchical and network models is that the organisational characteristics of the business become incorporated into how the database resource is structured. This means that any organisational changes in the company forces changes in, and redesign of, the data resource. The potential of object-oriented database management systems to play a significant role in business information systems depends upon whether the success of object-oriented programming can be usefully extended to the higher level challenges of data modelling and database management.

A relational database management system assumes that:

1 *a world of information* may potentially be required by a business;
2 there exists a *database engine* (or information system) that is able to translate (management) requests for information into logical instructions to modify the structure of the data resource into actions that add, delete or view data in the data stores, and also into instructions to produce reports and other documents which use the data in some manipulated form as information. The database engine works on mathematical or logical principles based on extensions of *set theory* called relational algebra and relational calculus and relies for its success on the data resource being appropriately structured; and
3 there is a *data resource* which is arranged into logical sets of data that have meaning for the business, and which can be effectively used by the database engine.

5.2.1 A world of information

It might be possible, but it would be difficult in the extreme, to develop a complete list of all possible information requirements for many, if not most, contexts in which information systems are used. In the past, the limitations on what information could be provided by the information system were often determined by the technology and the design of the database component. A relational model can provide almost any required information, in principle, provided the data are available in the database component, and the structure is well designed. The information requirements should consist of information required for management reports, decisions and other monitoring or control activities within the business.

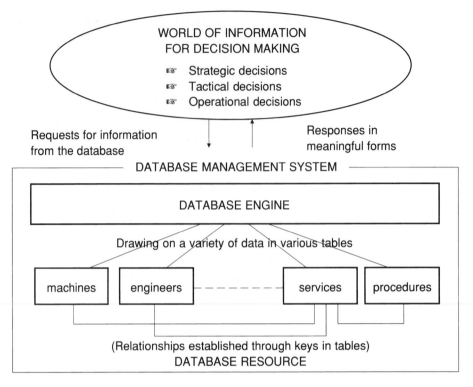

Fig. 5.1 Outline of an information system

5.2.2 A database engine

The relational database management system can take a request for information and then produce the required response by finding the relevant details in the data resource component. The 'engine' for most business managers is like a black box because they are concerned with *what* information is obtained, while computer or 'systems' professionals are usually responsible for *how* the information is obtained. In this introduction it is sufficient to note that it is very common now for systems specialists to use a logical language called SQL (Structured Query Language) with which they can 'talk' to the engine and precisely define what information they want or what modifications they want to make to the data, for example, to update a customer's account. SQL can be used by itself but it is commonly embedded in procedural database languages used in business computing.

5.2.3 The data resource is designed on mathematical principles

The data modelling techniques are a must if the information system is to work well and without problems because it is through knowledge of the business and intelligent use of the techniques that the data resource is organised into sets (called *tables*) that are suitable for use by the engine. The engine is designed to operate on mathematical/logical principles, requiring logical communication from the people who use the system and a logically designed data resource upon which to act.

5.3 INFORMATION: THE PRODUCT OF A RELATIONAL DATABASE

In Chapter 3 information was defined as consisting of facts or data that have meaning and relevance:

- to the person who needs them;
- to the role or roles that the person has in the business;
- to the decisions or acts that might depend on them; and
- that have the power to precipitate change.

Single facts or data, or even a single group or set of facts (such as the set of personal details that describe a passport holder) are often insufficient by themselves to provide information. Information can be the product of summarising facts, for instance, to see how a product group has sold over a certain period of time, or relating data to each other in various ways (such as when we can relate a specific passport holder's details to the details that relate to the document itself) or filtering out many facts to find some specific information. There are many sorts of processes that data can undergo in order to produce something that we can call information.

The relational database engine permits sets of data to be related and manipulated so as to produce a variety of types of information. In the following section the idea behind creating relationships between the sets of data will be explained and, therefore, how it is that this database model has the power to produce a vast range of information from a well designed but relatively lean data resource.

The relational model was the first database model to be based on clear principles. In essence, the model is quite simple and it takes into account the human ability to classify our world into meaningful groupings, while at the same time it requires a logical rigour that enables the logic to be translated into the mathematical world of the computer. What this means is that all the facts used in business which indicate the state of resources, such as the stock of products, how many hotel rooms are booked/vacant, etc., or how business activities are performing, such as whether sales trends appear to have been affected by a national advertising campaign, can be grouped together. Having grouped the facts into appropriate sets, such as the product, booking and perhaps invoice details, the relevant details can be sought and calculated with mathematical precision.

The relational model is explained only in outline in this text as an aid to understanding its basic characteristics. There are, perhaps, two sorts of considerations that have to be borne in mind as this topic is considered.

The first is that the mathematical or logical ideas which are the basis for the model are not particularly new but they represent a principled way of thinking and of representing aspects of reality such as the business world. The second consideration is that databases are part of the practical and essential life of businesses and organisations; any model to be used in this context has to be able to offer what the real world wants. There are, therefore, strong theoretical and practical reasons for understanding how and why this model has achieved its leading status today.

5.3.1 The language of relational logic

The language of relational logic allows us to talk about or describe someone or something in the real world by defining that person or thing by its attributes, i.e. all the elements of detail that make the thing what it is. A practical example of this would be if we look at a passport (*see* Fig. 5.2).

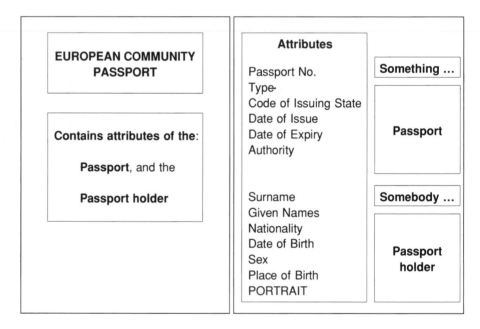

Fig. 5.2 The language of relational logic applied to a passport

In the example of the passport, it can be seen that, although the passport itself is designed to contain all of the attributes or details noted above (and more), they can be separated into two logical groupings or sets. One set refers to attributes that are primarily relevant only to the passport, describing only things to do with its role as a document. The other set refers primarily to the person who holds the passport, describing only things to do with the person, that is to say, the person doesn't expire on a certain date, neither does the document have a surname:

Passport	Passport no., Type, Code of issuing state, Date of issue, Date of expiry, Authority
Passport holder	Surname, Given names, Nationality, Date of birth, Sex, Place of birth, PORTRAIT

Each set of data in relational terms is called a relation (or *entity relation*) and relations are represented as two dimensional tables. The attributes are presented along the top as titles or headings of columns, while each row consists of the set of values appropriate to each passport or passport holder. However, if each of these sets of attributes were to form the basis of a database table then, although it would be possible to describe or identify each separate entity, the information that they are related would be lost. Therefore it is necessary to include within the logic the fact that passport holders are related to particular passports by including another type of relation which is called a *relationship relation*. The contents of the sets are determined to allow the relationship to be established through data modelling, which is covered in Chapters 6 and 7. To illustrate how a relationship relation works consider the examples shown in Fig. 5.3.

Passport holder

Surname	Given names	Nationality	Dobirth	Sex	Pobirth	PORTRAIT	Passport No.
Smith	Allison	British	2-3-56	F	Hull	Photo	57092341
Smith	Brian Fred	British	14-6-45	M	Brighton	Photo	*46233980*
Smith	Bryce	British	1-4-49	M	London	Photo	13289708

Passport

Passport No.	Type	Code state	Date issue	Date expiry	Authority
24578595	P	GRB	5-7-92	5-7-02	Gt Britain, etc
46233980	P	GRB	1-2-91	1-2-01	Channel Islands
20357955	P	GRB	2-8-93	2-8-03	Gt Britain, etc

Fig. 5.3 Two related relations!

The example above shows a table (representing an entity relation) for *passport holder* and one for *passport*, each with three sets of values in rows, called *tuples* in relational jargon, under the column headings (representing the attributes). This time we have included the attribute Passport No. with the Passport holder attributes. On the basis of the shared value in the common column, that is, Passport No. 46233980 we can establish that Brian Smith, who was born in Brighton, has a Passport with the Passport number 46233980 and that it expires on 1 February 2001.

In the database resource, all the values in the relevant row in Passport Holder and all the values in the corresponding row in Passport represent the same information that can be found in the document: Brian Smith's passport. The relationship relation was established through the common column Passport No., and specifically through the shared value 46233980.

The relational model has so much potential because so many relationships between individual data or sets of data can be represented within the logical framework of relational algebra or relational calculus. The case of the passport can, for example, be represented in relational algebra as something like a union of two sets where each has a common member (Passport No.). If the question is asked: 'When does Brian Smith's passport expire?' all the data needed to provide the information for the answer can be found in the union of the two sets. Relational algebra and relational calculus provide the basis for a complete array of logical operations that make it possible to create an almost endless variety of relationships between the data tables held in the data resource.

Because the database engine, which performs all these operations on the data resource, only responds to logical requests for information and logical instructions to change the contents, it means that it is necessary to know the logic to communicate with it. Examples of the sort of logic required are given below.

5.3.2 Relational logic: the key to working with the database resource

With the aid of some simple examples it is possible to show how the logical languages of relational algebra, and its working cousin SQL, are used to get information or make changes to the database tables. The above illustration of the passport is used. First, a quick translation of terms that are equivalent are given:

Relational algebra	SQL	Relational model
Data file	Table	Relation (or entity relation)
Field name	Column heading	Attribute
Record	Row	Tuple

The relational algebra (RA) terms are used for the illustrations which follow in order to be consistent. But before the logical operators can be used, certain assumptions have to be made known:

- the fields and files which contain the data we need must be known
- if the information needed is separated into related data files, then the names of the files involved need to be known
- once the names of the related files are known, the *common field(s)* through which the relationship is established also have to be known
- the desired structure of the request needs to be known.

1 **Information required – a list containing the names of all passport holders with their passport numbers.**

Logical operator: 'projection' which typically lists out the contents of fields:

Project GivenNames, Surname, PassportNo (passport holder): which reads 'List out the contents of the fields listed, in the data file called 'passport holder''.

Gives:	Allison	Smith	57092341
	Brian Fred	Smith	46233980
	Bryce	Smith	13289708

RA form:
   proj <list of field names> (<file name> or <result of RA expression>)

SQL form:
   SELECT <list of column headings>
      FROM <table>

2 **Information required – the passport details for all those passports authorised by the Channel Islands.**

Logical operator: 'selection' which includes only those records that meet conditions specified by value(s) in a field:

Select authority = 'Channel Islands' (passport): which reads 'List out the contents of any records where the value 'Channel Islands' is found in the field 'authority', in the data file 'passport''.

Gives: 46233980   P   GRB   1-2-91   1-2-01   Channel Islands

RA form:
   sel <condition> (<file name> or <result of RA expression>)

SQL form:
   SELECT <all column values>
      FROM <table>
      WHERE <condition>

3 **Information required – the names of all those passport holders whose passports were authorised by the Channel Islands.**

Logical operators: natural join, project, and select. 'Natural join' joins records in more than one file on the basis of a common field name where the values in that field match:

Project GivenName, Surname (*Select* Authority = 'Channel Islands' (passport)

Join passport holder: which reads 'List out the 'given name' and 'surname' of any 'passport holders' whose 'passport' was issued by the 'Channel Islands' 'authority''.

Gives: *Brian Fred Smith*

RA form:

> proj <fields> (sel <condition> (<data file relevant to the selection>) join <data file relevant to the projection>)

> Note that the common field (PassportNo) is left implicit in this formulation.

SQL form:

> SELECT <list of column heading>
>   FROM <table-x, table-y>
>   WHERE <table-x.common column = table-y.common column>
>   AND <condition>

Note that the common column is precisely specified but the term 'join' itself is only implied by the formulation.

There are many operators and many combinations of logical expressions that can be included in a request or instruction to the relational database engine. The three illustrations given above serve only to introduce you to the type of communication that is possible. The potential of the RDBMS to produce a range of information that is sufficient to meet business demands is great. It is possible to create new queries to satisfy new or ad hoc management requirements for information, because most queries could be expressed in a logical way. But without a good knowledge of what is in the data resource and its structure, plus a good knowledge of how to express queries logically, it would be difficult to exploit the full potential of a relational database management system.

The challenge here is not so much a technical one as a human one since the technology is capable of delivering most of what managers and other decision makers might want; most managers would find it time-consuming to have to learn the logic needed to interrogate the data resource on an ad hoc basis. The usual pattern of use is for computer professionals to provide managers with easy access to standard types of query, say through menu options, while writing queries in a logical form for individuals as necessary.

There are other methods of querying or updating databases, such as using some of the more software specific built-in commands or by using a technique called query-by-example. Many database software products have similar commands, and different software products may include similar forms of query-by-example, but it seems there is more attention being paid to SQL as a standard than to alternative techniques at present.

5.4 THE MANAGING ROLES OF THE RDBMS

We have seen that the database management system has an important role in taking requests for information and providing responses but this is only one of its important jobs. The database management system must have the facilities to:

- set up and maintain a data resource
- provide a programming environment and other facilities to build applications
- make sure the details it contains are trustworthy
- control what authority people have to use the system.

5.4.1 Setting up and maintaining the data resource

The data resource will consist of a number of tables of data. Each table has to be created as a structured computer file, much the same as creating columns with headings in a notebook to keep friends' addresses and telephone numbers in one place by the phone.

Name	Address	Telephone
Jenny	15 Main Street	0498
Simon	12 Arbutt's Lane	0223
Annie	95 Long Road	0223

Fig. 5.4   Example: friend's telephone book

Having acquired a suitable book, ruled it up and put headings on the columns, the structure of a document that is functioning as a database has been created. The 'address book' will only work well if the right sorts of things (data) are put into the columns, so if the telephone numbers are put in the 'name' column and vice versa the usefulness of the book will be reduced. When the lines for the column are ruled how much space should be left for each type of entry, such as for each friend's 'address' must be considered.

Creating a database table is a similar sort of task but when working with computers a little more precision about what is wanted is necessary, as is the need to know about their limitations; for instance, computers won't write a name in the margin if it is longer than the space allocated to 'name'. Once the table has been created and the necessary columns have been specified, the computer needs to be told what sort of data is to go in the columns (for example, numbers, alphabetic characters, dates, etc.) and an appropriate amount of space has to be allocated for the data needed to be put in each column.

When setting up the application for people to enter details into tables, it is possible to tell the computer to only accept the right sort of details for the columns. This is useful since it prevents some mistakes being made. On the other hand if the columns are not wide enough, then a person's full name or address may not fit in it and that can cause problems.

Changing business circumstances or a mistake in the initial analysis of the business data may mean that a new column has to be added or some *changes made in the structure of the database tables*. Usually, such changes can be made without major disruption of the data resource. Since the tables represent logical and discrete entities, there need not be any fear that changes in the structure of the company or in information requirements are going to necessarily influence the majority of the database tables. However, some changes would probably be needed in the development of new programs or reports to support changed managerial requirements for information.

Databases which are used by more than one person at the same time need to be sophisticated enough to prevent different business processes interfering with each other when they involve the same elements of the data resource. Different database products offer different degrees of sophistication but the essence of the challenge is that if, say, a bank processes a withdrawal from a customer's account then it should not be possible for another process to perform another transaction on the account at the same time, or in the wrong sequence. After all, if a person relies on a salary being available before paying a large bill and the large bill payment is processed first then he or she might end up in the red, which might happen if the processes had to fight for the customer's details at the same time or if they were processed in the wrong order. The answer to this sort of problem is to lock competing processes out while one is acting on the data.

Locking can be managed in different ways. One way of locking other processes out is to allow only one process at a time to access a particular table or tables that are related to a particular process, such as to produce information or to modify values or details in the tables. Keeping competing processes from accessing a whole table is not always necessary, so the database management software may permit single rows or specific columns only to be the subjects of locking; other processes are not barred from accessing other data, thus ensuring more efficient use of the data resource.

If access is just for getting information rather than changing any details, the system may allow more than one process to look at the data, that is, to read it, at once. Busy databases, where there is often competition for areas of the data resource, may experience instances where the competition between processes for the same data creates stalemates or deadlocks, where processes shut each other out. In such cases the database management system or, sometimes the application programs, will be designed to resolve the problem.

5.4.2 Building applications

An *application* is the term used when using a database, spreadsheet or other type of package for some (business) purpose. A *stock control system* is an example of a package which a company may want to use for:

- keeping track of what stock is on order
- tracking what stock comes from which supplier
- keeping track of how much stock is currently held
- tracking where stock is being held
- recording how much is committed, say, to a customer, etc.

The stock control system may also be used to get information for management reports that summarise the movement of certain types of stock or perhaps for identifying some areas in which stock appears to disappear. In a different context, a patient information system may be an application in a clinic or hospital in which all sorts of administrative and medical staff may enter details about the patient's treatment, and require information about them.

Relational database software packages usually provide a database programming language, application development aids and SQL or something similar. Programs are usually needed to create menu systems, reports, and other functions (such as obtaining data from bar code scanners) that make communication possible between the database and the real world.

Application development aids may help relatively inexperienced people to create simple applications without the need to program. They can also help experienced programmers to create applications quickly. Either way, a serious application takes a lot of serious thought and knowledge. Libraries of code and examples of programs in books are all helpful and may save time, but even with good programming skills, the final outcome is determined by knowing the business, understanding good management, knowing what information people really need and knowing how to communicate clearly with those who will use the application. In fact, it can be argued that good database applications are built by knowing as much about the people who will use the technology as about the technology itself.

5.4.3 Ensuring a trustworthy data resource

The information gained from a database can only be as trustworthy as the data that are used to support it. It is very important, therefore, that database management systems can ensure the resource is as accurate and dependable as possible. One kind of trustworthiness relates specifically to data that are entered into the resource, which is usually called *integrity*. Integrity checks can come in three common forms.

5.4.3.1 Entity integrity check

This check makes sure that for each new record, i.e. each new set of values, that is entered into a table, the value by which it can be distinguished from all others (i.e. the primary key value) must be included. The reason is that if the key is missing there is no way of locating the record (i.e. that instance of the relation). For example, if all the details of a particular passport were included except for the passport number, then it would be impossible to know to which passport the details belonged.

5.4.3.2 Referential integrity check

When different tables are related through the values in a common column, in one of the tables the column will contain the primary key (i.e. the values will identify each instance of the entity represented by it), for instance, each passport in the passport table is identified by the passport number. If any other tables contain those values in a column, those values are known as a foreign key because they are included to link to the records in the first table. The check consists of ensuring that the foreign key values really exist in the primary key column of the first table; for example, when a new passport holder's details are added to the table of passport holders, the passport number must refer to a passport whose details are already kept in the passport table.

5.4.3.3 Data-type integrity check

This type of integrity check was hinted at earlier when it was said that when programs are designed for entering data into a database, it is often possible to ensure that the computer detects when wrong types of data are entered by mistake. Data-type integrity should ensure that only the right type of data are entered into the right columns of a table. For example, the passport expiry column in the passport table should only allow dates to be put in it. More precise checks might ensure that only dates within a limited range could be accepted.

5.4.3.4 Backing-up and recovering data

The backing-up and recovering of data in the data resource is another aspect of trustworthiness. If a technical failure were to cause the loss of all the data held in a data resource, then it would be comforting for us to know that the data had been backed up and the details could be recovered. However, if, say, a bank's databases failed, it would not be so comforting to learn that backups are made only once every week. There might be a gain because there have been several withdrawals since the last backup or else, perhaps, a salary cheque was paid in since the backup and thus leaves the account holder short of money.

Backups and logs (recordings of all transactions since the last backup) have to be made as often as the kind of information system or application requires. Virtually all database management systems intended for use in larger business or industrial applications have facilities for backing-up and recovering data. Without such facilities the data resource could not be trusted to contain current, relevant data following a system failure.

5.4.3.5   Security

Security is another important aspect of trustworthiness of the data resource. Even in the case of a small information system on an individual PC, it may be a good idea to protect the system from prying eyes. One way of doing this is to protect the information system by allowing people to have access only if they have a password.

5.4.3.6   Controlling who uses the system

Password controls are useful, but experienced people who are determined to get into a system will usually manage to either discover the password or find a way around it. The controls should stop opportunists, provided the authorised users of the system don't make it too easy by leaving their machine or terminal unattended, or by leaving their password on a piece of paper in a drawer, or such like. When the wrong people get access to private or confidential data there is no guarantee that it will not be changed or simply, information will become known to people who have no right to know it.

Larger information systems usually have *different levels of access*. Those with the most authority have supervisory rights; not only can they change the structures of the tables and the values contained within them, but they can also determine who else has access to what. Access privileges are often associated with the need of an individual employee's need to know or change data in the database. A manager or other employee may only need to know about certain attributes of a person or thing, and may only be given access privileges to the relevant columns in the tables that they need to use. When people are given only part of the data resource to use or see, this is called a *view*; it is just like looking at a landscape of data through binoculars, only seeing part of it at a time. In this case the binoculars are fixed on a certain part of the landscape.

Databases that contain very sensitive information might be considered untrustworthy if passwords and views are considered to give insufficient protection from unauthorised people. Another facility that may be provided is the ability of the database management system to *encrypt*, or scramble the contents of the data resource, so that even if someone tries to get the data in an unauthorised way, the information they get will be scrambled. Only the right people with the right authority will be able to get information in its proper form.

5.5 DATABASES, COMPUTERS AND COMMUNICATIONS

It is assumed that relational database management systems are computer-based systems and that the RDBMS will exploit the computing technology by capitalising on its advantages.

5.5.1 Benefits that computers bring to database management systems

- They calculate quickly.
- They are good at mathematical and logical tasks.
- They are good at sorting data.
- They are good at representing numerical (and statistical) data in graphical form.
- They can be potentially or actually part of information or communication networks.

5.5.1.1 Speed of calculation

One of the reasons that many businesses have for employing computers is that many tasks can be done more quickly and accurately than if humans do them. In fact it would be very difficult indeed to do some tasks without using computers. For example, in large databases, such as those used by building societies and banks, customer accounts have to be kept up-to-date and statements sent out to all their customers. Without computers, the volume of work required to keep pace with all the transactions would be more than bank staff could manage. The ability of computers to work at high speed on large volumes of repetitive work is thus an advantage RDBMSs capitalise on.

5.5.1.2 Good at mathematical and logical tasks

In addition to the way in which the relational model can tap into the logical attributes of computers, the database management system also provides the mathematical facilities that allow columns of figures to be totalled, averaged, etc. Also, sorting operations which databases use extensively to update and search database tables are heavily mathematically-based, thus these strengths of computers make them the ideal technology for such applications. These are everyday business tasks that may need to be performed on the contents of a data resource and it makes sense for the computer that stores and manages the data to be used to do them. For example, if an invoice is sent out requesting payment so many days after the date on it, then the computer can calculate when such invoices are due for payment and *automatically issue* 'gentle' reminders, serious reminders or final demands if no record of payment is received. The computer is used to calculate and it can be programmed to do many tasks automatically, making decisions based on simple logical conditions.

5.5.1.3   Good at sorting data

Each time data are entered into a database table they are usually entered as the need arises; therefore, the order in which they are first stored tends to be random. For example, if it is important to have a list of customers in a certain area, in alphabetical order, the database management system can deliver such a list quite efficiently by using an index on the surname and/or other columns, and the contents of the table can then be represented as if all the customers with their details are in alphabetical order. The index provides a link between the records which are entered in a random order and the alphabetical order of names requested.

There is a number of different sorting techniques that have been developed in order to improve efficiency. When database tables become large, with perhaps millions of rows of data, where there may be many columns of data per table, the time taken to physically sort through the contents of the table could be considerable but such a task would be unthinkable if computers were unavailable.

5.5.1.4   Good at communicating numerical and statistical data

Recently, there have been increased expectations of computers. In the PC and mini-computer worlds computers are being given enhanced abilities to communicate with their users. One of the important qualities of 'information' is that it communicates well with the person who needs it. It is possible with some relational database software to represent trends and other numerical or statistical information in graphical form. It is also true that the numerical information can now often be more easily exported from database software and then imported into a spreadsheet for additional processing and better presentation.

5.5.1.5   Databases in communication

An almost hidden dimension of the database world is that many information systems regularly interact with others. National and international communications networks provide a hidden infrastructure into which are linked many databases. Sometimes a database system may include a central data resource and facilities, with distributed elements in separate locations where most activity is expected in relation to those elements of the data resource. In other cases, especially in the financial and banking world, financial data and information are rapidly transmitted across the world, with one information system updating another with, say, the latest trading position on a stock market, or a currency transaction, and so on.

The combination of communications and database technology have also given rise to facilities such as those provided by automatic teller machines, and more recently, the cash back option when paying with a cash card at supermarkets. We can look at what happens in database terms when using an automatic teller machine. First, a card is inserted and the machine checks to see if it is the right sort of card and that it is valid. Second, the machine asks for the Personal Identification Number, which is the password to be keyed in. Next it checks that the password is correct. Once the machine (or database management system) has checked the authority to access details of the bank account, it can then be asked for a current balance (information), a mini statement which details the most recent transactions (also information) or other options such as withdrawing cash with, or without a receipt. If cash is drawn out twice in one day the database will be able to show the second time that the limit has been reduced by the previous amount. Everything that the machine is able to tell about any transactions and the state of the account is information that has been requested or needed. The automatic teller machines are linked to a central database system that is updated daily via communication links.

A single PC can access remote databases through the use of a modem and, with telephone banking, simple transactions can be made through the use of a telephone handset. Access to, and use of, databases is often far nearer than is realised, as businesses like banks reach beyond the limits of the physical space of high street premises and the limits of regular banking hours, to give 24 hour services, some of which can be from the customers' own homes. These are some of the more obvious applications; successful business opportunities have been made possible through the powerful combination of database and communications technologies.

5.5.2 Limitations of computers in database management systems

- They are relatively inflexible and lack initiative.
- It is easier for people to adjust to them, than the other way around.
- Their limitations may only become slowly apparent.

5.5.2.1 Computers are relatively inflexible and lack initiative

There is a big difference between the detailed and precise workings of computers and the higher-level thinking and working that is characteristic of most managers and decision makers. The way we think often takes into account factors that are relevant, but not central to, a decision we have to make, or an action that has to be taken. When information is required from a computer it is necessary to specify exactly what is required, and it may be necessary to have to ask an information system a number of other questions in order to create the same range of information as a human might think of, almost without being conscious of it. Because of this difference, a failing of an information system can be quite frustrating.

5.5.2.2 People adjust to computers better than computers adjust to people

Computers, for the most part, do not learn. There may be a few exceptional cases in which they have been given a limited ability to learn but computers are no match for people when it comes to learning. While each individual who may use an information system is different, with a different perspective on his or her work, computers and other aspects of the business, it would make an information system hard to implement if screen designs, messages to the user, the help system, etc. were designed to suit each person.

Most information systems are relatively limited in scope, unexciting and often take some getting used to, but one thing is sure – the system will not adjust to us. It takes competent and knowledgeable management to insist from the start that a system is designed for relative ease of use.

Much research and experience has lead to greater understanding of the kinds of things that make computer-based systems harder or easier to use. The problem is that the people who develop systems are often so experienced in using computers that they forget that many users only want to know what is necessary for them to do their job with the minimum of distraction. Learning about the quirks of an information system is a distraction that can waste time and cause frustration.

Good design of what we call the 'user interface', or the 'human-computer interface' takes a lot of thought and knowledge of the subject. One of the problems for the thoughtful designer is how much experience of computers he or she can assume for the average user of the information system. The design and logical structure of the menus, how to make sure people don't get lost, how to make it quick and simple to go from one task to a closely related task without a lot of going through menus or screens or how to ensure people put the right data in are some of the factors that can make a big difference to how people view a system.

5.5.2.3 The limitations of computers only become slowly apparent

Database management systems are often quite demanding applications and can test the ability of the technology to give the kind of service that its users expect. Databases by their very nature grow and some limitations of the system may only become apparent when the system has been in use for a while. Typical limitations that are usually seen as slow or poor performance, or worse, result from:

- many people using the computer at once
- many people using the database management system
- many people trying to access the same tables
- database tables growing very large.

Many people using the computer at once. When many people use a computer at the same time, the power of the processor has to be shared among them, giving each one small slices of its time. Depending upon the types of task each person wants the processor to do, more or less power is demanded for the task. If a database management system is not the only application running on the computer, the system may be slowed down because the processor is busy trying to handle the other task(s) too.

Another general problem can occur when the database system is communicating with its users via a network. In this case even if some of the processing power is distributed to PCs, the volume of data traffic on the network passing between the data resource, database management system and the users, may slow the system down. On a single-user PC this sort of problem, of course, does not exist.

Many people using the database management system. A more specific problem sometimes occurs when many people try to use a relational database management system at the same time. This problem is connected with the relational approach in which data is held in many related tables. Some queries or modifications may require a number of tables to be active at once, but with a lot of people possibly each requiring a lot of tables which are held as files, the database or operating system software, or the computer's memory, may respond by taking more time to process the work.

Many people trying to access the same tables. The database management system has to have ways of preventing confusion and corruption of data in the resource when more than one process tries to access the same table or parts of a table (*see* section 5.4.1). One of the ways in which the problem is resolved is by making competing processes wait until the table, or part of it, is free. A heavily used data resource may have many processes competing for the same data, but the resolution of one problem can create a new one. In this case the resolution can slow the system down.

Database tables growing very large. Database tables grow; this is one of their benefits because the amount of information that can be drawn out from it is that much greater. However, the catch is that as they grow larger, they take longer to use and maintain. Each table may have indices attached to a number of its columns and, each time there is a change made to a table or a new row of details is added, the table and all the indices may have to be updated (depending upon the practicality of constant updating or the update policy employed). If it is assumed that one process may affect several such tables in a relational data model, then a slow deterioration in the response of the information system may be predictable unless sensible strategies are adopted to manage the problem.

5.6 SUMMARY

Most computer-based information systems in business use relational database management systems as their underlying technology. In this chapter an overview of the basic characteristics and functions of the relational database management system have been given. The potential power of the relational model has been touched on, but it has also been indicated that in some respects it still requires specialist knowledge to master the relational logic necessary in order to communicate with the RDBMS engine if ad hoc requests for information are wanted. It would also require familiarity with the structure and content of the data resource in order to frame the requests.

Relational database management systems are an extremely important business technology, and in the following chapters there is an examination of some of the techniques that are used to analyse and model business data and processes. If the data resource is not designed well it will not function as required and it will not be reliable, as a result, the performance of the business will suffer. It should be remembered that the development of information systems and the provision of information is, after all, for the managers and decision makers in a company. One of the responsibilities of managers is, therefore, to input their business knowledge and understanding into the analysis of the processes that deliver management information, and into the modelling of the data resources used by their business.

This chapter has provided the basic technical context against which the following chapters on analysis and modelling can be understood, but Chapters 1–4 provide the business and management context that is just as essential. The implementation of relational database management systems and their day-to-day operation may require specialist and technical expertise, but if management wants information systems that are going to serve their institutions well, then a strong business management bias with a view to understanding the role/purpose of information in business, has to drive the early (business analysis) stages of information systems development.

QUESTIONS

1 A business information system is what we often call a computer-based system which has the purpose of providing business information. Explain what the relationship of a relational database management system is likely to be to a business information system.

2 The word 'relational' in a relational database management system implies the mathematical notion of 'relation' and the idea of 'relationship'. Discuss these and what you see as being the relationship between them.

3 We have used the expression 'world of information' to suggest that it is impossible to limit the scope of information that a business might require in a rapidly changing business environment. Discuss this challenge for business information provision and explain why, in principle, the relational database management system can offer a partial solution.

4 A company's data resource(s) not only need to contain all the data that might have to be drawn on in order to provide information but the data needs to be organised or else they may not be found, inconsistent data may kept, etc. Explain why the organisation of data is important for the operation of a relational database management system.

5 Database management systems usually hold data of great importance to a business much of which can be confidential. Discuss four management functions of a typical RDBMS and give an example for each, suggesting what the consequences of not having such controls might be.

6 Explain how the database management system can help ensure the trustworthiness of the data resource.

7 Why are computers well suited to the sorts of tasks that database management systems often have to perform?

8 Why is it that businesses may only become gradually aware of the limitations of computer technology in database applications.

BIBLIOGRAPHY   Goldstein, R.C., *Database Technology and Management*, John Wiley and Sons, 1985.

Pratt, P.J. and Adamski, J.J., *Database Systems Management and Design* (3rd edition), Boyd and Fraser, 1994.

Elmasri, R. and Navathe, S.B., *Fundamentals of Database Systems*, Benjamin/Cummings, 1989.

Modelling business data: the top-down approach

6.1 INTRODUCTION

In Chapter 5 the basic principles and functions of a relational database management system were discussed. It was said that one of the important prerequisites for the system to function effectively is that the data resource '... is arranged into logical sets of data that have meaning for the business and which can be effectively used by the database engine'. In other words, the need to create a logically-based model of the business data is determined by what it takes for us to design a database system that can support the information requirements of a business. It will, therefore, be assumed that much of the business information required has to be derived from data held in the data resource of a database management system. The data model created forms the basis for the design of the data resource.

6.2 DATA ANALYSIS AND THE DATA MODEL

Data analysis means an examination of the data that are used in business contexts and their organisation into logical and meaningful sets that eliminate unnecessary redundancy and retain sufficient links to make sure that no connections between data are lost. The final representation of data sets together with the links between them that must be preserved is called the data model. The important thing is that the data model is constructed on the basis of principles and techniques that can be safely applied in virtually any business context.

6.2.1 Meaningful sets of data called entities

Each set of data should be meaningful within the context of the business in that it represents an individual entity of sufficient interest, from a business point of view, to record and store details about. Otherwise, an entity might represent some logical grouping of facts that relate to business activity. For example, a business may want to record and store details about entities such as its suppliers or customers and it may want to store details of entities that consist of some logical grouping of facts that relate, say, to invoices or orders. These 'things' are what the business needs to know about, since it needs to be able to identify its customers and it needs to be able to refer to invoices that it sends to its customers.

In Chapter 1 the word 'things' was used in the context of the business plan to refer to people, places, physical resources and products. *Things* is not a technical term and the only reason for us using it is to get across the idea that businesses deal with tangible resources and objects in the real world. Businesses usually do store details about these 'things'. Anything that a business spends money on, or receives money from, is likely to be important enough for a business to store details about. Documents and other formal means of recording what happens to these things, even documents that refer to the things and the transactions that involve them, also tend to be important for a company to identify by reference number and keep for subsequent use. All of these things tend to be good candidates for what is called 'entities' in the data model.

Entity is the technical term used for a set, or type of grouping, to which specific details belong. Thus 'entities' that a business spends money on might include raw materials, or any products or services provided to the company, while the specific details that belong to the entities would tell us, for example, what the raw materials are and how much stock we have of them, etc. A business should know where its money is going and what it is paying for. *Related entities* refer to the ability to relate, for example, which supplier is paid for what product, how much the transaction is for, as well as the need to know where these details are recorded – such as on a specific invoice/order. At a higher level, the payments made to suppliers for individual products are not relevant; instead they are included within documents like summary statements and yearly accounts. Some of these documents may also be stored as entities, or things to be referred to.

Note first that it usually takes a number of details to describe and identify each instance of a type of entity; for example, enough details to be able to uniquely describe each supplier, and each product or service provided to the business are needed. Often, one detail is specifically chosen to make it easier to refer to an instance of an entity; for example, invoices usually have a unique invoice number to make sure there is no confusion. Second, the relationships between entities like suppliers and the products that are to be paid for have to be stored in a data model even though a data model would almost certainly say that suppliers and products are separate entities with their own characteristics, properties or attributes. How this is done will be shown as the modelling techniques are applied to an example.

Typical definitions of the term 'entity'

The following are typical examples of definitions found in texts on database or information systems. Note, however, that some of these definitions do not appear to follow the custom of distinguishing between the terms 'data' and 'information':

Any object or concept about which a system needs to hold information is known as an entity type (or entity for short). (Weaver, 1993, p. 39)

An entity is a topic, task, object or event of interest to the organisation (and within the area of the system) and about which information is kept. (Crinnion, 1991, p. 96)

Entities are things of interest to the organisation. They may physically exist ... they may be transient ... or even represent aspirations. In practice, if you want to store information about it, it is likely to be an entity. (Adapted from Downs, Clare and Coe, 1992, p. 123)

Entities, then, are things. In the data analysis context, entities are things about which information is to be recorded. The things may be objects, such as a person or car; or events, such as a birth or a goal being scored; or activities, such as the production of oil from a particular well ...; or associations, such as the fact that a particular man is married to a particular woman ... (Bowers, 1993, p. 25)

An entity model views the organisation as sets of data elements, known as entity types, which are the 'things' of interest to the organisation, and the relationships between these entity types (usually referred to as entities). (Avison and Fitzgerald, 1988, p. 67).

Despite the free use of the term 'information', in many of the definitions, it is, nevertheless, useful to maintain the distinction between the terms 'information' and 'data'. The term 'data' will be reserved for the details kept about entities, while 'information' is reserved for that which is meaningful and relevant for decision-making. 'Information' may include, for example, relevant, selected data, summarised figures or statistical projections in the form of graphs which are based on the data.

6.3 FOUNDATIONS FOR THE ANALYSIS OF BUSINESS DATA

The concern here, then, is about what it is necessary to know in order to create a data model. A good foundation for data analysis and modelling requires knowledge of:

- what is important to business
- management information
- systems ideas or principles as a basis for data analysis
- how to use analytical techniques
- some idea of the principles of operation as well as the limitations of database technology.

Unless the analyst knows what to look for there cannot be analysis of anything. Analysis means applying specific criteria against which experience or things in the real world are measured. For example, to analyse a set of sales figures it would have to be decided what the significant criteria are – the sales of particular products, product groups or comparison of weekly, monthly or quarterly sales against previous years or previous months. On the other hand, it could be the sales by areas, by sales representatives or retail outlets etc. It all depends upon what is considered important to know or what it is necessary to know at the time.

When athletes are tested for banned substances, the tests can only show results for drugs included within a certain range because the criteria used in the tests relate only to specific types of substances. Analysis without criteria would simply become unfocused observation and reveal little of importance for management. Knowledge is needed so that facts that are significant to focus on, what measures, tests or criteria are appropriate to judge the facts by, can be recognised.

6.3.1 Knowledge of what is important to the business

Any specific business is an instance of business in general and, in that sense, knowledge of what motivates or drives business is useful in trying to understand what, in principle, any business should be trying to achieve. Knowledge of business principles and business practice is the 'yardstick' against which the practices of an individual company are evaluated. Quite clearly, knowledge of a particular industry or type of business in which various general business practices have become more specialised is also very helpful in knowing what is important to that industry or business. Such knowledge can be very important when attempting to decide what things to do with the monitoring of the business activities that are important enough to classify as entities. For example, someone who manages a plumbing wholesalers would know about what things are important to know about the business. The manager would know what facts about entities are important such as how various plumbing supplies are classified, measured and how they can be differentiated from each other, as well as knowing about things or entities that are of more common business interest such as customers and suppliers whose details the business would want to keep.

6.3.2 Knowledge about management information

One of the main purposes of information systems is to provide information to assist managers in understanding how the business is performing. The information may help managers to make better decisions or to take action about situations that the information reveals. If the types of activities or resources, that are important for managers to know about if they are to manage properly, are understood, then they will be in a better position to determine what resources they should keep data or details about and what documents are used by the business to record what activities they feature in, such as invoices which record what products or services (resources) have been sold (a transaction, i.e. an activity) to the customers.

In Chapter 3 it was discussed how it is that managers need different types of information according to the purpose for which it is needed. It was said that some decisions managers make require information about how the business has been operating over a period of time and it may be that it is meaningful to the business to classify certain kinds of products in groups so that something can be discovered about trends in consumer demand. For example, certain kinds of sports equipment might be classified by designations such as 'track', 'field', 'water', etc., because it could then be possible to tell when sales start to rise in relation to the beginning of their regular season of activity. Such information could indicate when it is best to build up, or reduce, stocks in order to maximise sales and minimise residues of groups of seasonal products. It is only higher-level management interest in the products that sees any value in treating sales of individual items as indicative of sales of a family of items that might be classified as, say, 'field'.

Because there are different levels of management which may require different information about business processes, or items such as products, it is necessary to make sure that a data model includes all the necessary details about the entities that will enable managers at all levels to be given the information they need.

6.3.3 Knowledge of systems ideas as a basis for data analysis

Systems ideas provide the unifying basis for this approach to data and process analysis. Chapter 8 looks in considerable detail at how systems ideas allow a diagnostic approach to process analysis to be taken which can help give significant understanding of important management and business issues that relate to providing management information in a company. Just as it is possible to analyse processes which are used to deliver information from a process perspective, it is also possible to model the data that would be needed to deliver that information.

Systems principles which are often (wrongly) associated with the idea of attempting to understand complexity by decomposing it into smaller, thus simpler components, are used here to support an approach to analysis which can be used to build a complex model from analysing and modelling well defined and well understood (sub)systems. This approach can be based on the systems principle of 'holism', which means that the data analysis and modelling are undertaken within a systems context that recognises the place of information delivery (sub)systems within the wider context of the business. For example, where would one begin an attempt to model the data resource required for, say, a hospital? Such organisations are very complex and to begin to build a coherent information system to help monitor their activities, a systemic approach is required, by which is meant that an analytical approach is needed as an aid to recognising and responding to the complexity it reveals. The systems (or systemic) approach provides the best thinking tools for analysing and understanding complex structures and tackling the task of providing information systems that are appropriate to the complex environments in which they function. A systems-based analysis should help to see what is important to the performance of the different activities (or sub-systems) in the hospital and this should help to identify the entities from which information about their performance will have to be drawn.

6.3.4 Knowledge of how to use analytical techniques

It is very hard to create a data model unless there is a reasonable awareness of the top-down or bottom-up analytical techniques. In this chapter, a discussion and explanation of the top-down approach which uses the Entity-Relationship modelling technique is given. The process has beeen modified slightly to try and give a little more insight into how it works and what it is modelling. There are few texts that actually attempt to work right through an example and suggest steps for doing so, but there will be a chance to examine such an example in this chapter. For interest, the same example is followed for the bottom-up data modelling in the next chapter, and for the process modelling in Chapter 8. The techniques do not guarantee a correct solution because better solutions come with greater understanding of the business context or of how to make best use of the computer technology, but some principles that will, hopefully, give a clearer grasp of the analytical or modelling process itself are provided. A knowledge of the rules of chess will not guarantee a win, but there is the freedom to think more about how to get the result wanted.

6.3.5 Knowledge of database principles and limitations

Few people would become involved with data modelling unless the intention is to create a data resource for a database management system. It would be unrealistic to think that some concession to database technology or understanding of its limitations does not influence how the problem of data modelling is considered. Having said that, the manager or non-specialist gains most advantage from knowing only a few general principles – issues of implementation are for the specialists.

The sort of knowledge which can influence the design is, for example, where, instead of saying that an entity such as a 'customer' has the attributes {name, address, telephone, etc.}, if known how a database searches for facts, the attributes would be separated into smaller, meaningful parts that can be searched for (more efficiently) in their own right, such as {surname, initial, given-name, street, town, county, post-code, telephone, etc.}. Also the absolute age of a person (such as an employee) would not be included, when it is known that most computers will be able to work out the current age of someone if the date-of-birth is provided.

The rigidity of a mathematical machine can sometimes be a blessing or a nuisance, but it can also take the uninitiated by surprise when designing what attributes of an entity would be necessary in order to provide a given range of information for managers and other users.

The foundations for analysing and modelling business data have to be based on knowledge of different factors, all of which help to clarify the process and what is being aimed for. Data analysis is not, and cannot be made, easy, but it can seem easier when it is known what foundations are needed.

6.4 THE TOP-DOWN APPROACH

A distinction is, perhaps, needed here between taking a top-down approach to modelling and starting with a high-level view of a business, which might seem the right place to start a top-down analysis simply because it is at the top. Taking a top-down approach does not necessarily mean literally beginning the analysis at the top of anything, rather, what is meant by *top-down* is that a model is being imposed, as it were, from the top, or the understanding of the way things ought to be is given as much importance as that of the holistic context in which the process or (sub)system plays a role. In the case of a top-down approach to data modelling, it is already known what characteristics the model should have. The characteristics, in this case, would be that it is reasonable to think that all the data that an information system would need could be represented as minimal sets and that it should be possible to represent any relationships between these sets in a systematic way. The aim, therefore, in top-down data modelling is to discover what things or entities the business (system or sub-system) will need to store details about in order to provide the information needed to run or manage it, and how to ensure that all relationships between the entities are represented in a way that is consistent with the logic of the relational model.

Simplistic scenarios, though useful vehicles for teaching, may make it appear as if data analysis can really be approached by starting at the highest level of a business; in a real business, starting a data analysis at the highest level may be totally unrealistic because the sheer size and complexity of some businesses would make the task incredibly difficult. Remember, if business knowledge is the key to good data analysis, starting at the highest level of a large complex business would imply the need for an adequate knowledge of how that company operates from the highest level downwards. We are not convinced this is a reasonable or even possible task. However, starting the data analysis at the highest level of an organisation is unnecessary.

The systems approach to business analysis, and in particular the holistic principle, allows a modular view to be taken so that it is possible to identify systems and sub-systems at different levels within the company. The advantage of this for data analysis is that the top-down model can be applied at a point where a sub-system suitably defined by its boundary can be identified. After all, the need for a well designed data model is driven by the need for information, and the need for information is driven by the need to be able to manage and control business activities, and most activities can be modelled as systems or sub-systems. The natural place to begin a data analysis, then, would seem to be where a system or sub-system and the information needed to control or manage it can be identified.

6.4.1 Assumptions behind a top-down approach to data modelling

The top-down approach assumes:

1 *a business activity or context* for which *a system or sub-system* can be modelled that delivers the information needed to exercise management control;
2 sufficient *knowledge* of the context to identify what aspects ought to be *monitored*, what information is, therefore, needed and what can be done with it to exercise *effective control* in the context;
3 that if it is known what information is necessary for good control, the development of a *data model* by identifying those *things* or *entities* that the system would need to hold details about in order to provide the information can be begun; and
4 that the data model developed is based on simple logical concepts and will provide the data resource for a Relational Database Management System (RDBMS).

Most of the highlighted terms have already been discussed elsewhere in the text but as a reminder, the familiar terms are explained briefly and the newer ones introduced more fully below.

6.4.1.1 A business activity or context

A data model is not developed in a vacuum. The business context and what it is that management wants to achieve in that context should be considered. It is necessary then to determine how the activity or context can be modelled as a (sub)system, i.e. what goal or standard management wants to achieve and what criteria are, or could be, used to evaluate its performance. For each business activity that is monitored there will be information sub-systems that have an interest in its performance. An information sub-system will have the purpose of delivering some specific information about the activity; it will need a way of obtaining the necessary data, of processing it and of producing the information in a form that is suitable for those that need it.

Lower-level operational activities are far easier to recognise and model as systems than higher-level tactical or strategic activities. As an example of a lower-level activity, consider a travel agent who can tell which seats are currently booked on a flight because flight bookings are modelled as a system in which the goal is a full flight and the actual bookings are monitored. As a result, the travel agent can get information about which seats remain available when prospective travellers inquire about booking a flight. Airlines may use the information to try and fill seats just a few minutes before departure by allocating them to standby passengers at a cheaper rate. This lower-level situation is clear, well understood and is a regular occurrence; consequently, the range of information required is limited but the data resource has still to be designed properly to support the requests. In practice, airline booking systems are specially tuned in order to provide rapid responses to booking agents and carriers from all over the globe.

On the other hand, at a higher level, the proprietor of an ice cream manufacturing business may be forced to examine trends in his sales and to look for greater manufacturing and distribution efficiencies if confronted with an aggressive new competitor. He may need to develop *new* business strategies to survive in a tougher business environment. Responses to changes in the environment often mean changes in the requirements for information, and thus changes in the monitoring activities. The manufacturer would have to initiate new activities to get the information he needs to make plans and develop his business further. He may want to investigate his sales more carefully to look for overlooked patterns of trading over the last year or two. He may want to look more carefully at trends of consumption of different kinds of ice cream, of the growth, or decline, of different sorts of outlets for the sale of ice cream, etc. If the proprietor asks good questions he will get useful answers – on which he can base new plans. For every good business question, he requires some monitoring activity from which he can get the information (answers) he needs. He can only get the information if a suitable data resource is available from which information can be drawn. This higher- level context is more complex, the information required to manage it has to be thought about carefully and the data resources needed to support the new situation should be adequate if they have been designed well.

6.4.1.2 Knowledge, monitoring, information and control

The type of knowledge needed in any particular instance is related to the level of decision making that is relevant. Strategic decision-makers need more knowledge of the environment in which the activity occurs than lower-level decision-makers do. The better the knowledge managers have, the better they will know what information is important for controlling and managing the activities they are responsible for. Information consists of a set or combination of key details that are arranged or summarised in a way that meaningfully communicates with the manager and has the potential to make a difference to the kind of decision or action that has to be taken.

6.5 TOP-DOWN MODELLING WITH ENTITIES

The top-down data model is often called the *Entity Relationship* (ER) model. The focus of this approach is on the entities and the relationships between them. It may be helpful to recognise three distinct kinds of entities and, by knowing the characteristics of each, it is easier to discover both what they are and how they relate to each other. Entities can be divided into *natural, document*, and *design entities*.

Natural entities. This first type is the more *natural* kind of entity which represents objects, or even events, in the real world. For example, in a retail business, customers, suppliers and stock-items are tangible entities about which the business person is likely to want to keep details.

Document entities. Document entities represent the kinds of things done, or used in order to keep track of what is happening in the system, that is, they monitor and control business and organisations by the use of data. The kinds of entities in this case would be *documents* (paper or computer-based) which contain details concerning, or refer to, the real world entities, for example, invoices, orders, etc. Both the details that refer to the real world entities and the details that refer to the documents that discuss them, are likely to be important to the organisation. For example, an invoice will refer to specific items that have to be paid for and the company pays on the basis of specific invoices. Sometimes document entities may refer to other documents too, for example, an invoice might refer to the order which requests the products being invoiced.

Design entities. Finally, there are entities that are generated, as it were, for the purposes of developing a good data model or a good *design*. These entities sometimes do not seem to have an obvious counterpart in the 'real world', though, on reflection, it is often possible to recognise indications of their existence in existing documentation. Top-down modelling tends to produce entities in order to resolve many-to-many relationships and bottom-up modelling may produce entities to resolve problems of redundancy, etc.

6.5.1 Top-down data modelling in action

An application of the top-down modelling technique to a simple example is given below. The purpose of this exercise is to provide insight into the modelling process rather than to suggest a recipe which will succeed in every context, though it is hoped that it will be generally useful.

6.5.1.1 Steps for identification of entities

1 Identify the business/organisational context of interest, for example, a specific strategic, tactical or operational decision/action point.

2 Identify the information that would be needed in order to support the decision/action.

3 Determine the 'natural' real-world entities about which information would be needed for the decision in question. Ensure there are one or more attributes, sufficient to identify the specific instances of each real-world entity.

4 Determine any documents that are relevant to the decision/action point or that refer to the natural entities identified in this context.

5 Model the relationships between appropriate *natural* and *document* entities using entity relationship diagrams. Consider whether all of the original entities are relevant to the provision of the information required in the decision/action context and eliminate those outside the boundary of interest, i.e. that do not influence/affect the decision. Documents can be important in deciding which entities are related.

6 Where direct many-to-many relationships exist between natural entities, and the same entities are linked via one or more document entities, eliminate the direct many-to-many relationship between the natural entities. The likelihood is that there will be a many-to-many relationship between one or more of the natural entities and the document entity.

7 Examine any many-to-many relationships between natural and document entities and create a 'design' or 'link' entity to resolve each many-to-many relationship. The entity name should be as meaningful as possible in the context and may well be suggested by some term used on the document. If a document entity is in more than one many-to-many relationship with natural entities, check to see whether one design entity will also resolve any of the others before assuming that it is necessary to create more design entities.

8 Examine any one-to-one relationships to see whether both entities are really necessary or whether the relationship is more complex than at first thought.

6.5.1.2 Applying the top-down modelling technique

Step 1: identify the business context

The business context is a manufacturing business and, in particular, the production manager is concerned about an apparent long-standing inability of the factory to produce the required number of units within specified periods of time. One way of addressing this problem is to keep a check on the down-time of machines and to examine how long it takes to get the machines running again. The manager thinks it would be useful to have an information system which would allow him to check the maintenance history of the machines so that he can tell when and why they go down and when they are ready for operation again.

If the information system works well, the manager should be able to get a number of different kinds of information from quite a small data resource. For example, he should be able to tell if certain makes or kinds of machines seem to have recurrent problems; he may be able to see an association between the age of the machines, make links between down times and patterns of usage or types of failure or he may find that the maintenance staff do not know how to tackle certain problems well without special training, etc. He should be able to tell if some kinds of problems take a particularly long time to fix, which may be due to the difficulty of the work or, perhaps, a poor internal or external supply of spare parts. Some engineers may seem to do a quicker job than others, and some may do a worse job, and so on. This information is important because unless the manager is able to find out why the machines, and hence the factory fail to perform properly, he is not in a position to address the real problems. Only appropriate information can reduce the number of possible problems – based on guesswork – to those which are in most need of urgent attention – based on information gained by monitoring the situation.

Step 2: identify the information needed to support the decision

As seen already, there are many possible kinds of information that could be required so, in this case, *one possibility* will be looked at.

EXAMPLE

> The manager has heard from a colleague in another, similar factory that the high pressure hydraulic hoses on some Armstrong machines are underspecified and higher specification ones prevent problems. The manager wants information that could tell him whether there is any evidence to confirm whether this problem exists and, therefore, whether higher specification hoses should be fitted to the machines. The information required should identify whether any high-pressure services have been carried out, to which machines and how often. He also might want to identify which engineers have been involved and seek their opinion.

Step 3: determine the natural entities

In this step, 'natural' real-world entities, with which the information is concerned, are sought. Knowledge of the business context is useful in this process of identification because it is not always easy to sort out what is significant from what is not so significant. For this analysis and modelling it is necessary to recognise what is significant, such as what things are significant to model as entities in this specific context and for this specific purpose. In step 2, the required information concerns whether a high pressure hydraulic service is carried out on a machine by an engineer. It is, therefore, necessary to know details about machines, about what kind of service is given and about engineers. It helps to know that, for safety reasons, the company has specified service routines so that, for instance, if there is a high pressure hose fault, the 'procedure' means that the high pressure system is checked and specified high pressure parts are replaced even if they look all right. The natural entities are, therefore:

- machine: it is necessary to know which machines are relevant to the problem
- procedure: it is necessary to know if a high pressure hydraulic service is performed
- engineer: the manager may want to talk to the relevant engineers.

Whether there are any other entities or natural things of interest in this context may well need considering. One candidate that might be considered is the high pressure hose; the hose is of potential concern and it is a thing of significance in the context. It is excluded here because a service is performed on a machine and the high pressure hose is part of that machine. If looking at how many of each spare part were used over a period, then the hose would be an instance of a spare part. The company has to buy the spares, and the hose is therefore of significance as an instance of the entity 'spare part', but it is not the focus of this context. What *is* of interest is how often the high pressure system fails and thus causes the machine to be inoperative and we can find out about this problem without reference to the part itself.

Step 4: determine relevant document entities

The relevant document entity is a maintenance chart which is kept with each machine. When the machine fails in some way a production supervisor fills in brief details on the chart and contacts maintenance for an engineer. When the engineer completes the service, he fills in his part of the chart and reactivates the machine. (*See* Fig. 6.1 for an example of a maintenance chart.)

MAINTENANCE CHART

Machine make: Armstrong   **Machine No:** 123
Model No: A5000c   **Machine type:** Press
DoManu 1989

Procedure	Reason	R date	R time	F date	F time	Engr
Hi pr hyd	C/o hi pr	4/6/91	0947	4/6/91	1015	FH
Full hyd	Reg hyd	1/11/91	1300	1/11/91	1510	SSo
Relay	C/o elec	2/3/92	1610	3/3/92	0920	FH
Hi pr hyd	C/o hi pr	15/3/92	0850	15/3/92	1230	SSo

Fig. 6.1 Example of a maintenance chart

Step 5: modelling the entities and their relationships

Once it has been decided what the relevant natural and documentary entities are for the business function, each entity type is represented by a symbol such as a box (whatever the diagramming convention – be consistent). Relationships between the entities are represented by drawing lines between related boxes. Although only one line is usually drawn between the entities, the line in fact represents a pair of relationships; one going each way. It is important to note that relationships are established on the basis of the possible relationships between actual *instances* of the entity types represented by the boxes. Each relationship must be labelled to indicate the nature of the relationship, as well as indicating whether it exists as a 1:1 (one-to-one), 1:m (one-to-many), or as a m:n (many-to-many). The following worked example will explain the first stage of the process.

Figure 6.2. shows the pair of relationships between a document entity – the maintenance chart – and a natural entity – the engineer. Document entities often refer to more than one natural entity, and sometimes mention other document entities too; thus they often provide the key to the patterns of relationships between entities. In this example, it can be said that each maintenance chart may contain the signatures of many engineers (i.e. the engineers who carry out the procedures recorded on the chart). Also, since an engineer may carry out procedures on other machines, it can be said that each engineer may sign more than one maintenance chart. The two relationships are summarised by the one line in which the many (crows-foot) ends indicate each of the 'many' ends of the 1:m relationships.

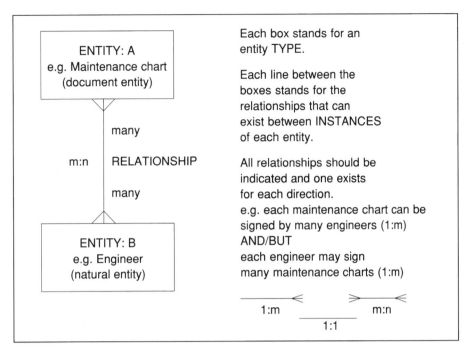

Fig. 6.2   Entity relationship modelling (ERM) conventions

Step 5.1: model natural and document entities using the entity relationship diagram technique

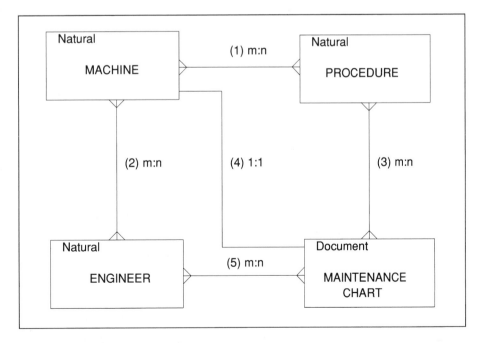

Fig. 6.3   Example of ERM technique: step 5

Step 5.2: label the relationships

Relationship (1) m:n   Machine/Procedure

This is a many-to-many (m:n) relationship; this is determined by examining, first, the relationship between the machine and the procedure. Each machine may receive more than one maintenance procedure, say, over a period of time. The relationship in this direction is thus one-to-many. Going from the procedure to the machine it is possible to determine that each procedure may be applied to more than one machine, therefore, this is also a one-to-many relationship. The resulting one line summary of the two relationships between the two entities gives a many-to-many relationship.

Relationship (2) m:n   Machine/Engineer

As with the above pair of relationships, the same principle applies, i.e. each machine may be serviced by more than one engineer. The other relationship of the pair is certainly one-to-many in that each engineer services many machines. The resulting summary relationship is thus many-to-many.

Relationship (3) m:n   Procedure/Maintenance chart

This is the first relationship to have been looked at that involved a 'natural' entity and a 'document' entity. Using the same principle as before, it is possible to determine that each service procedure may appear on more that one maintenance chart; each maintenance chart may contain entries for more than one service procedure. The summarised relationship line will show, in this case, also that there is a many-to-many relationship between the two.

Relationship (4) m:n   Engineer/Maintenance chart

Each engineer will make entries on more than one maintenance chart, and each maintenance chart will, very likely, contain records of service procedures signed off by more than one engineer, that is to say, the service could be signed off by a different engineer each time. The resulting relationship is therefore determined to be many-to-many.

Relationship (5) 1:1   Machine/Maintenance chart

Each Machine has one maintenance chart. Even if the original chart were damaged, lost, or full of service entries and needed replacing, a new chart would in effect just be a continuation of the old, for a maintenance chart would be identified on the basis of the specific machine to which it referred, i.e. probably by the same value as the machine number, as in the example '123'. One-to-one relationships are not normally considered useful in data modelling and the relationship should be examined to see if both the entities are really necessary. Knowledge of the context and of the type of relationship that exists between the entities can help sort out such problems.

If it is assumed that each machine received a new maintenance chart each year as a result of the way the factory's maintenance was organised, then the relationship would be different and there would be a relationship of one machine to many charts. In the example, it is necessary to be aware that one entity is a natural entity and the other a document entity. The role of the document entity is to keep track of the service history of each machine and thus provide a link between the service procedures performed on the machine, the engineers who perform them and the machine in question. The only reason for wanting to keep details about the document is so that a record can be kept of this history of events.

Note that the document itself appears to be acting as a data resource on which details of the service history are recorded. In a computer-based system the role of some documents may be taken over by the technology. For instance, the details can be more effectively stored in a well designed data resource, information can be gained more efficiently from the data resource, and information can more easily be manipulated and integrated into reports for good communication. Thus it is necessary to distinguish between stages in developing a data model. First, the analysis starts on the basis of what natural and document entities are currently needed to produce some specified information. Second, the top-down modelling logic which produces design entities is applied – these exist only because this is an attempt to create a logical model. Third, if the logical model is used as a basis for designing the data resource, the role of some of the documents may be taken over by the computer-based system and may, therefore, be eliminated from the model.

Step 6: examination of many-to-many relationships and the creation of design entities

The *natural* and *document* entities have been sought, but now it is necessary to identify entities that are necessary for the purpose of good design. We know that these *'design'* entities are necessary because good design does not allow many-to-many relationships. This means that each set of many-to-many relationships that we have identified has to be resolved. In practice, it is common to find there are some documents or procedures in the organisation that already reflect this 'design' need.

There are good theoretical, business and implementation reasons for eliminating many-to-many relationships but concentration here will be solely on the practical problem of developing the model.

Step 6.1: resolving the many-to-many relationship between natural entities

Each pair of many-to-many relationships will be examined in turn.

Step 6.1.1 Relationship (1) m:n   Machine/Procedure

One thing to remember about data modelling is that it is the data that the organisation *uses* which is being modelled. While this may seem to be an obvious remark, notice that both of the above are 'natural' entities and not 'document' entities. Organisations, however, usually *use* documents to tell them about what is happening to the natural entities. In this case, it can be seen in Fig. 6.1 that both the machine and procedure entities have a relationship with the same 'document' entity. The machine/ maintenance chart relationship is a one-to-one relationship which will be looked at again, while the other relationship, procedure/maintenance chart, is another many-to-many relationship. Figure 6.1 suggests that the organisational interest in the relationship of machine to procedure is via the 'document' entity, maintenance chart, rather than the direct many-to-many relationship established through the modelling process.

The direct many-to-many relationship link will be removed from machine and procedure in favour of the indirect relationship via the 'document' entity, maintenance chart (*see* Fig. 6.4).

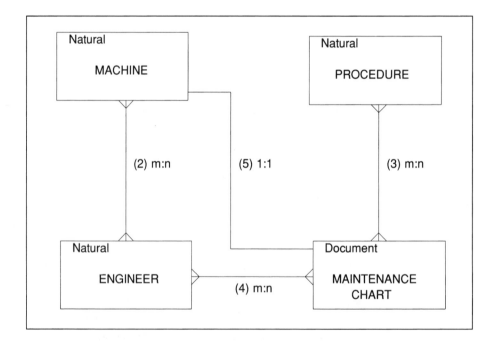

Fig. 6.4   Example of ERM technique: step 6.1.1

6.1.2 Relationship (2) m:n   Machine/Engineer

Here is the second many-to-many relationship between two 'natural' entities that also have a common link with the 'document' entity, maintenance chart. Again the same approach will be adopted and the direct relationship between the 'natural' entities will be eliminated in favour of the indirect link between them via the 'document' entity, maintenance chart (*see* Fig. 6.5).

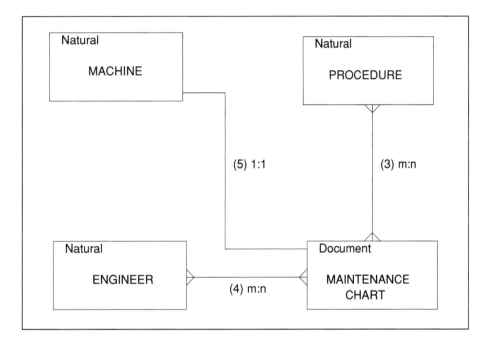

Fig. 6.5   Example of ERM technique: step 6.1.2

Step 7: resolving the many-to-many relationship between natural and document entities

Step 7.1 Relationship (3) m:n   Procedure/Maintenance chart

This model has been simplified and there are now no direct many-to-many relationships between 'natural' entities, but this and another similar relationship have to be resolved between 'natural' and 'document' entities.

So far, what each entity type consists of has not been considered. Each entity is composed of attributes which must:

1 allow unique identification of any instance of the entity type, for example, the identification of one specific customer from a data resource which perhaps contains details of thousands of customers;

2 include all, and only those details about an entity which are required to produce specified information in the context; and

3 in many cases, contain details that preserve the links between related entities.

In the approach adopted here, interest is limited to those attributes of entities which are significant within the specified context, that is, those which are significant for the specific decision/action point.

It should be possible to identify each instance of an entity from the specific details or values represented by one, or a combination of attributes which would provide a unique reference for it. It could be possible, for example, to identify a particular machine by the number *123* which is the value of its 'machine-no' attribute. Whether the entity is identified by one or a combination of its attributes, such attributes are called the 'identifying attributes' of the entity, because singly, or together, they allow identification of one specific instance from all the rest of its type.

One way of resolving the problem of many-to-many relationships is to create *design* entities, where the identifying attribute(s) from each pair of the relationship is copied to the new intermediate 'design' entity. An instance of a design entity will therefore provide a link between specific instances of each of the linked entities. where they are related. For example, in this case, knowledge about specific (high pressure) service procedures carried out on specific (Armstrong) machines is wanted. Each instance of a design entity (i.e. a service) has to include the identifying attributes from the many-to-many pair but, in order to be able to identify a specific instance of the 'service' entity, it will be necessary to include additional attributes to distinguish one procedure recorded on one maintenance chart from any others.

If, as is often the case, the relationship between the entities is established through a document, then the identifying attribute of the document may have to become one of the identifying attributes of the design entity. Remember that as a minimum requirement the attributes for each relating link or design entity have to be able to distinguish one specific instance from all others.

If the identifying attribute of the procedure entity is taken, which could be the 'description' details of the service procedure, for example, *Hi pr hyd serv*, and combined with the identifying attribute(s) of the maintenance chart, which may be the machine's number, for example, *123*, then part of what is needed to identify any instance of the new service 'design' entity is achieved. To be able to identify absolutely a specific service procedure on a particular machine, it would also be necessary to have, say, the date and time when the engineer signed it off, for example, *15 September 1992 at 12:30*.

The new 'design' entity can now be identified by four details: the machine no (123), the service procedure (hi pr hose), plus the date and time when the service was finished, that is, the Fdate (15/3/92) and the Ftime (1230). This 'design' entity can reasonably be called the service entity since each service consists of a specific type of procedure. It is easy to forget, when going through the modelling process, that an understanding of the context of these entities is significant. Thus considering the purpose of the document and design entities is an aid to thinking through the problem.

The entity model is now modified to include the new 'design' entity (*see* Fig. 6.6).

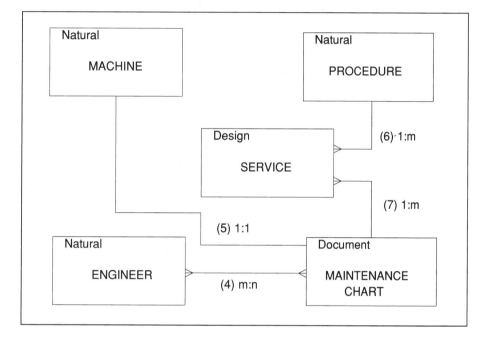

Fig. 6.6   Example of ERM technique: step 7.1

The new entity model now shows the many-to-many relationship between procedure and maintenance chart has been replaced with two one-to-many relationships. Relationship (6) 1:m Procedure/Service says that a particular procedure (for example a hi pr hose procedure) could be the subject of many services (for example on 4/6/91 and 15/9/92) or, for that matter, on various machines at different times. Relationship (7) 1:m Maintenance chart/Service says that each maintenance chart may contain records of many services, for example on the sample chart there are four. Each service, however, will only be ·recorded on one maintenance chart and each service can consist of only one procedure.

Step 7.2 Relationship (4) m:n   Engineer/Maintenance chart

A careful consideration of Fig. 6.6 shows that if each service line on the maintenance chart is used as a basis for our new 'design' entity service, then the *Engr* entry included within the service line can tell us which engineer signed off any specific service. The many-to-many relationship between engineer and maintenance chart can be resolved by using service as the link between them (*see* Fig. 6.7).

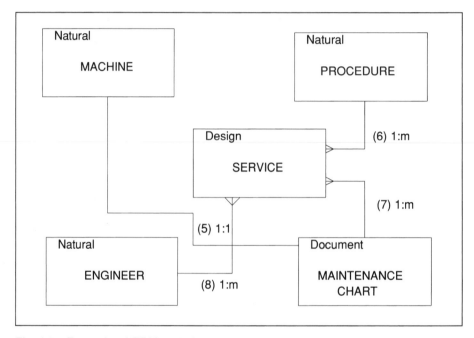

Fig. 6.7   Example of ERM technique: step 7.2

Figure 6.7 now shows that Relationship (8) 1:m Engineer/Service has replaced the many-to-many relationship between engineer and maintenance chart. Relationship (8) says that each engineer may sign off many services (for example, engineer *FH* has signed off two services on the sample chart) but each service can only be signed off by one engineer.

Note that, without knowledge of what we are trying to achieve in the business context, it is not at all certain that the advantage of using the service 'design' entity as a link between two sets of many-to-many relationships would have been seen. By modelling without under-standing, two 'link' entities could have been created.

Step 8: resolving one-to-one relationships

One-to-one relationships need to be carefully examined in the light of the business context, with regard to the types of entities involved and their role in management control.

Step 8 Relationship (5) 1:1   Machine/Maintenance chart

There is a clear difference between the entities in this relationship: one is a 'natural' entity and the other a 'document' entity. Machines are important as physical, 'natural' resources for the business. They have specific physical attributes, and other attributes which imply specific details about the physical attributes. For example the machine may be made up of a set of specific components, but attributes like the model number and date of manufacture may imply particular specifications of some of the components. On the other hand, each instance of a maintenance chart consists of a 'document' whose purpose is to record the service history of a specific machine, and to be a source of information about the services for maintenance or production personnel. These entities are definitely not the same thing.

Of interest is that the 'document' entity, maintenance chart, physically contains almost in its entirety the 'design' entity, service. In the absence of a computerised information system, businesses tend to use some documents as data resources from which information about other entities can be obtained. In this situation the factory is organised so that each machine has its own maintenance chart as its own data resource concerning maintenance history. A computerised information system could eliminate the need to keep individual sets of records of service history with each machine, by storing the records of all services of all machines in a single set as a database file. The physical 'document' entity, maintenance chart, that functions as a service data resource for

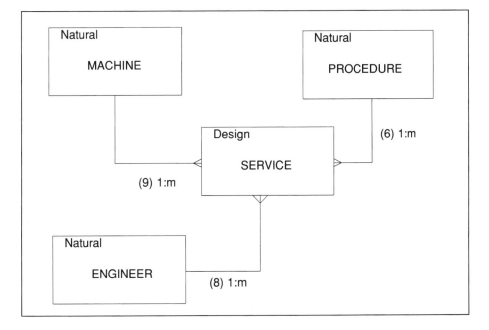

Fig. 6.8 Example of ERM technique: step 8

each machine, can be replaced in a computerised system with the 'design' entity, service, which has a similar function to the original 'document' entity. This link entity only needs to include the machine number which identifies both the machine and the chart, to enable us to identify a specific service with a specific machine, procedure and engineer.

The new Relationship (9) 1:m Machine/Service says that each machine may receive many services but each service can only relate to one particular machine.

Understanding the business context helps thinking through the top-down data modelling process and to identify the necessary entities and their relationships to each other, thus developing a well structured data resource.

6.6 BUILDING A MORE COMPLEX DATA MODEL

The approach adopted here means that it is necessary to consider building – or synthesising – a more complete data model to support requirements for information needed to manage a defined (sub)system of a business. Imagine that a tool store in the factory, in which expensive test equipment is stored and checked out on loan to the engineers. Like many such factories they experienced mysterious disappearances of the equipment before starting this system. A simple data model will be assumed for this system along the lines illustrated in Fig. 6.9 in which there are three entities represented: engineer, test-item, and test-loan. Each item of test equipment is recorded – in its system – as a separate loan and the engineer who books it out is considered responsible for its return in good condition.

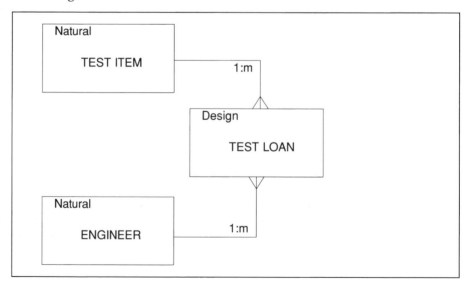

Fig. 6.9   Example of ERM for loans of test equipment: part B of composite model

The entity relationship model depicted in Fig. 6.9 can be combined with the model shown in Fig. 6.8 to build up a more complete picture of the set of data required by each entity and to build a more complete picture of the relationships that exist between different entities. On the face of it the only entity which is common to each model is the engineer. However, if it is also assumed that the engineer has to check out the test equipment for each specific service, then it will be necessary to ensure that the relationship between a loan and a service is reflected in the data model. (*See* Fig. 6.10 for a composite model that reflects the set of relationships discussed.)

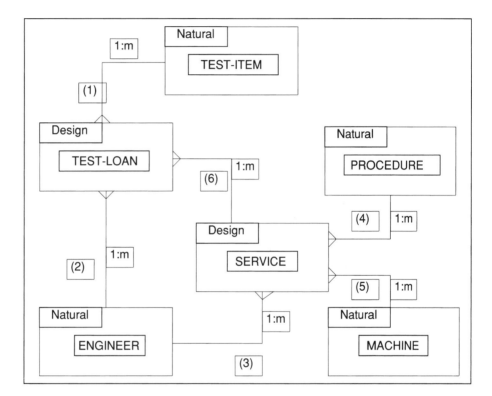

Fig. 6.10   Example of a composite ERM which combines the models in Figs 6.8 and 6.9

The composite model shown in Fig. 6.10 contains the following *relationships* and *assumptions*:

1 Each test-loan can only be for one test-item. Each test-item can be checked out for many test-loans (over time) – this assumes that there is a regulation which says that a test-loan cannot cover more than one test-item being checked out under that loan;

2 Each test-loan can only be checked out by one engineer. Each engineer can make many test-loans – this assumes that an engineer may take out many test-loans at the same or different times, unless a limit is set

for the number of test-items that any engineer can have out at the same time;

3 Each engineer can carry out many services. Each service can only be carried out by one engineer – this assumes that only one engineer is needed for each service, unless the service is signed off by the engineer who is considered responsible;

4 Each procedure can be used in many services. Each service can only consist of one type of procedure;

5 Each service can only be carried out on a specific machine. Each machine may receive many services;

6 Each test-loan has to refer to a specific service. Each service may require the loan of more than one piece of test-item – this assumes that the management thinks it better for an engineer to account for why the test-items are being checked out, rather than for test equipment to be specified as part of the service details. Otherwise the model could (and would) have to resolve the relationship as a many-to-many because we could say that a particular service could require more than one test-loan.

Note that the addition of the test equipment model suggests that more details about the engineer ought to be required. Only the engineer's initials are required on the maintenance chart, but in the new context we are conscious that valuable equipment should only be checked out if, say, the engineer supplies a full name and perhaps a signature which can be verified.

It should also be said that the principles of analysis and resolution of problem relationships, embodied in the 'steps' above, seem to apply equally to a data model as it is being built up into a more complete structure.

6.7 SUMMARY

Once a model has been developed which seems suitable for the business context, it must be ensured that each entity has an adequate set of attributes in order to supply appropriate information for the contexts in which it is used. For example, each entity type machine will have to include attributes such as the machine number so that any instance of a machine can be distinguished from all the other machines. Other attributes of the machine will have to include the maker, model number, date of manufacture and any other details about the machine which would be needed for this context.

Note, however, that different management contexts will often need information about some of the same entities, new relationships may be discovered and additional attributes will increase the set of attributes that comprise an entity. Thus as more decision-making situations are identified, a fuller picture of the world of business information emerges.

The original goal was to enable the production manager to find out whether high pressure hoses have caused problems with Armstrong machines. The manager reasons that if he looks at the maintenance charts for these machines they will record any instances of high pressure hose services, and thus confirm the problem raised by his colleague. The top-down data model developed for this context indicates that the service entity which logically takes the place of all the maintenance charts would play the important role of allowing the linking of a particular service procedure, for example, the high pressure hose procedure, with any machine which is made by, for example, Armstrong. It is also possible to identify which engineers have signed off each of these services on the Armstrong machines.

Through this simple example, the essence of top-down data analysis has been demonstrated using ERM. The technique and the result with the bottom-up approach which is explained in Chapter 7 can be compared. Both types of analysis have their strengths and weak points, but together they comprise a powerful combination. It is important to note that in both cases important insight comes from consideration or knowledge of the organisational/business context of analysis. It is also important to keep in mind that the purpose of the exercise is to model business or organisational data, not just to complete an exercise. Recognising the patterns of relationships between entities and meanings that are associated with them are important to the development of a good, useful data model.

QUESTIONS

1 A medical doctor is expected to *know* something about human anatomy and physiology, something about illnesses and something about medicines, otherwise patients ought to feel nervous if they should happen to get sick. A manager or systems analyst is expected to have relevant *knowledge* when analysing business data or processes. Discuss what sorts of knowledge would be appropriate and how analysis or modelling could be affected if the foundations of knowledge were inadequate.

2 Explain what is meant by a top-down approach to analysis and modelling.

3 One of the assumptions that we have made in our approach to analysis is a business context for which an information product or products are needed for monitoring and management control. Explain why this approach has been taken.

4 Explain the nature of the relationships between the 'natural', 'document' and 'design' entities and indicate how it is possible to understand this view of entities in terms of management monitoring and control.

5 A librarian in a local library wants to know the frequency with which books that have been in the library for more than five years have been borrowed on

a yearly basis over the period, with a view to purging some books that have had very little interest shown in them. Produce a top-down data model (or, 'an entity relationship model') based on this information requirement.

6 Imagine the librarian mentioned in Question 5 decides to check on the borrowing patterns of people in the town and decides that she wants to know how frequently borrowers from different areas borrow library books, with a view perhaps to better targeting when 'marketing' library services in areas where interest seems poor. Produce a top-down data model based on this request for information and synthesise it with the model produced in question 5.

BIBLIOGRAPHY

Arison, D.E. and Fitzgerald, G. *Information Systems Development,* Blackwell, 1988.

Benyon, David, *Information and Data Modelling,* Alfred Waller, 1990.

Beynon-Davies, P., *Relational Database Design,* Blackwell, 1992.

Bowers, David, *From Data to Database* (2nd Edn), Chapman and Hall, 1993.

Crinnion, J., *Evolutionary Systems Development,* Pitman Publishing, 1991.

Curtis, G., *Business Information Systems,* Addison Wesley, 1989.

Downs, E., Claire, P., Coe, I., *Structured Analysis and Design Method* (2nd Edn), Prentice Hall, 1992.

Skidmore, S., Farmer, R. and Mills, G., *SSADM Version 4 Models and Methods,* NCC Blackwell, 1992.

Teorey, T.J., *Database Modelling and Design* (2nd Edn), Morgan Kaufmann, 1994.

Weaver, Philip, L. *Practical SSADM Version 4,* Pitman Publishing, 1993.

Modelling business data: the bottom-up approach

7.1 INTRODUCTION

Chapter 6 provides an introduction to data modelling from a top-down perspective which is often referred to as Entity Relationship Modelling (ERM). This chapter looks at the complementary bottom-up approach. The main concern in both cases is that what is wanted is an information system that is capable of delivering business information which managers and other decision-makers can use to support the decisions that they have to make. While the top-down approach attempts, on the basis of knowledge of the business and of business functions which have to be monitored, to determine what things or 'entities' are significant enough to hold details about, the bottom-up approach attempts to start with the data or details and tries to determine from them what the entities are.

There are three possible sources of data, or starting points, for a bottom-up analysis. One source of data could be the output of a top-down analysis where entities have been established and a set of attributes has been allocated to each. A bottom-up analysis may well discover additional entities hidden in those already established through the top-down approach. Another source of data could be database tables – often used to illustrate the bottom-up modelling principles – although it is really the kinds of items that are included as data in a table that are focused on. The third possible starting place is with documents that the business currently uses to monitor its activities. In this chapter a worked example of bottom-up data modelling is given in which the source of data is a document.

7.2 THE BOTTOM-UP APPROACH TO DATA MODELLING

A bottom-up approach usually means starting with evidence found in the real world. As noted above, however, the reality for data modelling is that there are three possible starting points for bottom-up modelling. One 'real world' source would be the documents that refer to the resources, products, services or other documents that feature in the activities of the business. Other starting points tend to develop after some analysis has already been carried out since items of data are organised as attributes of entities or into columns in a database table.

The analysis aims to create sets of data items that include all the necessary elements and none that are unnecessary. The focus of each set is an element (or combination of elements) to which all the others relate as dependants; it is important therefore, to understand what the elements mean in relation to each other and in the context of the analysis. It is also important to ensure that links are maintained between sets that are related.

In Chapter 6 section 6.3 it was indicated that data analysis is not just a matter of following a technique in order to get the right answer, but that there are a number of foundations or aspects of knowledge which can be drawn on if it is intended to develop a good data model. It will be necessary to read section 6.3 before proceeding with a bottom-up analysis. Chapter 4 section 4.3 also gives some guidance on how the scope of the context of analysis can be constrained. Limiting the scope of the analysis to what is manageable and understandable can be as useful in bottom-up data modelling as it is in applying the top-down approach.

7.2.1 Basic terms and concepts used in bottom-up data modelling

The terminology of top-down modelling is usually distinct from that used in bottom-up modelling, even though some of the terms have an equivalent sense. The basic equivalencies are:

Top-down model	**Bottom-up model**
Entity	Entity, Relation, Table
Attribute	Attribute, Item, Element
Identifying attribute	Key (*see* text for types of key)

Keys. The concept of a key is necessary to the modelling process. A key is one or more characteristics of a type of thing that will enable identification of any specific instance of the thing. For instance, to find someone's telephone number in a telephone directory, using the surname as a key may be considered. The problem is that many people can have the same surname. If the initials are included as part of the key, then it is possible to narrow down the search for the number but, even then, often more than one person with the same surname and initials may be found. A combination of surname, initials and address will, however, normally be a sufficiently good key to find the appropriate telephone number. The characteristic(s) or attribute(s) that allows identification of a specific instance of a thing in a table is called the *primary key*.

Other 'keys' will be discussed in context, but the essential thing to remember is that keys are the identifying characteristics of things and, in a relational database management context, these are the *key* to accessing more description or details about the things that are associated with the key. For example, the key to registered vehicles is the registration number – each number is sufficient identification to find out the rest of the details about the vehicle, such as its type, colour, engine capacity, etc., as well as to whom it is registered.

Functional dependency. The relationship between a primary key and the other descriptive characteristics or attributes of a thing is described as one of functional dependency, in which the other descriptive characteristics are said to be functionally dependent upon the primary key. For example, if you went abroad for a vacation and your passport was stolen, you might go to the British embassy with your passport number, which you wisely kept safe for such an emergency. Before you are issued with a temporary passport, the officials might want to check that all your characteristics match those recorded on your passport. With your passport number they locate all your details and are able to confirm that you match the details they hold about you. Recovery of all your details depends upon having your passport number; all your details are functionally dependent upon your passport number. It can also be said that the passport number *determines* what the rest of the details are.

Since bottom-up data modelling is often talked about in the context of databases, some common sets of database terms have been included in Fig. 7.1. Figure 7.2 illustrates the basic structure of a database table as a reminder of some of the concepts discussed in Chapter 5.

Entity relationship model (top-down)	Entity type	Entity instance	Attribute/Data item
Relational theory	Relation	Tuple	Attribute
Relational database	Table	Row	Column
Common database terms	File	Record	Field

Fig. 7.1   More commonly used sets of database terms

It is an unfortunate fact of life that not only are there different sets of terms used for data modelling and for talking about databases, but these are not always used consistently. Familiarity with the concepts however should aid understanding in a discussion conducted in another dialect.

Table. The term 'table' is used when referring to the arrangement and contents of the details in a database, for example a database of customers, suppliers or, as in the illustration, a database that contains details of machines in a factory. Each design entity tends to become a table and the attributes of the entity become the names of columns. Also, each row of values represents one instance of an entity. An assumption is made that each cell (at the intersection of a row and column) may only contain one meaningful value. It would be possible to have too little or too much detail in a cell. For example, if in a table containing customers' details, a column heading were *Street* then the value in a cell could be *11 September Gardens*, but it would not be meaningful to put just *11* or just *September Gardens*, since the intention is to record the smallest practical level of detail about the customer's address. On the other hand, it should not be possible to put the whole address in a cell since, if a business wants to mail-shot customers in a certain area, it would be very difficult for the computer to find which customers lived there because the *Town* element would be lost in the rest of the address details.

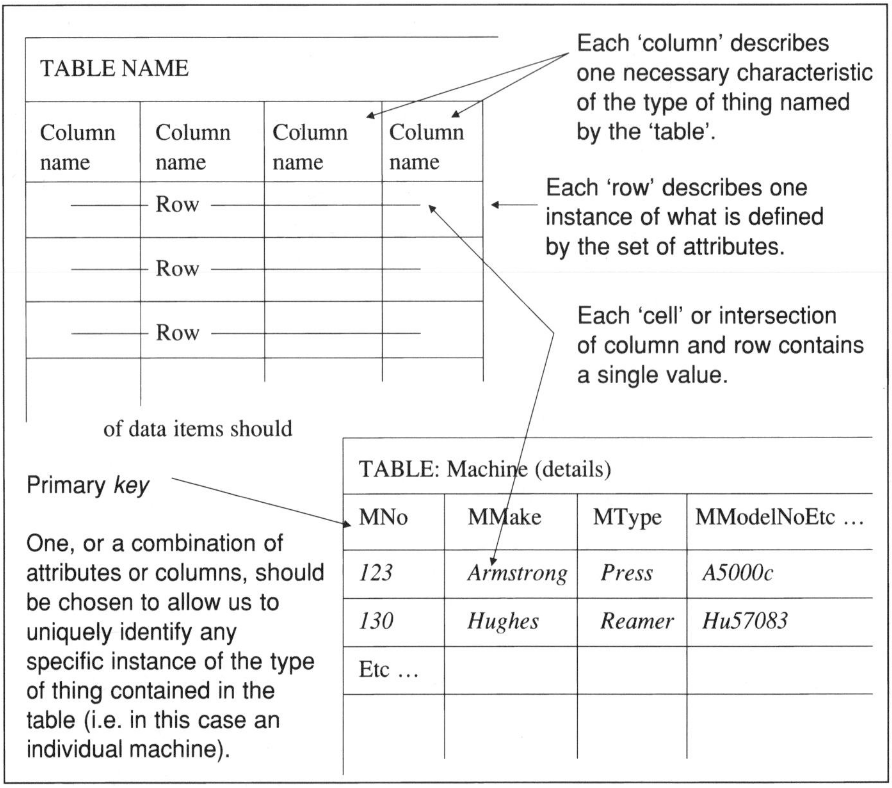

Fig. 7.2   The basic structure of a database table

In Fig. 7.2 each row identifies and describes a specific machine, while the columns give the elements of detail that are necessary to keep about the machines if answers to all the questions about the machines can be given that the manager and others in the business need.

7.2.2 The aim and purpose of the bottom-up approach

First, it should be said again that the reason for developing a data resource for a business – or part of a business – is so that the information needed to manage the business can be derived from it. Data resources are there because information is needed. The information will, however, only be useful if the data resource is used to store new details – such as to add a new customer's details, change details – such as a customer's address or credit level, manipulate details – such as produce monthly statements of customers' accounts, or delete details – such as when a customer closes an account. In other words, the database management system has to keep the data resource up-to-date as it monitors and stores details about significant transactions and states in the company.

It is in this context that data modelling is considered important. The aim and purpose of the approach is to ensure that potential problems in keeping the data resource current and accurate are designed out, while the possibility of gaining an almost limitless variety (in the context) of information is designed in.

The main way in which bottom-up data modelling tackles the issue of designing out problems is to ensure that each table contains only those attributes that are strictly necessary, while containing no less attributes than required by the information demands; in effect, a minimum necessary set of attributes. However, one of the main roles of the system is to provide information, therefore, no significant details should be lost. The bottom-up approach has to ensure, therefore, that as part of the modelling process the minimum sets cannot result in any data getting isolated and lost. Principles for relating tables to provide information are thus also designed into the modelling process.

Another way of expressing the purpose of bottom-up modelling is to say that it is a technique that is designed to reduce redundancy (i.e. unnecessary duplication) of data in a database, without eliminating duplication that is necessary in establishing links between related tables of data.

7.3 PUTTING BOTTOM-UP MODELLING TO WORK

To use this technique it is necessary to be sure that the components are at hand to make it possible. Many of the prerequisites have been discussed in Chapter 6, and in a sense, this follows on from it. The main assumptions listed below are basic requirements and there is no escaping the fact that business understanding is a necessary ingredient, just as much as an understanding of data modelling techniques.

7.3.1 First assumptions

It is assumed that:

1   the analysis/modelling starts with a document on which there is data, the output of a top-down analysis (i.e. an entity relationship model), or some sort of table of data;

2   the scope of the analytical context is well defined and manageable (*see* Chapter 6, sections 6.3 and 6.4);

3 there is enough understanding about the meaning of the attributes (or data) in relation to each other to enable a decision on which attributes are functionally dependent on what, or to put it the other way, which attributes determine the values of which others; and

4 it is understood how to apply the modelling steps.

7.3.2 The modelling steps

The following steps are based on an established practice called *normalisation*. As an introductory text, the interest here is only in illustrating how it is possible to analyse business data and produce a data model using only the sources discussed above as a starting point.

Four useful steps

1 Examine the initial document or table and choose one, or possibly a combination of characteristics or attributes of the subject of the table that would enable a unique identification of any specific instance of the subject. In a table for books, the ISBN number would be enough to find the other details of a specific book, such as the author, title and publisher).

2 The analyst should examine a document to see if it contains one or more sets or groups of data that refer to entities other than the document itself such as details about a customer or some products on an order or a list of telephone calls on a quarterly statement. If there are such groups then take note of which quality(ies) or attribute(s) in the group is(are) sufficient to uniquely identify an instance or member such as the customer's account number or the product code. The group (sometimes called repeating groups) should be separated out and the identifying quality or attribute *plus* the identifying value of the original document represent the primary key of the separated group(s). For example, if the product group is separated off into a group called, say, order line, and each product on the order has a unique product code, then the key to that group would be something like the order-number – which identifies the document – plus the product-code – which identifies each product on the document.

   In a table of data, such groups could only be represented in one of three ways but each would be problematic. Take, as an example, an order for three products. For each product the following details appear on a line: product-code, product-description, product-quantity, unit-price, and price (extended):

   (a) One design option for the table would be to include necessary order details plus one group of columns which represent each of the product details. Thus if we want to store the details (values) for the three products each cell might store three values for each of the product details. Fortunately, this option is not allowed since only one value per cell is permitted – in any case, it would cause confusion at the least if it were attempted.

(b) Another possibility for using the proposed table design would be to use a new line each time there is a new product listed on an order. The problem with this solution is that it would be necessary to repeat the rest of the order details every time there is more than one product mentioned on an order. The reason this solution is not allowed is that, if the order number is the key to finding an individual line on the table, there would be as many lines for as many instances of an order number as there are instances of a product on an order. The ability of a key to identify a specific line would then be lost, therefore, this solution is also not viable.

(c) The only other option would be to include in the design of the table, the group of columns that relate to the products for as many times as would be necessary to represent the maximum number of product types on an order. This might be a viable design but it also means reserving space in the database for the maximum number of products, whether all that space is used or not. For example, just one product may be on an order, but storage space could be allocated for, say, ten products. This is not a good solution because it is undesirable to waste storage space.

These three possibilities have been mentioned since, if looking at a table with a view to resolving such problems, it can help to recognise possible ways in which they could appear. It is, therefore, necessary to look for one or more embedded sets or groups of data that could potentially become tables in their own right. These 'repeating' groups of data are formed into a separate table and one or more of the data elements must be chosen to serve as a primary key together with the primary key of the table from which it came.

The resulting key is thus not a simple key, but a *composite key* comprising the primary key from the original table plus a suitable characteristic from the separated out set. The composite values should make it possible to uniquely identify any specific row in the new table. The original primary key provides the link between related rows in the two tables. When primary key values are used in another table to establish the relationship between them, the data element is known as a *foreign key*.

3 Re-examine the original document or table (i.e. the original table minus the 'repeating' group). If the primary key consists of two or more elements (attributes) see whether any other elements (attributes)

depend on only one part or element of the key. If this is the case create a (new) table and *copy* that attribute or part of the key and *transfer* the attributes that depend on it alone to the new table. The link between the two tables is preserved by the copied part of the key. As far as the new table is concerned, go back to step 1.

4 Examine the document or original table again and now check to see if there are any elements that do not depend on the key but, instead, depend on an element that is not part of the key; this too is an embedded set or group. If you find a set like this, the element which determines the others is *copied* as a primary key to a new table, while the dependent elements are *transferred* to it. The relationship between the new set and the original document or table is preserved through the key element which was copied.

Go through the same steps for any new tables. If any of the above steps lead to new tables being created, it means that entities that were not at first suspected have been discovered.

Note:
- A first table is often suggested by some document (in the 'real world') that contains a collection of details that relate to the context for analysis.
- Remember that some data items discovered should possibly not be included at all, if, for example, the value of one data item can be *worked out* from the value of another. For example, because the age of an employee can always be worked out from the date of birth, the data item 'age' would be unnecessary.

7.3.3 Applying the bottom-up modelling technique

The same data source will be used for the modelling process as was used in Chapter 6 on top-down data modelling. It may be interesting to compare the two techniques. Typically, the bottom-up technique will identify entities that would not be discovered by the top-down approach alone. The strength of the bottom-up technique is in revealing cases of unwanted redundancy which would otherwise give problems in the effective operation of the database. Each step of this worked example will be discussed. The context of the modelling process is the same as that given in Chapter 6:

The business context is a manufacturing business. In particular the production manager is concerned about an apparent long-standing inability of the factory to produce the required number of units within specified periods of time. One way of addressing this problem is to keep a check on the down time of machines, and to examine how long it takes to get the machines running again.

The manager thinks it would be useful to have an information system which would allow him to check the maintenance history of the machines so that he can tell when and why they go down, and when they are ready for operation again.

... there are many possible kinds of information that could be required, so in this case we will take *one possibility*. The manager has heard from a colleague in another similar factory that the high pressure hydraulic hoses on some Armstrong machines are under-specified and higher specification ones prevent problems. The manager wants information that could tell him whether there is any evidence to confirm whether this problem exists, and therefore whether higher specification hoses should be fitted to the machines. The information required should identify whether any high pressure services have been carried out, to which machines, and how often. He also might want to identify which engineers have been involved and seek their opinion.

The reason for identifying the context in this way is also discussed elsewhere in Chapters 4, 6 and 8, but it is sufficient to note here that within this context the pivotal source of data is the document 'maintenance chart'.

MAINTENANCE CHART

Machine make: Armstrong   **Machine No:** 123
Model No: A5000c   **Machine type:** Press
DoManu 1989

Procedure	Reason	Rdate	Rtime	Fdate	Ftime	Engr
Hi pr hyd serv	C/o hi pr hose	4/6/91	0947	4/6/91	1015	FH
Full hyd serv	Reg hyd sys	1/11/91	1300	1/11/91	1510	SSo
Relay serv	C/o elec fail	2/3/92	1610	3/3/92	0920	FH
Hi pr hyd serv	C/o hi pr hose	15/3/92	0850	15/3/92	1230	SSo

Fig. 7.3   An example of a maintenance chart

Taking the above maintenance chart as the starting point for the bottom-up analysis, it is assumed that this document contains details or data that are of some importance; furthermore it is assumed that the maintenance chart is something that can serve as a basis for providing some of the information about machines that is crucial to the management of manufacturing resources. The first step is to look at the kinds of data contained in the document:

Maintenance Chart (MachMake, *MachNo*, MachType, ModNo, DoMan, SProc, SReas, RDate, RTime, FDate, FTime, Engr)

To understand what these characteristics mean (it is easy to forget the meaning of cryptic names if you are working with hundreds of similar items), what they represent is noted below:

MachMake	The name of the maker of the machine.
MachNo	The individual number of each machine in the factory.
MachType	The type of machine.
ModNo	The model number of the machine (useful for identifying parts).
DoMan	Date of manufacture (useful where modifications to a model are significant).
SProc	The standard service procedure routine designated by the term. A standard procedure is normally invoked by one of a set of causes or reasons for a machine's failure.
SReas	The reason for initiating the routine service procedure.
RDate	The date when the request for service was made.
RTime	The time when the request for service was made.
FTime	The time when the service procedure was signed off.
FDate	The date when the service procedure was signed off.
Engr	The identification of the engineer who signed off the procedure.

Step 1: identifying the subject of the table or document: the primary key

Examine the initial document or table and choose one, or possibly a combination of characteristics or attributes of the subject of the table that would enable a unique identification of any specific instance of the subject. These identifying characteristics or attributes are called the *primary key*.

If this collection of characteristics or data items which make up the maintenance chart is examined, it becomes necessary to ask which one of them (if only one is needed) would enable a unique identification of this particular chart from all other maintenance charts. The one which seems most obvious is the machine number since, presumably, no other maintenance chart should refer to a machine with the same number.

The result of this examination for step 1 is to choose as the primary key attribute:

MachNo

It should be noted that the machine number refers to both the actual machine as well as the maintenance record associated with it.

There is thus a table called Maintenance Chart with the following set of characteristics or data items:

Maintenance Chart (*MachNo*, ModNo, MachMake, MachType, DoMan, SProc, SReas, FTime, FDate, RDate, RTime, Engr)

Step 2: looking for sets of details that do not refer to the document/table itself

The document or table should be examined to see if it contains one or more sets or groups of data that refer to entities other than the document itself such as details about a customer or some products on an order or a list of telephone calls on a quarterly statement. If there are such groups then a note should be taken of which quality(ies) or attribute(s) in the group is (are) sufficient to uniquely identify an instance or member such as the customer's account number or the product code. The group (sometimes called *repeating groups*) should be separated out and the identifying quality or attribute *plus* the identifying value of the original document represent the primary key of the separated group(s). For example, if the product group is separated off into a group called, say, order line, and each product on the order has a unique product code, then the key to that group would be something like the order-number (which identifies the document) plus the product-code (which identifies each product on the document).

From Step 1 the following set of characteristics or data items are given:

Maintenance Chart (*MachNo*, ModNo, MachMake, MachType, DoMan, SProc, SReas, FTime, FDate, RDate, RTime, Engr)

Step 2 suggests something needs to be done with the table because, for each occurrence of the primary key value, *MachNo*, there is a set of characteristics or data items which 'repeat' or have many values. In fact, each time a new service is recorded on the chart a new line of service details is added to the set or group, e.g.:

SProc	SReas	RDate	RTime	FDate	FTime	Engr
Hi pr hyd serv	C/o hi pr hose	4/6/91	0947	4/6/91	1015	FH
Full hyd serv	Reg hyd sys	1/11/91	1510	1/11/91	1300	SSo
etc . . .						

Other machines may or may not have the same kinds of service procedures performed on them and the maintenance records might look very similar. In the example the significant thing is that these service procedures were performed on this machine. However, if all service procedure details were to be stored in one database for all machines, a table containing details of all the maintenance services would also need to identify which machine each service was performed on. The group that has been identified is called the service entity or table.

Once this subset of data has been identified (sometimes called a *repeating group*), it is necessary to go back to step 1 and identify the primary key for the group. For the service table, either the *SProc* (service procedure) or the *SReas* (the reason for the service), plus the *RDate* (the date when the request for service was made) could be chosen. The SProc or the SReas both seem reasonable choices to help identify a particular service entry on a maintenance card, but first the relationship between the two elements or data items should be examined to see if there is a reason to choose one rather than the other. In this case it is preferred to include *SReas* as one of the identifying elements in the primary key because the *SProc* depends upon the *SReas*. The date on which the request for service was made is included to enable an account for the possibility of the same service elements having to be recorded on different dates for the same machine. Remember, the machine number is included in the new table to ensure the relationship between the service procedure and the machine is not lost.

The key of the new table is therefore:

MachNo, SReas, RDate

which gives us the new table Service:

Service (*MachNo, SReas, RDate,* SProc, RTime, FDate, FTime, Engr)

and the original table Maintenance Chart is now reduced to:

Maintenance Chart (*MachNo,* MachMake, MachType, ModNo, DoMan)

It seems reasonable to give the name *service* to the new table since it indicates quite accurately the nature of the contents. Not only is it important to ensure that the data are allocated to their correct tables, it is also important to retain links between related tables, such as we have done above by including the key of the original table in the new table(s) taken from it.

Step 3: re-examining the original key and if it contains more than one element seeing if other elements depend on only one part of it

Re-examine the original document or table (i.e. the original table minus the 'repeating' group). If the primary key consists of two or more elements (attributes) see whether any other elements (attributes) depend on only one part or element of the key. If this is the case create a (new) table and *copy* that attribute or part of the key, and transfer the attributes that depend on it alone to the new table. The link between the two tables is preserved by the copied part of the key. As far as the new table is concerned, go back to step 1.

Now examine the table Maintenance Chart to see if step 3 can be applied to it:

Maintenance Chart (*MachNo*, MachMake, MachType, ModNo, DoMan)

The third step requires an examination of the elements which make up a composite primary key and to look for any other elements that do not depend upon *all* the characteristics in the key. In this case, since there is only one element in the key, it is possible to skip this step of the analysis for this table and move on to step 4.

Step 4: checking to see if there are elements that do not depend on the primary key but instead depend on a non-key element

Re-examine the document or original table, and now check to see if there are any elements that do not depend on the key but, instead, depend on an element that is not part of the key; this too is an embedded set or group. If a set like this is found, the element which determines the others is *copied* as a primary key to a new table, while the dependent elements are *transferred* to it. The relationship between the new set and the original document or table is preserved through the key element which was copied.

The original table from step 3 looks like this:

Maintenance Chart (*MachNo*, MachMake, MachType, ModNo, DoMan)

An examination of this table suggests that yet another table may result. It is striking that there are two characteristics or data items that could be determined by one other. If the model number is distinctive enough it might identify the maker; the model number would also be likely to identify what type of machine it is. If, by knowing the model number of the machine, it is possible to determine its maker and what type of machine it is, it is also possible to say that the make and type of machine are functionally dependent upon the model number. If there is no reason to doubt this relationship then the following tables are left.

The original document is reduced to:

Maintenance Chart (*MachNo*, ModNo, DoMan)

and the new machine type table is:

Machine Type (*ModNo*, MachMake, MachType)

The *ModNo* element in the new table is the primary key since both of the other elements depend upon it. In the original table the *ModNo* is the foreign key which establishes the link between the tables. However, in practice, it would not be usual to apply the technique in a purely mechanistic manner and wider knowledge would be used to question whether the entity called Maintenance Chart is really the subject suggested by its primary key and other data elements. The fact is that the attributes tell something about specific machines while the maintenance chart simply records the services performed on those machines. The Maintenance Chart should, therefore, be renamed simply Machine and the role of the document maintenance chart is to be taken over by the service table in the database. Hence:

Maintenance Chart (*MachNo*, ModNo, DoMan)

becomes:

Machine (*MachNo*, ModNo, DoMan)

The following tables have now been identified and separated out which were embedded in the original document/table:

Service (*MachNo, SReas, RDate*, SProc, RTime, FDate, FTime, Engr)
Machine Type (*ModNo*, MachMake, MachType)

and the original document has been reduced to:

Machine (*MachNo*, ModNo, DoMan)

The document/table Machine has been simplified sufficiently to ensure a good foundation for development of a database, however, it is necessary to go back to step 2 and apply the analytical techniques again to the tables which were separated out. Step 1 was carried out on the new tables when they were first separated out.

Re-application of steps to new tables
Step 2 applied to the new tables. Possible repeating groups of data or characteristics are sought in the *Service* and *Machine Type* tables, but neither appears to have such embedded sets. Move on and apply step 3.

Step 3 applied to the new tables. The only table that has more than one element in its primary key is the *Service* table. This table is examined to see if any non-key elements depend on less than the whole key. The non-key element *SProc* (a standard service procedure) depends only upon *SReas* (one of a set of reasons for machine failure that invoke it) in that each standard service procedure can be initiated by a specific range of faults or problems which come within the scope of the procedure.

Following the step through, SReas is copied to another new table and the element that depends upon it, SProc, is separated off. This new table may be called the Cause/Procedure table.

The only other possibility for reducing the Service table further in this step would be to suggest that RTime is dependent only upon RDate, however, it is not easy to see any benefits in pursuing the analysis this far.

The Service table:

Service (*MachNo, SReas, RDate,* SProc, RTime, FDate, FTime, Engr)

has now become:

Service (*MachNo, SReas, RDate,* RTime, FDate, FTime, Engr)
Cause/Procedure (*SReas,* SProc)

The justification for identifying Cause/Procedure as an embedded table inside the old Service table would be that there would be no need to record the required procedure each time a cause or reason for service is recorded since it is possible to look up which procedure is needed in the Cause/Procedure table.

Step 4 applied to new tables. It might be possible to suggest that Ftime (the time when the service is finished) depends upon FDate (the date when the service is finished), but as above, this degree of analysis adds little of use to the data model.

No further application of bottom-up data modelling techniques is suggested by the contents of the tables and the application of the modelling steps to them. The original table based on the analysis of the document Maintenance Chart was:

Maintenance Chart (*MachNo,* ModNo, MachMake, MachType, DoMan, SProc, SReas, FTime, FDate, RDate, RTime, Engr)

The result of applying the modelling steps (and using knowledge) are the tables:

Machine (*MachNo,* ModNo, DoMan)
Machine Type (*ModNo,* MachMake, MachType)
Service (*MachNo, SReas, RDate,* RTime, FDate, FTime, Engr)
Cause/Procedure (*SReas,* SProc)

Note that the application of the bottom-up technique of data modelling has been demonstrated on a very small corpus of data. Only one document was taken as the basis of the analysis, but a number of tables could be identified within the scope of details contained in it. The focus has been on the relationships between the data items or elements.

The result of applying the bottom-up technique is that there are four tables or entities. The difference between this technique and the top-down is that there has been a failure to identify an entity for engineer which was recognised in the top-down analysis, but a machine type was identified which was not found using that analysis. However, if the maintenance chart had included a detail such as grade of engineer, then the bottom-up technique would have revealed the need for another table. The fact that such a significant difference in result could rest on the inclusion, or not, of one data element on a data source should highlight the importance of remaining aware of the realities of the business or modelling context. It is important not to be so occupied with the modelling process that its purpose is forgotten.

The techniques applied in bottom-up modelling are more mechanistic than those used in top-down modelling. The result, not surprisingly, of applying each technique is similar but not the same.

Note that a primary key of one table that occurs in other tables as either a dependent item or part of a key, is called a foreign key in those tables, e.g:

Data Item	Primary key in.	Foreign key/ Partial key in	Foreign key/ Dependent data item in
ModNo	MachineType		Machine
SReas	Cause/Procedure	Service	
MachNo	Machine	Service	
MachNo/SReas/RDate	Service		

Machine (*MachNo*, ModNo, DoMan)
MachineType (*ModNo*, MachMake, MachType)
Service (*MachNo, SReas, RDate*, RTime, FDate, FTime, Engr)
Cause/Procedure (*SReas*, SProc)

A further examination of the new tables does not indicate any further tables need to be created.

7.4 SUMMARY

The bottom-up data modelling technique is complementary to the top-down approach. As has been seen in the discussion above, each has its strengths and limitations. In practice, most people who are experienced at data modelling will consider the implications of both approaches and thus, for example, would be influenced by the need to eliminate unwanted redundancy when using the top-down (entity relationship) modelling technique.

One significant aspect of data analysis and modelling is that it is a two stage process. The first stage uses systems ideas to help focus and constrain the scope of the analysis. This allows clarification of the context for data modelling. The second stage is to apply the data modelling technique(s) within that context with a view to building a more complete data model through further diagnostic requests for information that is relevant to the business (sub)system for which information is required.

In Chapter 6, the chapter on the top-down approach to data modelling, it was suggested that entities that are discovered or 'thrown up' as a result of the analysis can be called 'design' entities. Those design entities primarily come about through the resolution of many-to-many relationships between entities. It should be noted, however, that the 'design' entities thrown up in bottom-up analysis are motivated by the need to eliminate redundancy in database tables. It will have been observed that because of this difference in what is looked for (i.e. the analytical criteria), each approach is 'blind' to some entities recognised by the other.

Chapter 8 discusses principles and ideas that are relevant to modelling business processes that are intended to deliver management and decision-making information. A similar, and hopefully, consistent philosophy underpins all of the modelling chapters.

QUESTIONS   1   Explain the main differences, and comment on any similarities between the assumptions made in top-down and bottom-up data modelling.

2   The related idea of 'keys' and 'functional dependency' are important to bottom-up analysis and in the development of a database scheme. Discuss what these ideas mean and why they are so significant to the production of information.

3   In Chapters 2, 3 and 6 we drew attention to the relationship between knowledge and information. In Chapter 7 we emphasised the importance of knowledge in top-down analysis and modelling. Discuss what sort(s) of knowledge are particularly relevant to bottom-up data modelling and note whether and/or how they differ from the top-down approach.

4   If we accept that the bottom-up data modelling approach is complementary to the top-down approach, comment on the difference(s) in the 'design entities' that result.

5   Summarise in your own words the purpose and results of applying each of the modelling steps.

6   Distinguish between 'primary' and 'foreign' keys and explain with an example how these keys are used.

BIBLIOGRAPHY   Benyon, David, *Information and Data Modelling*, Alfred Waller, 1990.

Beynon-Davies, P., *Relational Database Design*, Blackwell, 1992.

Bowers, David, *From Data to Database* (2nd Edn), Chapman and Hall, 1993.

Skidmore, S., Farmer, R. and Mills, G., *SSADM Version 4 Models and Methods*, NCC Blackwell, 1992.

Teorey, T.J., *Database Modelling and Design* (2nd Edn), Morgan Kaufmann, 1994.

Business process modelling

8.1 INTRODUCTION

In this chapter the focus is on *business process modelling*, but it is not unreasonable to ask *what* precisely is to be modelled, and *why*, before asking *how*. In attempting to answer these questions the approach will be based on the premises proposed when systems principles were introduced in Chapter 4.

1 Systems ideas provide a valuable set of diagnostic criteria that help us to ask sensible questions about how (effectively) a business is functioning.
2 Systems ideas provide a very useful means of relating business activities to information systems design and development.

The reason the approach to process modelling is based on these same premises is that they are highly relevant to the important questions of what, why and how to model.

There are all sorts of business processes that can be analysed or modelled, but within a business it is assumed that processes can be grouped and related to each other as patterns of activities that have purpose. Most businesses can quickly appear to be very complex institutions when we begin to look carefully at all that happens and at all the relationships that exist between the activities. But it is possible to begin making some sense of the complexity if the systems principles are applied as a set of 'diagnostic thinking tools' with which it is possible to systematically build a picture (or model) of how a business achieves things. Perhaps at the outset, the aim in this chapter is not to focus on the detailed technical specification of processes for computerisation, but more on how to ensure that analysis and design is sensitive to, and integrates the concerns of good business management, as well as the need for good, accurate and accessible information. The idea in this chapter is to facilitate clear and practical consideration of what is wanted, what sorts of things to expect of an information system and about some of the management implications of the processes needed to gain information.

In a general sense, it can be said that whatever is done by anybody or by anything in a company, at any level as part of its mission or purpose, constitutes a process. Processes may range from being quite simple to very complex and, significantly, whatever the process is, it can be modelled as a (sub)system. By taking a 'systems' approach it is possible to get a much better understanding of the part being modelled for the whole business and vice versa. Process analysis and modelling as part of information systems development are best treated as an activity in which systems principles provide the foundation for (all) the thinking and practices traditionally associated with it.

The implications for moving from a more traditional view of a process model to regarding process analysis and modelling as an application of systems principles will now be considered. Even though the primary aim is to examine processes that are involved in the production of information, from a practical point of view, it would be unhelpful to ignore the systems principle of holism which is a reminder that an information (producing) system cannot be isolated from other – often related – (sub)systems working in parallel. Only in this way can sense be made of the questions from which everything started. In other words, in terms of the systems principles, it could be said that keeping an holistic perspective on modelling a (sub)system gives a better understanding of the (sub)system, and thus what questions should be asked about it.

It should be noted at this point that the approach to process analysis corresponds approximately to the stage in systems analysis and design which focuses on analysis of the current system, that is to say, the way the business currently does things. The next stage in standard approaches is to develop a logical model of what happens, in which the focus changes to how the business might carry on all the necessary data processing that it currently does, plus what it needs to do, in an ideal world of effectiveness and efficiency. The assumption built into the traditional systems analysis and design approach to the development of an information system is that the improvements are going to be based on an effective and efficient computer-based system. This approach leaves open the issue of what type of solution is the most appropriate and concentrates more on understanding how management information is delivered in a company, where there are weaknesses and what issues of information provision might require management attention. The 'right' solution can only be based on an holistic understanding of the formal (and informal) systems in a business: information systems form some of these and need to be understood in context.

8.2 PROCESS ANALYSIS AND MODELLING FROM A 'SYSTEMS' PERSPECTIVE

Process analysis and modelling takes commitment from management of time and human resources, since it is an activity that would have to happen in addition to normal working responsibilities. The motivation for the task would normally be a decision to create an information system for a particular client base within the business. In a hospital it might be a nursing information system, a patient information system, or perhaps a management information system for business managers. Process analysis would be just part of a more comprehensive information system development project. Such projects can cost vast amounts of money, and it is usually thought that there is less risk of project failure if the discipline of a standard method of structured analysis and design is adopted. There are a number of established methods of structured systems analysis and design, each with its own preferred diagramming techniques and strengths. The differences between the methods are not substantial and for the most part they are more like variations on a theme. Virtually all of them have the same basic idea of what a process is.

8.2.1 Typical components that make-up or describe a process

- Purpose
- Way(s) of achieving the purpose
- Input(s)
- Output(s)
- Resources

As it stands, these components could describe, in principle, almost any process, whether the process relates to a business function, an information function, or a production function. There is a clear similarity between the way that a process is described and the way that a (sub)system is described. In Chapter 4 it was stated that a (sub)system has a purpose; it is organised in a particular way so that it can achieve its purpose; it should normally produce something (an output), and that it requires resources (human, physical and document or data). It is reasonable to think that a process, understood in the above terms, is a type of (sub)system, even though the typical systems analysis and design perspective of a system is quite narrowly focused. We will argue for a more holistic, as we have defined it, analysis of business processes and procedures based on the systems principles we outlined earlier.

It ought to be noted here that the idea of the systems hierarchy implies that there is one component of a (sub)system that is not recognised as a component of a process. If it is accepted that a process is a type of system, then it would be necessary to say too that one optional component of a process is a process (or a set of processes); the idea of a structure that can contain within it a structure of the same type is what is sometimes referred to as 'recursion'. A process that contains processes could be called a complex process, thus an information process could be represented as shown in Fig. 8.1.

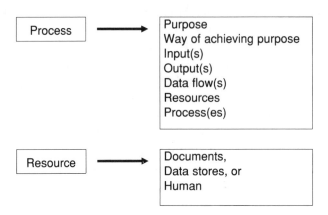

Fig. 8.1 Typical components of an information system

The difference, therefore, that should be made clear between the more traditional view of process modelling and this approach is the inclusion within the components of a process of the optional element of a process (or processes), and the extension of the idea of a resource component to include all business resources that are relevant to the scope of the analysis.

Systems ideas seem to comprise the one essential common language that allows discussion and thinking in a principled way about the issues of management control and performance in business, as well as the tasks of analysis and design for information systems that should support these management responsibilities. They also offer an insightful set of thinking tools and help identify business realities that can often be ignored by the somewhat narrow view adopted by traditional systems analysis and design methods.

The process components will now be considered in greater detail.

8.2.1.1 Purpose

Some assumptions that could be made about the purpose of a process from a systems perspective include:

- A process has a purpose, thus anything represented in an analysis or model as a process ought to have an identifiable purpose, otherwise it might be questioned whether a process exists at all.
- The purpose of a process is closely related to the overall purpose of its own hierarchy.
- In the context of information systems the purpose of the process is related to some aspect of providing information.
- There are likely to be correspondences or close relationships between the information processes and the business processes they are returning information about. It is important to be able to distinguish the purposes of each (sub)system.

One of the implications of accepting that a process (or system) has a purpose is that when a situation is analysed, anything which does not have a purpose should not be represented as a process. It is as important to know what not to include as part of an analysis as it is to know what to include.

EXAMPLE

> A laundry business offers laundry and dry-cleaning services to hotels and guest houses, and a sales and marketing office is located in three large cities within a thirty mile (50 km) radius. The business began as a reasonably equipped medium-sized laundry and it later acquired a dry-cleaning business which had two processing units on industrial estates near two of the cities. The main offices are at the laundry, but each site has a manager and an office to handle customer accounts, staff wages and supplies. Like many businesses, it has grown and changed its shape, but the way in which it is organised and run incorporates patterns from the past.

At the beginning of an analysis of this business there are many questions which will have to be asked. To illustrate the issue of purpose, it is necessary to begin to make some choices. A systems approach to the analysis would suggest that although we are looking at one business, there are a number of distinct hierarchies that operate within it. If interested in business information, then the first concern should not, for example, be the authority hierarchy or what departments exist within the company, but rather what information is required within the organisation for decision-makers and what processes exist to provide it. Someone with a good knowledge of business and systems principles should be able to ask analytical questions which would reveal whether the current business information systems were effective, efficient and adequate for good management of the company.

If interested in information systems, then a distinction should be made between the sort of information system that monitors the laundry and dry-cleaning processes and the sort of information system that provides business information because the purposes of the (sub)systems would be different.

8.2.1.2   Way of achieving the purpose

Assumptions that can, and cannot, be made, from a systems perspective, about the way of achieving the purpose include:

- If there is a process then there must be some way of achieving it.
- The way of achieving it may be influenced or determined by the management style or culture.
- The way of achieving it may be influenced or determined by the presence or absence of technology, or by the type of technology available to implement the process.

- When analysing a business process we document the way the business performs, or would have to perform the process.
- When modelling a business process we may document how to perform a process better, or how one would perform it, but systems principles should not determine how to perform anything, only what process, in principle, would need to exist. The way in which it is performed is a matter of management style and/or technology.

The way or means of achieving the purpose of a process or (sub)system is closely associated with the purpose, but it should be remembered that there may often be more than one way of achieving it – some ways being better than others. Particular businesses and particular management styles often have preferred ways of organising fairly standard business activities.

EXAMPLE

A hotel may have a very cumbersome manual method of booking in its guests. An analyst may study and document how the hotel performs this business activity. One solution might be to computerise the procedure so that the cumbersome method can be automated and speeded up, but another solution might be to consider how to do the task(s) more effectively and thus improve the way the purpose is achieved. The best solution, however, could be to improve the way in which the task is done, giving full weight to any advantages that could be gained through the use of computer technology. All the systems principles would say is that if 'booking in guests' is one of the desired business functions (or processes, or (sub)systems) then there should be a way of doing it. The systems principles will, however, cause the analyst or manager to look carefully at the relationship of that function to other activities in the business, including, for example, an information system that reports on occupancy levels for management purposes.

8.2.1.3 Inputs and outputs

Assumptions about inputs and outputs that can be made from a systems perspective include:

- An input is a resource that is drawn on by a process, while an output is the product of it which may become a resource that is drawn on by another process.
- When one process is contained within another (that is, when one (sub)system is contained within another) then the input or output of a lower process may appear to be the input or output of a higher.
- When the output of one process is the input of another, then the two processes are highly interdependent (or 'tightly coupled').

The inputs needed by a process are determined by what outcome is required. When information is needed about a business process it is necessary to make sure that there is data available about the process from which the information can be produced. The information itself might become part of the input for another process which, say, presents it as part of a summary report for a higher-level manager.

EXAMPLE

> Take the case of a nursing manager who observes what appears to be a distressing reaction by a patient to a new course of medication. She wants to know which doctor prescribed the drug for patient 'x' and whether that patient has a history of drug allergy.

A good patient care information system may be able to provide all the information that the nursing manager needs. The information required by the nursing manager would be an output of the system, but to get the output, someone needs to have already provided the details upon which the information is based, as input. Perhaps each time a doctor prescribes medication for a patient, he or she keys in the prescription on a computerised hand-held device which later is used to update the patient care information system.

If the nursing manager followed the progress of the patient and his reactions to medication over a period of time, she might discover either a pattern of patient reactions to certain types of medication, or a pattern in which a certain doctor is keen to experiment with unusual medications. Either way the information gained after each incident, having been acted upon at the time, subsequently becomes input data for the new information (output of a pattern-seeking process) about the pattern which is discovered.

EXAMPLE

> An executive wants to know what her schedule is for the next day. The process of providing this information is called the 'executive schedule production process'. Her personal assistant (PA) has to prepare a standard list of meetings, contact names, telephone numbers and addresses for people she has to entertain or visit; she will be provided with any briefing material relevant for the day. The information will be gleaned from company memos, notes in the office diary and any additional relevant details in the executive's personal diary. The PA performs a number of sub-processes in order to complete the process. Each time the PA interrogates one source, that is a sub-process; when the PA adds new details to the list that is another sub-process and so on. Finally, the PA completes the schedule as the last of the sub-processes in the series that lead to that point. The output of the last sub-process in the series is also the output of the 'executive schedule production process'.

This is just a simple illustration of how the output of a sub-process (that is, a process within a process, or a sub-system within a (sub)system), can be coincidental with the output of the process of which it is a part.

8.2.1.4 Resources

Assumptions about resources that can be made from a systems point of view include:

- In contrast to the standard position in structured systems analysis and design that the only resource of relevance is data, our systems perspective would say that all business resources that are relevant to providing required information products should be included as part of a business analysis or a process model.
- Resources may include human, technical, data, or any other resources that are necessary for the successful implementation of a process.
- Resources are most closely identified with processes at the lowest level of the hierarchies that use them. Further analysis may allow more generalised statements to be made about their use.
- Specific resources may well be the focus of competition between processes in the same or different hierarchies.

As indicated above, a traditional view of process analysis is concerned with the resources that an information system uses; these resources are understood to be entities (in the analysis and modelling stages) and become implemented as databases to be used by a database management system. The systems view would include the traditional interest in entities, but it would take into account the other types of resources as well.

EXAMPLE

If it takes a clerk two hours each week to interrogate a manual system in order to provide some financial or sales information on a regular basis, then this fact is relevant to the utilisation of human resources in the business. Furthermore the documents used by the clerk for the purpose are presumably being monopolised while in use. The clerk and the documents are instances of human and document resources that are being used in the process of providing the financial or sales information. If this is analysed in more detail the specific data used on the documents might be identified, and questions might be asked regarding what other physical resources are relevant.

EXAMPLE

> To go back to the personal assistant in a previous example, the PA was a human resource that was required by the process, just as the diaries and any other sources of data were document resources of some kind. The PA would have many responsibilities, and every one competes for time and attention, which is to say that the PA is a human resource which a number of processes may compete for or need to share.

How common is it for management to assume that human resources have almost limitless capacity to process more and more work? Specific humans or staff positions are often used as a resource for a number of processes in the same hierarchy of activity. But, in addition, the same human resources are almost always operating in more than one hierarchy. Each hierarchy may not just compete for the person's time, but the type of competition is not necessarily fair.

EXAMPLE

> Some police constables are recruited to fulfil a crime prevention and detection role in area X of a large city. Suppose the constables are good at their job and make a number of arrests and issue a number of cautions. Each day before they start their patrolling activities they have to file reports on the previous day's work. The more successful they are, the more time has to be spent on administration. However, as more time is spent on administration, less time is spent on patrol, and their performance seems to deteriorate.

If what they did was analysed it would soon be apparent that two important tasks compete for their time: one is what is supposed to be a set of primary activities that fall within a 'protection and detection system hierarchy', while the other comes within what could be called a 'protection and detection information system hierarchy'. But the officers are also part of other hierarchies that compete, if not for time, then for loyalties. They may see themselves as part of an authority or political system hierarchy up which they are anxious to climb. Impressive reports (information about their policing activities) may facilitate the climb to a greater extent than good policing (if defined on the basis of crime prevention and protection). This could lead to a working pattern in which performance in report writing takes precedence over performance in the community.

They may resolve the competition for their time and energy by assigning an importance (or significance) priority to each system hierarchy in which they function. They may have the power to determine which system hierarchies are more important, or the management may restrict their ability to choose. One thing for sure is that competition for resources, when identified by applying these systems principles, should be addressed as a management issue, since otherwise dysfunctional performance may not be recognised, understood, or addressed.

8.2.2 Analysis of business information processes: a management responsibility?

In the previous section a systems perspective on what could reasonably be considered typical attributes of a process was taken. Perhaps the way in which this approach differed most from typical approaches to process analysis is in considering a range of resources as significant for information systems analysis and design; to ignore the use of resources that are significant to the effective performance of business processes is not in the interest of the company. However it does raise the question of why business processes are analysed: what are we really interested in?

It is assumed that the prime interest here, from a management point of view, is how the business currently produces specifically requested information and how the processes that provide it relate to other business processes that affect them or are affected by them.

When this information was discussed in Chapter 3 it was suggested that information consists of meaningful facts that:

- are significant and relevant to the person who needs them
- are relevant to the person's position or role within the business
- are relevant to the decision or action that might depend on them
- have the power to precipitate change.

It was also explained in Chapter 3 that business information can be broadly classified into three types that reflect the types or levels of management decisions or actions that it supports, that is to say:

- strategic information for strategic decision making
- tactical information for tactical decision making
- operational information for operational decision making.

It can hardly be said that management control in a business is adequate if the types of decisions that have to be made (operational, tactical and strategic) cannot be supported with appropriate information. It is in this context that information systems are looked at, whether manual or computer-based, and diagnostic questions are asked about the ability of the system to deliver suitable information. Obviously there are no absolute distinctions between the types of decision making since in reality there is a continuum with no clear boundaries between them. Also, there may not always be an absolute match between the type of information required and the decision it may be supporting. Nevertheless, it is helpful to realise that information tends to differ in quality and type according to the purpose for which it is required.

The value of the information gained from the analysis will only be as valuable as the questions asked. One of the problems with asking questions is that while it seems such a natural thing to do, asking good questions takes a lot of practice, care and knowledge.

8.3 DEVELOPING FOCUS AND CLARITY IN PROCESS ANALYSIS

It is now known, in theory, what a process consists of, so it might seem that this is a good point to take on the challenge of process analysis. But it is necessary to know more, in order to undertake analysis with confidence. It is difficult to even begin a good analysis unless the scope and purpose of the task is clear. Most businesses and other organisations are very complex institutions and analysis has to start with asking some questions, but it is necessary to know *what* questions to ask and *why* to ask them. If there is no clear purpose and focus to the investigation then a lot of time can be wasted and confusion will arise: what is needed are good, proven principles to help gain the best understanding of what it is necessary to know within complex business organisations. The systems idea of holism gives a perspective on the complex set of relationships which a process may have with the business context in which it is located. A boundary can be set so that it is possible to focus on that process, thus limiting the scope of the analysis to understanding the process and how it relates to the processes that are relevant to it.

8.3.1 A holistic approach to process analysis

A very common practice in process analysis and modelling is to first take a very high-level view of a business, for example, one which represents the mission of the particular company in the business world. Then the analysis proceeds to break up the business into segments that seem more manageable than the whole thing. Eventually, the analyst focuses more on what data are used in the business, and the processes that use and create it. There are two observations that can be made. The first is that there seems to be an assumption that analysis has to start at the top, that is to say, the highest level of the business or organisation. The second observation is that it seems to be recognised that the whole business may be too complex to analyse without breaking the task down into smaller manageable parts.

The problem with the first point is that there is no clear or direct relationship between a very high-level view of a company and lower-level views that have any relationship to data and information in the organisation. The second point appears to assume that analysis has to proceed in a one way direction, which is downwards from a higher-level view to a lower-level decomposition of the more complex higher-level view. It may be natural to think that analysis has to include decomposition, but it can be argued that if we are seeking to understand something better by analysing it, then the analysis should consist of an examination of a process in order to understand it better. This would certainly include an examination of the thing in terms of the meanings or significances of its relationships within an holistic context; there is no particular motivation to focus the analysis on decomposing the thing into simpler parts; in fact, the idea of emergent properties (*see* Chapter 4) could suggest some understanding is lost through decomposition.

An analytical approach that is more concerned with developing a greater understanding of a (sub)system (or process) is preferred, for example by considering tactical level management concerns, rather than one that sees analysis only as gaining detailed knowledge of lower (operational) levels of activity. Systems ideas suggest this approach could be based on the holism principle explained in Chapter 4, that is:

- Holism recognises vertical (higher and lower) relationships between subsystems (or processes) in a hierarchy.
- Holism recognises horizontal relationships between sub-systems at the same level of a hierarchy.
- Holism recognises depth relationships between sub-systems in different hierarchies in a business.

A traditional process analysis which is meant to document data flows in the organisation would possibly have taken into account the fact that

EXAMPLE

Figure 8.2 illustrates three partial sub-systems which are currently operating in a medium-sized plastic moulding business. The company supplies nationally known store chains with festive novelties and fancy tableware. Every so often the company goes through a new product search process as it looks for some new ideas to supplement variations on standard seasonal products. Of the three sub-systems (or processes) focus will be on the product development information system.

At first glance it may appear that the sub-systems are relatively independent of each other, but a closer look is necessary. The highlighted box depicts a monitoring process which is part of the company's philosophy of regarding meaningful parts of the organisation as cost centres. The monitoring in this case is intended to provide regular updates on the progress each designer is making on the projects, and how much time is allocated to each. The report containing these details has to be completed by 3pm every Friday afternoon in time for inclusion in a summary of progress and costings from all cost centres to be considered at an executive directors' meeting on Monday mornings.

Product designer 'Fred' is responsible for three current projects, one of which is an urgent job for a large retailer. This project is in a testing phase and when Fred is not busy drawing and modifying the design of the product, he is busy setting up the moulding machine for another prototype, or evaluating the result. On top of this he has just received a memo telling him to come up with some 'new' ideas for a brainstorming meeting which is supposed to take up all day next Friday. He wonders how he is meant to complete his report!

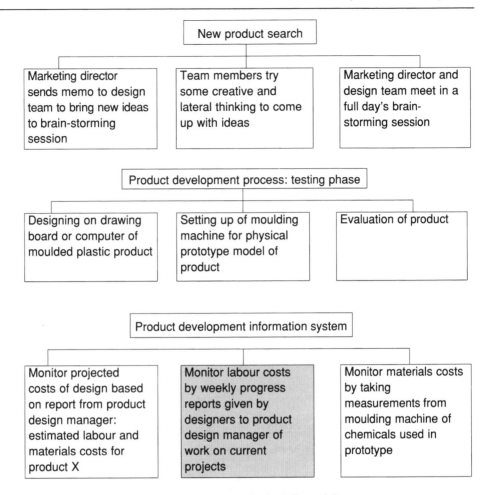

Fig. 8.2 Locating a process within a holistic 3-D model

certain details are entered on to a report by designers and that those details become part of a summary report. But there is more to the effective running of the business and to the provision of information than simply documenting data flows.

In systems terms there are three parallel (sub)systems, each with its own purpose. One of the (sub)systems is actually designed to monitor one of the others (the product development information system monitors product development processes) so, in that sense, there is a clear relationship, but even the third (the new product search process) impacts on both the others. These (sub)systems are in a depth relationship. Each of the (sub)systems has its own hierarchies into which it either fits as a sub-system or/and it has sub-systems below it, that is to say, it is part of a hierarchy or pattern of vertical relationships. Also, all three evidence at least three sub-systems (or processes) which may relate in a logical sequential order, or they may be an unordered, but necessary, set of sister activities.

When there is an awareness that any process analysed or modelled can be located in a 3-D matrix of relationships, the principle of holism is recognised. The management information gained from such an analysis is considerable but, taking a 'holistic' perspective on every process to be analysed or modelled seems to expand the enquiry rather than focus it. This is a serious question that requires consideration of another principle – the system boundary.

8.3.2 Defining the scope of process analysis through boundaries

The concept of a system boundary is another idea that is very important to analysis or modelling of processes. Processes may be simple or complex, that is to say, complex processes, like any (sub)systems, may contain components that are (sub)systems too. Apart from the potential complexity of a process itself, it has been indicated that the holistic context of a process within a business creates an awareness of the complexity of relationships that can affect its performance. It is important, therefore, that there is a clear focus to the analysis and that *only* those factors which are relevant for this purpose are included within it. One way to keep a clear focus and to limit the consideration of related factors is to determine what the boundaries are, or could be. The following approach for defining the scope of analysis or for deciding where boundaries might be is suggested.

8.3.2.1 Boundary and purpose

If there is clarity about *what* is being analysed, and *why* it is being done, the task will seem easier. It has already been said that one of the components or attributes of a process is that it has to have a purpose. Having said that, it is not always easy to identify the purpose. Some guidelines might help.

Setting the boundary by the overall purpose of a business system

It is accepted that the business process analysis concerns one particular systems hierarchy in the business, for example, a management information system. The *overall purpose* of the management information system is to provide management information. In this text alone, enough about management, decision making and information has been discussed to provide criteria sufficient to judge, with some confidence, whether a management information system is fulfilling its purpose. Any processes that are not part of the overall purpose of providing management information are therefore not directly within the scope of the analysis.

Setting the boundary by the specific purpose of a specific sub-system

It is possible to know reasonably clearly what purpose a system hierarchy has. The analysis may be initiated with some sub-system (or process) at a lower level in the hierarchy. In this case, whatever purpose the lower system has, it has some role in providing management information which is the general purpose of the system, but within it *the sub-system has a more specific role or purpose* that contributes to the general purpose in some way. The relationship between the specific purpose and the overall purpose is parallel to that between a subsystem and a system; purpose is an inherent component of a (sub)system (or process). Whatever lies outside the specific purpose of the (sub)system being analysed is not directly a focus of the analysis. The scope of our analysis can be further limited by the type of purpose we have for analysing it.

Setting the boundary by purpose in analysing the (sub)system

Another aspect of purpose, therefore, concerns the purpose in analysing the business processes. Every dimension of a (sub)system may not need to be considered in an equal amount of detail; interest may be more to do with effectiveness, with efficiency, with management issues or with computing. The clearer we are about what is wanted from an analysis, the better we can focus on the questions we ask managers, or other employees of the business.

EXAMPLES

1. Concern could be shown regarding the ability of a business to provide, say, management information and, if so, how it does it. That is to say, the data available would have to be documented, as well as the way in which they were organised and what processes would be needed to provide the management information required. The ability of the system to deliver the information must however depend upon more than just the simple logic of the situation, it must also depend upon the availability or accessibility of the human and data resources concerned and upon the availability of processing resources, etc. The purpose of the enquiry may not include specific consideration of the means of delivering the information.

2. Interest might be shown in whether a current manual system is effective and efficient, whether a computer-based alternative might offer significant benefits or whether a reorganised manual system would be adequate. In this case, an analysis would document the current system to see what data are available, how they are stored and what processes are used to deliver the chosen information. It would also be necessary to consider how human and other resources are used, whether there might be better logical alternatives, etc. The purpose here has more to do with performance.

3. Interest might only be in how data is processed, what processes are used and where it is stored. The fact that a management information system is being considered may be of secondary importance to documenting data flows in the organisation. In such a case it is possible that one might record what documents or data flow in and out of, say, a sales office, or an accounts department.

Of these examples the first focuses on the ability of the business to provide management information. Many businesses would have to say that they would find it hard to readily provide much tactical or strategic information. A process analysis would help to identify the extent of such A problem, and thus highlight a management responsibility to address it. The purpose of the analysis would determine how much peripheral information is looked for, such as whether competition for human resources to provide the information would cause other systems to degrade. This is clearly a management issue and not primarily a computer-related one. The boundary would include consideration of the use of human and other resources in the processes analysed but it would exclude consideration of other systems unless, for example, they would make competing demands for resources shared by a management information system.

The second example is more subtle in that, if concerned with an effective system for providing information, it would be necessary to consider more than whether data is available, but also, for instance, whether it is reliable. An efficient system would be concerned about accessibility of all resources needed to provide the information, as well as how good the processes for getting the information are. The computer dimension is clearly significant as a potentially useful technology, but the issues are still very much management ones. The boundary again is in part set by a focus on a management information system, or a part of it, but it also has to allow fulfilment of the purpose, which is to get information about those things which will show something about the effectiveness and efficiency of the information system. This means looking carefully at the resources, including a probable data analysis.

The third example, on the face of it, seems more concerned with taking a snapshot of a company's use of documents and data at a particular moment in time. It is hard to imagine what purpose the task might have except to provoke questions about the purpose and use of documents and data. Explanations could range from 'received business knowledge' which reflects long forgotten practices (sensible or not) to criticism which may or may not be justified given fuller knowledge. But, obviously, such a purpose excludes anything that relates to business or management performance, and the boundary can therefore exclude any consideration of management-related concerns.

Traditional approaches to process modelling within information systems development have tended to have more in common with this third example than the two before it. The important thing was that all necessary current processes were represented in an apparently computer-based, logical and efficient system, turning data into required information.

Diagnostic requests for information can set boundaries

An approach which has been tried, with some success, is to assume that if a manual or computer-based information system exists in a business, then its purpose, not surprisingly, is to deliver information. On this basis, it is possible to go further and assume that if the system is meant to deliver management information, then it should be possible to ask for a range of management information appropriate to the business context. With some business and management knowledge, and involvement from decision-makers in the business, it is possible to identify a minimal set of requests for information about the operation of the business, ranging from, for example, wanting to know about current information on stock positions and sales of ranges of products to wanting information about sales trends of certain types of lines over the past three years.

The requests become diagnostic in that each is a test to see whether and/or how the information system delivers the required information – in other words, discovering whether there is data to support the information requirement, whether there is a sub-system to deliver it and what the business implications are for delivering it, such as, the demand on resources committed elsewhere. A request defines the boundary of a process that can be specified in terms of a *purpose* (to supply specific information in response to the request), a way of *achieving the purpose* (the sub-system that would deliver it), *inputs* (the data that would be needed), *output(s)* (the information itself), and *resources* (in this case the documents, people and other relevant business resources needed to fulfil the purpose). This approach allows the analysis and creation of models based on focused, understandable and business-motivated information deliverables. From the individual analyses a composite picture can be built of either the capacity of a current system to deliver information, or of the sort of information system that might successfully be integrated into a business. Analysis and diagnosis are very different processes from developing a model as a basis for the design of an information system.

8.4 APPLYING PROCESS ANALYSIS AND MODELLING TECHNIQUES

The purpose of analysis and modelling is to try and get a better knowledge of the information producing processes, including the effects of their interaction with their immediate business environment. To increase understanding, analysis has to reveal the things about the processes that matter, and there is also a need to understand the significance of what is seen. Usually, the subject of the analysis will seem to contain a confusing mass of possibilities and the task can make us feel insecure and unsure of how to proceed. The following sections show how analytical techniques have been applied to a simple scenario; the analytical process has been discussed to encourage consideration of some of the issues and, through that consideration, a way may be found through similar problems.

8.4.1 The business context

Taking the same basic example for the analysis as that used in Chapters 6 and 7 on data modelling, the business context is a manufacturing business and, in particular, the production manager is concerned about an apparent long-standing inability of the factory to produce the required number of units within specified periods of time. One way of addressing this problem is to keep a check on the down time of machines, and to examine how long it takes to get the machines running again. The manager needs an information system which will allow him to check the maintenance history of the machines. He currently has a manual system of recording the relevant details, from which he can extract the information he needs.

Within this context there are many possible kinds of information that could be required, so in this case we will take one possibility: the manager has heard from a colleague in another similar factory that the high pressure hydraulic hoses on some Armstrong machines are under-specified and that higher specification ones prevent problems. The manager wants information which will tell him whether there is any evidence to confirm whether this problem exists, and therefore whether higher specification hoses should be fitted to the machines. The information required should identify whether any high pressure services have been carried out, to which machines, and how often. He also might want to identify which engineers have been involved and seek their opinion.

8.4.2 The analysis

The business context will be taken as the basis for an analysis and each of the above criteria (analysis components and systems ideas) will be used as a practical check list. One of the main goals will be to see whether anything of value to the business can be learned and, specifically, anything affecting the production manager's ability to manage in relation to the type of problem framed above.

8.4.2.1 Purpose

One of the first things to find out is whether a process has been identified. If one has, then it should have a purpose. In this case, the purpose is to deliver some information which will indicate to the manager whether a problem might exist with high pressure hoses on the Armstrong machines.

Unfortunately this is not a well defined purpose for an information system – it is not precise enough. The request for information needs to be repackaged in a way that makes sense for an information system; that is to say the request needs to be defined so that it is possible to ask what details would allow the manager to infer there might or might not be a problem. The repackaged request might be something like 'please give me a list of maintenance calls to Armstrong machines over the last two years in which the high pressure system required an overhaul'. (It helps to know that for safety reasons the company has specified service routines so that for instance if there is a high pressure hose fault, the 'procedure' column on the maintenance chart means that the high pressure system is checked, and specified high pressure parts are replaced even if they look all right.) Now this is a purpose that is reasonable for an information system, that is to say, the purpose is to provide some specific information requested by the production manager.

MAINTENANCE CHART

Machine make: Armstrong
Model No: A5000c
DoManu 1989

Machine No: 123
Machine type: Press

Procedure	Reason	Rdate	Rtime	Fdate	Ftime	Engr
Hi pr hyd serv	C/o hi pr hose	4/6/91	0947	4/6/91	1015	FH
Full hyd serv	Reg hyd sys	1/11/91	1300	1/11/91	1510	SSo
Relay serv	C/o elec fail	2/3/92	1610	3/3/92	0920	FH
Hi pr hyd serv	C/o hi pr hose	15/3/92	0850	15/3/92	1230	SSo

Fig. 8.3   A document resource: maintenance chart

8.4.2.2   Way of achieving the purpose

Under the current manual system of getting information that relies on data contained in the maintenance records for each machine, there is a standard practice. It is necessary to know that each machine has a maintenance chart which is kept by the machine in a suitably protected environment. Because of the odd error in the past when charts were removed and later found themselves on the wrong machines, they are not now allowed to be taken away. Therefore, any interrogation of the charts requires one of the service engineers to be detailed to go to each location with a clipboard and pen to note down any necessary details. In this case, there are five Armstrong machines at different positions in the factory.

It is beginning to become apparent that there is a way of achieving the purpose. The process of delivering the information includes within it a number of lower-level processes which means the process can be described as complex. It is necessary to know what lower-level processes are involved, then to work out whether there are significant groupings or patterns of relationship between them. The processes it is necessary to know about will be all those things that need to happen to ensure that the requested information can be delivered.

The information request is diagnostic in that a number of useful facts are discovered about how such a request has to be handled. The typical employment of a maintenance engineer to obtain and process the data and the amount of time involved are just two serious aspects that management might consider. Furthermore, other information requests that include the interrogation of the maintenance charts would also invoke the same pattern of activity – the same way of achieving the purpose.

8.4.2.3 Inputs and outputs

Normally, in the context of an information system, information would be thought of as being the output, while data would be the input. In this case, the output, in terms of content though not presentation, has been specified and this is enough to tell what data needs to be available as input to the process.

At any point where data are *input* or enter the process, there will be a sub-process or processes for that function. Because we are interested in understanding the implications of processes for the business, we will also be interested in issues like how reliable, or efficient, the process is, how labour intensive it is, how well it fits in with other working activities, how it is viewed by those who are involved with it, etc. If the maintenance charts have not been kept up to date, then clearly there will be serious problems in trying to provide the information; similarly, there will be problems if any cards have been lost or damaged. If the maintenance engineer fails to copy down the details accurately or clearly, there will also be some difficulty. If there is any problem with getting the data into the information system then it threatens its viability.

The *output(s)* in information terms is usually the information itself but, since one of the important qualities of information is that it should communicate, there is also concern about the form, as well as the content, of it. The final form of the output has to be produced by some sub-process: in a manual system the priority concern for the final document might be content rather than form, but in a computer-based environment content can often be easily represented in a variety of forms to assist with good communication. In the example, it is unlikely a maintenance engineer would have the time or skills to represent the information on a single sheet of paper as a bar graph showing numbers of high pressure services per machine or by plotting the frequency of high pressure failures over the two year period. Unfortunately for the engineer, these more effective ways to communicate information ought to be considered the norm. The information process should be evaluated on its ability to produce good quality information in all its dimensions, that is, accurately, on time, effectively, etc.

8.4.2.4 Resources

We are interested in all the resources that are used by the process if it is to produce the information. Of particular concern are the resources that have significance for the effectiveness or efficiency of the business. In the example, there are *document* resources which contain the relevant source data, that is, the maintenance charts. Another significant resource is the maintenance engineer who, as a *human* resource, has to spend some of his time walking around the factory, checking the maintenance charts, making a copy of relevant details and writing up the results.

Time is a type of resource and is usually an important issue for business, but time is a commodity that can be attached to most processes. Time is, therefore, a factor like *cost* with which processes are evaluated and their significance to the company is considered. Other resources could be included such as the clipboard and writing pad; that is to say anything that the engineer uses in the process of producing the information.

Since the analysis of the process is concerned with gaining understanding about the process, the use of resources is looked at carefully. One of the questions that the systems idea of holism poses is whether any of the resources used by the sub-system represented by the process in the example, are also used by other sub-systems. Two significant resources are the maintenance chart and the maintenance engineer. It must, therefore, be asked whether they are used for anything else and if there is likely to be competition for them by other processes (or (sub)systems) which must be managed. In the case of the document, there is little competition for its use, but in the case of the engineer, both he and others may resent the time he spends on monitoring the use of machines, rather than making sure that they are in good repair which is a different system. The purpose of the two systems hierarchies are distinct, even if they both have something to do with the machines, and they both want to use some of the same resources. If something is not done to manage the situation, the business will not get optimum performance from either system.

It would be reasonable to assume, in the example, that the manager actually decides he needs more information than he originally thought. He remembers that there are another ten presses that also have high pressure systems and it has occurred to him that he ought to see whether the Armstrong machines are showing evidence of any more problems with their high pressure systems than the other makes of machinery. He, therefore, wants comparative information which means the engineer has to find more time – time stolen from his primary role as a human resource in a maintenance system – to be used as a human resource in the maintenance information system.

8.4.3 Focusing the scope of the analysis

The analysis proceeded on the basis that interest was shown in the production of some specific information, i.e. 'Please give me a list of maintenance calls to Armstrong machines over the last two years in which the high pressure system required an overhaul'. Because the manager wants information about the maintenance of some machines, it is known that the request belongs somewhere within an information system. As it happens, the information system is very crude. The fact that the necessary data are stored (on maintenance charts) anticipates their use for information. The way of producing information seems to rely totally on the availability and processing ability of human resources. Without having to analyse such a system completely it is possible to locate the example as a specific request for information within an overall purpose of providing information about part of the business. The scope of the analysis can be limited to what is required to provide information for the request. Insecurity may abound because, say, the whole maintenance information system has not been analysed, but then it is unlikely to be a coherent whole. Nevertheless, the request is diagnostic because quite a lot has been learned about the 'system' and its place in the business.

It is possible to build up knowledge of how the 'maintenance information system' works and also what information can be provided by testing the system with more carefully chosen requests. How many diagnostic questions are asked, and what sorts of requests are made will depend upon what we really want to know about the 'system'. There should be some purpose for the analysis.

One problem with many real world information systems is that not only have many of them never really been designed well, but they are rarely complete, and changes in information requirements are often met in ad hoc ways simply to overcome the problems. This is not so much a criticism but a statement of realities. There may be little point in attempting a complete process analysis of the current state of a large complex business; it is worth asking what the purpose of developing a model of an existing system might be. In the example, the production manager could want to analyse how the information system works because he gets embarrassed because of the time it takes him to get information to share with his colleagues and he wants to see where the problems are before deciding on how to address the situation. He may already have decided that a computer-based information system is needed, and the purpose of the analysis is to systematically build up a picture of what already happens, before considering how a computerised system could be organised within the working environment. There are many possibilities, but the scope and focus of the analysis and model building can be constrained by the purpose or reason for the analysis.

8.4.4 Diagramming techniques used in process modelling

There are a number of diagramming conventions that are commonly used, but differences in the appearance of the diagrams only disguise the common ideas on which they are based. This text will not cover all data modelling and process modelling techniques in detail, but rather will give some understanding of what they are about. The main technique of interest in process modelling for information systems is called Data Flow Diagramming (DFD).

We will follow the diagramming notation that is typically used by methods such as the Structured Systems Analysis and Design Method (SSADM) and organisations like Learmonth and Burchett Management Systems (LBMS). Other methods and organisations often have their own preferred ways of representing the same things.

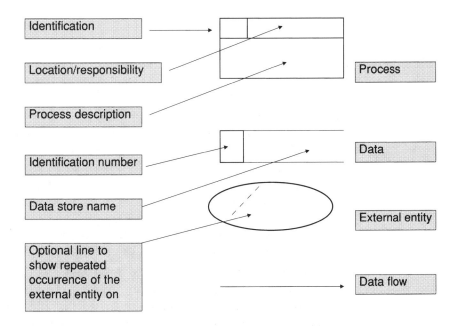

Fig. 8.4   A common data flow diagramming notation

The DFD symbols shown in Fig. 8.4 can be related to the components of a process which was discussed earlier in the chapter. A brief explanation of each of the symbols will be given and comments will be made on their use.

8.4.4.1 The data store

When making a DFD for the current information system, a data store can represent anything from a collection of invoices in a filing cabinet, or a patient's chart in a hospital on which his or her temperature and pulse readings might be recorded, and medications might be noted, to a customer database file held on a PC in a small business. Some data stores are permanent and some are just created for temporary reference. Usually the identification number has the letter M for manual stores, D for digital (computer-based) stores and may include a T for a temporary store. More than one representation of a single store (to make a diagram easier to read) is noted by a double line at the end of the box.

8.4.4.2 The data flow

The data flows should be labelled to indicate what data are being created, changed or used by a process. The main purpose of labelling is so that the diagram communicates clearly with the people who are meant to read it. Watch the use of arrows on the flows to and from data stores. Usually an arrow to a store means data is sent to it, while an arrow from a store means the data is being looked at by a process and an arrow with a head at each end means a process is using and changing the data in a data store.

8.4.4.3 The process box

Each process box is meant to represent a (sub)system or process at some level of an information system hierarchy. Typically data flow diagramming is begun at a high level in a business, and the DFDs are used to represent different levels of analysis and decomposition in a top-to-bottom direction (*see* Fig. 8.5).

The top level, level-0, or 'context' diagram has just one box and usually indicates the highest level at which the analysis or modelling process begins. Some authors say it defines the scope of the analysis which implies that perhaps the context is part of a system, thus representing a significant sub-system; others say that the context diagram should try and capture the entire system as a single process. Most, if not all, writers do not distinguish, especially at a high level, between the functional (sub)system that the information system is monitoring and the information system itself and, furthermore, many writers do not distinguish between the data that is used to provide information and the documents that contain data. Unfortunately, SSADM seems to encourage the documentation of physical flows in DFDs which depict items that are neither documents nor data. Because of these inconsistencies it is hard to be clear about the purpose of DFDs, and context diagrams can vary a great deal in how much detail they contain, being either too vague or too detailed and arbitrary to serve much of a useful role. If a context diagram is representing a process, then regardless of the level the DFD should presumably contain all the typical components of a process, but in a diagrammatic form.

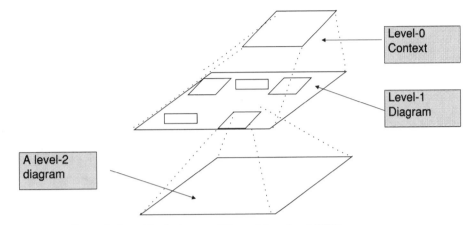

Fig. 8.5 The relationship between different levels of DFDs

Figure 8.6 illustrates a context or level-0 DFD which reflects the approach to process analysis. The diagram captures the essential components of a system and it infers its clear purpose which is to provide information. An examination of the inside of the process box reveals:

- in the top left segment is the box identification number, which, in this case is zero;
- the top right segment has been given the label 'maintenance information sub-system'. Different authors and analysts use the segment in different ways; some tend to put locations of the processes

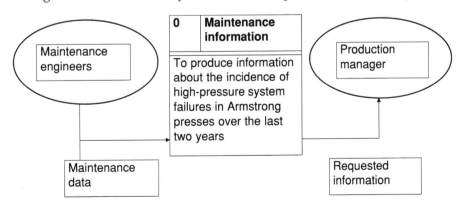

Fig. 8.6 Context diagram for maintenance information sub-system

such as department names, others put company positions or roles that are directly responsible for the process. At the context level the segment is often left blank. The segment has been used to indicate that the process belongs within the maintenance information system as a sub-system;

● the large bottom segment contains the purpose of the process.

The other components on the diagram are two oval shapes to indicate 'external entities'. External entities are people who interact with the process in some way but who have no direct role in the process. In the example the production manager is represented as one external entity. He is, as it were, the consumer of the information product – he wants the information that the process is meant to deliver. Sometimes the external entity that wants the output of a data/information process is called the 'data sink'. The other external entity is called maintenance engineers. The reason for this is that the original source of the maintenance details are the maintenance engineers who enter the details on the maintenance charts. The external entity which supplies the data is sometimes called the 'data source'.

The last components to be commented on are the data flows. In this high-level diagram it is sufficient to state what sort of data are input to the process, and what sort are leaving the process as output.

The level-1 DFD is taken to be the level-0, or context diagram which has been 'broken down' into a number of major processes; some suggest between five and nine. To state that there should be a limit is to imply that the motivation for doing so has to do with presentation rather than anything to do with the analysis or the business itself. It is suggested that the motivation for breaking down a complex process into smaller entities should come from an understanding of the business or a clearly motivated analytical decision. But how is it decided what processes should exist at this, the first level of decomposition? This is discussed further below.

Whereas the context diagram aims to communicate the single primary purpose of the system, the level-1 diagram presents a more detailed view of the subsystem (or process) in which the lower-level simple or complex sub-processes are shown as process boxes. The original context box is now represented by the boundary. Part of the difficulty of decomposing or breaking down a process into lower-level processes, is deciding on what they should be, that is to say, just how or whether some lower-level processes should be organised into one or more coherent and meaningful complex sub-processes, or whether they should be represented as single, simple ones. The process box of level-0 is still a process box at level-1, except that it is represented by the boundary and lower level processes within it are now exposed. An examination of the contents of the boundary of the maintenance information sub-system follows:

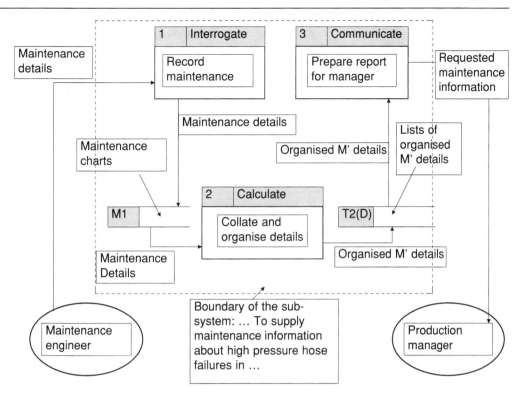

Fig. 8.7   Level-1 diagram for a maintenance information sub-system

1   The process is represented as *three lower-level processes*. The first
process, *Interrogate*, represents one of the roles of an information
system which is to get data about, or monitor a business function. The
job of recording the details on the chart could either be done by the
engineer who performs the 'business function' of maintenance, or by
the machine operator who could write it down for him. Some analysts
might use the position of the person responsible such as *Machine
operator*, while others might say *Engineering section* to represent the
responsible department.

The second process, *Calculate*, is not well named, but it represents a
complex process in that more than one simple lower-level process is
contained in it. In the example, it is the process that is focused most
on actual data processing or manipulation. Other approaches may
well decide to include more processes within the boundary of the
sub-system, or they may decide to group lower-level processes in
different ways. Whatever principle is adopted by the analyst in
breaking down processes, it should be as clear as possible and well
motivated.

The third process, called *Communicate*, is responsible for providing
the final output of the sub-system, that is, the information in a form
that is meaningful and relevant to the manager who wants it.

2 Also within the boundary are *two data stores*. The store M1 is a manual store which represents the maintenance charts on which the maintenance data are found; the store T2(M) represents a temporary manual store which denotes the results of gathering the maintenance details and sorting them into some sort of logical order in preparation for making the report to the manager.

3 *Each data flow* either between the environment of the boundary and inside it, or between components within it, is labelled with the essence of the data that is passing between the components. These flows are the inputs and outputs of the processes within the boundary. Where input enters, the boundaries of the process and the lower-level process that handles the input coincide: a similar situation exists for the output of the process.

Outside the boundary are the *external entities* shown in the oval shapes, not to be confused with the 'entities' of data modelling. The production manager initiates the whole process and wants the output of the (sub)system, while the maintenance engineer is the person who examines the machines and provides the original data for the system that is monitoring maintenance activity in the factory. A data model may identify engineers as a resource about which details need to be held, in which case facts about the engineers may be kept in a data store, but the engineer as a human resource who is essential to the process of providing information, is different to the data resource which contains facts about him.

8.4.5 Decomposing processes

As processes are 'broken down' or 'decomposed' into sub-systems, the relationship between a process and the processes it contains are maintained by the identification number box in the top left corner. So a process at level-1 that has the identification number 2, when broken down as an amplified level-2 diagram, would keep the number 2 on the lower-level processes, but it would add another part to give identification numbers such as 2.1, 2.2, etc. 'Calculate', the second process in the example, could be expanded into a level-2 DFD which would detail the processes and other components which are assumed by the 'Calculate' process box.

There is no set rule or simple principle which helps us to know for sure how to break down a higher-level DFD into lower-level ones. There are some factors, however, which might help us to make better judgements. The rationale for breaking up a process into lower-level processes should come from a combination of factors, including the business context, systems principles, and from the patterns that we see being built up through the use of good diagnostic questions or requests. In contrast some observations on DFDs are questionable, for instance if a method suggests that a DFD should contain between, say, six and ten processes, then the motivation for this is somewhat arbitrary and, not well motivated. Sometimes DFDs contain some information-related processes together with processes about the system that is being monitored. This is a confusion of hierarchies and it makes it very hard to tell what sort of process or sub-system is being analysed.

DFDs are diagrams that are used to document and communicate the results of our analysis; they are not the analysis itself, but they can help analysts or managers to clarify thinking. Analysis usually begins with hypothesis, that is to say, some assumptions are made about the process being analysed, but as more is learned through the analysis some assumptions may be changed and understanding improved. When analysing processes, as indicated above, it should be because we want to learn something specific about the business and its ability to provide information; the reason for using DFDs as an analytical devise should be to help do the job better. The use of DFDs should communicate important statements about the perception of the (sub)system; therefore when a process is decomposed into lower-level ones, there ought to be a clear rationale for how and why it was decomposed as it was.

There follows an examination of three possible factors that could influence how a process is decomposed:

- business factors
- systems factors
- emergent factors.

8.4.5.1 Business factors

Business processes do not exist in a vacuum; each is an instance of the way a business achieves its purposes. Certain management styles, certain types of organisational structures (*see* Chapter 2), and even certain businesses may have preferred ways of doing things. These ways will tend to be generic and individual processes will often fall into typical patterns of doing things. A good analysis may capture generalisations in the organisation or groupings of sub-processes when processes are broken down. For example, if it is necessary in some bureaucratic organisation to fill out a form, get it countersigned and then give it to a certain person, for certain categories of information, then an analysis may pick up on how information is categorised and how that relates to the way in which the system produces it. These sub-processes might usefully be summarised as a single complex process in a lower-level DFD, just as we might have been able to classify or categorise the information by some of its characteristics.

8.4.5.2 Systems factors

Systems principles may provide some clarity in the analytical task by acting as a reminder that, whether looking at simple or complex lower-level processes, it should be possible to define them in terms of their necessary components. It is not at all uncommon to see processes appearing on DFDs that would be very hard to justify on the basis of these criteria. For example, if a higher-level process is broken down into sub-processes, resources and data flows, then one thing that the systems ideas should do is to show that whatever is represented as a process box, it should be possible to account for it as a meaningful, coherent element that has all the components of a process.

8.4.5.3 Emergent factors

It may seem a little strange to think of building up while breaking a (sub)system down, but when using a 'diagnostic' approach such as discussed here, there should be an awareness that each such 'diagnostic' request for information may be designed to give us additional insight into a greater whole. Thus, if we were to build up (or synthesise) a picture of an information sub-system through the use of diagnostic requests for information, each request may add to the understanding of how the business produces the information it needs. New information may complement information gained through analysis of related processes which then enables better capture of important generalisations about the way the business delivers (say, management) information, and this could help us sort out whether some sub-processes would be more meaningfully represented as simple or as complex processes at particular levels of decomposition. The new emergent factors are different from the business factors in that if there is an awareness of the *business factors* it may be possible to start with a hypothesis about what is significant, but in the *emergent* case the significance becomes more apparent as the result of more analysis, or new diagnostic requests. Business knowledge may allow certain assumptions to be made about what is believed to be important, but we ought to be aware of what assumptions have been made, and ought, probably, to test them in the course of analysis. For example, suppose the production manager in the example used earlier wants to check which machines have received a full service during the last year so that he can plan some scheduled down-time for those that still need one. His request for information would probably initiate an information production process similar to the one that we analysed previously. The new request might however identify a problem of getting to the maintenance charts when some machines are in operation. A good analysis ought to pick up on a problem that could add perhaps hours to the delivery of maintenance-related information.

8.4.6 Annotating DFDs

A DFD is not necessarily self-explanatory. DFDs need some sort of commentary or annotation in order to convey significant facts that are not included within the diagram. If the standard diagramming conventions are used, the use of human and physical resources would not be included, neither would the issue of competition for the resources, or factors to do with effectiveness or efficiency of the process(es). All of these important management issues could well be identified by analysts or managers involved in the business process analysis.

Diagrams are helpful if they are better at conveying information more effectively than text. Relatively simple, clear and uncluttered diagrams are more effective than those that contain a lot of detail, thus it is a good idea to complement the diagrams with what they cannot or do not show and what would be valuable in understanding the process in its business context. DFDs may be suitable for illustrating the decomposition aspect of analysis, but they are not so good at drawing attention to those aspects of process analysis that help us to understand the relationships that hold between the process and its business context.

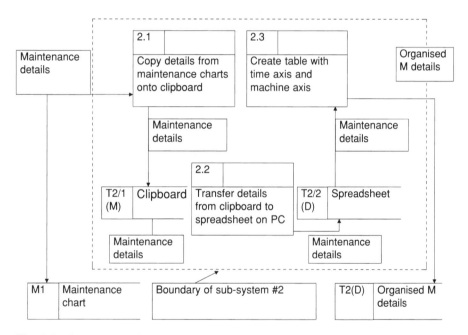

Fig. 8.8   An annotated level-2 diagram for a maintenance information sub-system

8.4.6.1   Resources

Human: maintenance engineer has to walk around factory copying details from maintenance charts on to clipboard. He also has to type the details into a spreadsheet and organise the details into a table suitable for a secretary to include in a report to the production manager.

Competition: the engineer's main job maintaining the machines.

Time factor: significant since one such request to provide information can typically take up half a morning.

Cost factor: derived from (time * rate) plus cost of lost production due to down-time delay if he is taken away from a maintenance job.

Physical: PC is located in the secretary's office, but is used by the engineer to enter maintenance details and he organises the details on a spreadsheet since he understands the details. The secretary prints a hard copy and includes it in a standard report.

Competition: the machine is used by the secretary for word processing and other duties. Usually the secretary allows the engineer to use the PC when he is ready, but if she has deadlines he has to wait.

Time factor: the engineer is not trained to use the PC and he probably spends twice as much time as he needs to, and can take up to an hour to produce a crude table.

Cost factor: derived from (time * rate) plus any time lost by secretary in her duties, and/or time lost by him if waiting.

Documents: maintenance charts are the only permanent documentary resources used in this process.

Competition: none of consequence.

Time factor: not applicable, except that when some machines are in operation, the charts cannot be accessed for safety reasons.

Cost factor: not applicable

8.4.6.2 Emergent properties

Desired: the information as requested.

Undesired: failure to meet maintenance schedule, or increase in overtime to get schedule back on track.

8.4.6.3 Efficiency and effectiveness:

The process does *not* appear to be very *efficient* in that a lot of time is spent:

- collecting the data, i.e. walking around the factory floor to as many machines as are relevant to the request process;
- copying across data, i.e. copying from the charts to the clipboard to the spreadsheet, and later to the report. This is time consuming and prone to human error;
- manipulating data, i.e. requiring the use of a human resource untrained in using spreadsheets to manipulate and communicate (say, graphically) effectively.

The process is *reasonably effective* in that when information is requested it is delivered (at some point).

Note in this level-2 diagram the top right segment of each process contains no information. The purpose of each process is included in the large lower segment, but it is not clear at present what information in the upper segment would benefit the reader or business manager. It would be possible to attach some resource information to each process, and some analysts include information related to the person who is responsible for the process, or where it is performed. Other analysts leave the segment blank presumably because they feel the relevant information is inherited from the process that has been broken down. Whatever information is included within the segment it should be well motivated and should be consistent.

Where a circle is used to represent a process, as is the case with a number of American approaches, there is no equivalent to the top right segment.

8.5 ANALYSIS, DESIGN AND PROTOTYPING

The focus of this chapter has been very much on analysing business information processes and developing models of how they deliver the information. The importance for management of understanding the capabilities and limitations of the systems that are used to deliver information has been stressed, and the approach to analysis is that it is seen as a means of gaining greater understanding, which in turn should lead to more effective management. Analysis of business information processes is not regarded as primarily a job for analyst-programmers or systems analysts because the clear implication would be that the purpose of the analysis is to provide a computer solution and, by implication, to ignore the human and management issues. If these issues are ignored then sight has been lost of what the information is for. There are many ways in which computers can benefit a business and this will be looked at in Chapter 9, but, it has also been seen that through using 'systems principles' the way in which we understand some of the complexity of organisations can be clarified, thus revealing problems that require management action, not the universal panacea of a computer-based solution.

Analysis is not particularly useful unless it tells us what we need to know; this approach to analysis can tell us much of what we need to know. There is a danger that traditional approaches may tell us not so much what we need to know but what we want to know, which is to provide a solid basis for the design of a computer-based information system. Analysis and design are two very different activities and experience in the computer industry should be a warning that there is still a lot to learn about how to design systems in complex environments. For that reason, design is outside the scope of this text, although some brief observations about prototyping will be made as an approach to gaining more understanding as well as paddling in the shallower waters of design.

8.5.1 Prototyping as analysis

A prototype is not usually regarded as the real thing. Prototypes of aircraft or new cars are built to give life to an idea. The ideas may be fully worked out in terms of design, etc. but designs have to be tested. Positions of warning lights, controls, use of space, visibility, practicality, aesthetics and a host of other factors have, in the end, to be tested out using real people. Even the ability of an aircraft to perform safely in the air, ultimately, requires people to risk their lives on the design.

Experience from the prototype allows the design to be modified in numerous possible ways until at some point a design may be made to put the prototype into full production. The prototype, by eliciting responses from those who would use the product, assists in analysis by raising questions to be asked and issues to be addressed that previously had not been considered, or about which more thought is needed.

Major differences between prototyping an aircraft or a car and prototyping an information system are that:

1 there is more known from the start about some of the key characteristics of a car or aircraft and, in fact, virtually all such vehicles are variations on a theme;
2 the prototype is followed by production of many copies and the development costs are recouped through subsequent sales.

The closest comparison to this in software development is the design and prototyping of application packages such as word processing, spreadsheet, or database software. Much money is invested in their development and the costs are recouped through subsequent sales in the same way as the products above. Each information system, if it is intended to integrate well into the business, is as unique as the business and the people who work for it. It is not the usual practice to buy an 'off the shelf' information system, even though some companies may adapt their working practices to try and fit a system that has been successful elsewhere. This at least avoids the risk associated with the development of a new system.

A different approach to prototyping has been adopted by many information systems developers called rapid prototyping. Some of the assumptions behind this approach are:

1 users (i.e. people in a business who would use the system) may not know what a new system might be capable of, nor what sort of limitations a computer-based system might have, thus it is hard for managers, etc. to adequately specify what they might want of a

system (at least to an analyst's satisfaction) even if they have a fairly clear idea of what information they habitually need;

2 it is easier for users to offer constructive criticism about something they can see and experiment with, than to give precise descriptions of what they think they need;

3 it is good for users to feel that their views and concerns are important to the developers of the system, it is also good that users like managers and systems designers dialogue and learn to understand each other's worlds;

4 it helps systems designers because they could never elicit with questions alone what contributions users might be able to make to the design of a system;

5 it helps systems designers because when users experiment with a prototype the designers can use objective criteria such as, how long it takes to learn a function, how many errors are made, what kind of errors users make, whether there is a pattern to the types of problems that arise, etc.

In short, prototyping can be considered as a way of asking unvoiced questions about what users of a system want or need and about how they would interact with it, rather than as a way of discovering whether a proposed solution will 'do'.

8.5.2 Prototyping as design

While analysing users' responses to prototypes to find out some of what users need or want of a system, the result should be to influence the design of the system so that it will provide the information that is needed in the way it is needed. Some ways in which prototyping is an aid to design are considered.

1 Negative reactions or unintended responses by users can be used to refine how the system looks and feels to the user(s). Usually these responses will be at the level of one screen's impact on the user at a time. However, the overall logic of how the users actually locate the parts of the system that interest them can be missed if the user focuses on immediate detail. It is hard to keep the whole design in mind when confronted by menus, requests for information, or reports presented one screen at a time.

2 It is possible to prototype just part of an information system to give users a realistic feel for how it would respond and communicate. By giving the prototype limited functionality the designer can keep costs to a minimum, gain user confidence, and get valuable information from the user to feed into the design.

3 The prototype may give the users some sense of what could be expected from a new system, and may help them to more clearly define

what they can realistically demand from it once they see its potential.

8.5.3 Prototyping and the use of the diagnostic technique

Earlier in the chapter, the technique of using diagnostic requests to test the ability of a business to deliver management information were discussed. On the basis of such a request it was possible to illustrate the design of a data model in the previous chapters and, in this chapter, DFDs were used to model how the business delivered the information.

A similar approach has been successful with students when prototyping, in which composite data models have been developed within limited contexts by using diagnostic requests for information relevant to these contexts. The models serve as bases for the design of data resources suitable for prototyping. Given an appropriate business setting for the context and the assumption of supporting technology, DFDs can document the processes needed for a prototype to deliver information products for a set of requests. The challenges of design pose different questions to those addressed while considering analysis. Some of the challenges of design are discussed in the next section.

8.6 CHALLENGES AND PROBLEMS OF DESIGN

It almost goes without saying that information systems are not designed in isolation from the business contexts for which they are intended. Thus, some practical choices need to be faced. One may be to upgrade a current computer-based system, another may be to try and upgrade on an incremental basis or bit by bit, and yet another choice may be to try and develop a complete system which will take over from the old. All such choices have potential advantages and drawbacks even if it were assumed that the best possible analyses had been carried out. The eventual choices are strategic decisions that involve weighing up factors like the costs, the time dimension, risks, and potential benefits of each possibility. The size and complexity of the task and the longer term approach to dealing with information provision in complex environments are still major challenges for systems professionals, and the track record in the industry is not convincing enough to imagine that enough is known to meet these challenges with confidence.

Some of the more obvious challenges are discussed below.

8.6.1 Complexity

Faced with a complex business environment for which an information system is desired, it seems unlikely that analysis and design can proceed in anything but an ad hoc way, unless some sense can be made of the complexity, in business terms. The risk factor associated with large complex projects is high. From the perspective of systems ideas we would have to conclude that the greater the degree of complexity required in an information system, the greater the scope for emergent properties (*see* section 4.2.2.3) to arise. That is to say that if emergent properties can be associated with each system or sub-system where the desired products may be the desired emergent properties, then experience teaches us that other, unwanted and/or unpredictable emergent properties are also apt to appear.

8.6.2 World of information

Earlier in this text, it was said that the scope or range of information required by managers and others to monitor and manage business activities potentially amounts to a 'world of information' (*see* section 5.2). As businesses respond to changes in demand, make changes in their own structures, take new initiatives, and so on, information requirements change too. Even if a snapshot were taken of a business at a point in time, the information required to support all decision making at all levels could be very large in terms of quantity and variety; there could also be all kinds of constraints on it.

The challenge here is how to tackle a problem that can have no totally satisfactory answer; not all the information can be provided for all the decision makers in a company.

Computer-based information systems are best at providing only certain sorts of information; if they store appropriate data they should be able to produce information from it when required, or if it is quantifiable then they should be able to manipulate it. Qualitative information, suggestions or opinions are harder to extract.

Computer-based systems cannot provide all the information that every potential user wants. Even if we tried to provide all the information that the people need, it would be impossible since needs change. If only some of the information can be provided, then what should be provided? Choices based on relevant practical criteria and compromise between what is desirable and what is possible have to be made. For example it is known that computers can store and rapidly search through large quantities of data for information, whereas it would either take people a long time to do the same job manually, or it would be impossible. It is known that in a well designed database management system the computer's manipulation of data is a lot more error free than if the processing were done manually. If historical data are held in a database, business trends and other higher-level analytical management information can be relatively easily produced, but in a manual system similar tasks might be impracticable, thus denying managers vital business information. Computers are therefore better at managing large stores of information, but it is probably easier for an executive to keep his own list of contact numbers.

An information system may not be the best vehicle to deliver information that needs to be packaged in individualised ways for meetings with clients or boardroom presentations. For such purposes it might be better to download a selected set of data from a database management system to a spreadsheet package on a PC. The superior ability of the spreadsheet to manipulate data together with its good graphics facility can then be used to repackage the data as information that communicates really well. It is probably better for individual people to control the form of information that requires context specific presentation and communication, even if the information system is used for pre-processing or to filter the data in the data resource (thus reducing the individual's workload).

Choices about who needs what information also have to be made. Two common problems with this are that on the one hand it is difficult for anybody to remember what information they need for every aspect of their job, but on the other hand people are just as likely to ask for information that would be nice to have, but not necessary. If responsibilities remained static it might be possible to make good choices, but this situation is rarely the case.

A distinction needs to be made between information that is required on a regular basis and individual requests for it. It is clearly easier to plan for regular requirements for information than it is to plan for the unknown. While a relational database management system can, in theory, respond to an almost infinite number of different information requests, in practice each request would have to be logically structured (or framed) so that the system could handle it. Specially trained staff would need to translate many such requests into the appropriate forms.

Prototyping: in some cases rapid prototyping can develop incrementally into a complete system, but it is more usual for prototypes to have limited purposes. Prototyping can have great value from the point of view of the potential users of a system because they feel included in the development process, and the designers can gain valuable information, but the focus is primarily on what individual users see of the system: how it is presented to them and how they would use it. Prototyping contributes little or nothing to how the data resource is designed, and not a lot to how a system would relate to other business activities with which the users may be involved. If the issues of data resource design, and designing a system to meet major information requirements are the body of the design task, then prototyping has to do with choosing the right clothes or wardrobe for the environment.

8.7 SUMMARY

In this chapter some of the fundamental ideas, principles, and motivations for the analysis and modelling of business processes that have a role in producing information for managers and other decision makers have been explained. It has frequently been stressed that even though the analysis of business processes has been seen as a task for business systems analysts, managers are the ones who might benefit most. If the primary purpose of information systems is to provide information to assist in the decisions and actions that are management's responsibility, then managers also have a responsibility to ensure that they know what these systems cost them in terms of the performance of other business systems with which they interact. It is possible to cut through some of the complexity and apparent confusion of purposes and processes in business by using some of the insights of systems thinking, and by applying the principles in a consistent manner.

We do not apologise for our strong emphasis on the primacy of business, and of understanding information-related processes from a business or management perspective. Good analysis should help managers manage better, and good business process analysis should help systems analysts to reject the rather narrower approaches that have contributed to creating the gap that now must be bridged.

QUESTIONS

1 What do we mean by a 'model' and how can a model help us to think about or intervene in the way a business monitors its performance?

2 Clearly, if we are interested in process analysis then it helps if we can identify the object of our concern. Describe, using a non-information based example, the essential components of a business process.

3 Our particular interest in this chapter is in the modelling of business information processes. Explain the principles of an information-based process that provides some management information about a business process such as that mentioned in question 2.

4 Discuss the significance of 'purpose' in setting a boundary or limiting the scope of (process) analysis.

5 Decomposing or breaking down a complex process into its constituent parts (i.e. (sub)processes and resources) should reflect our understanding of what ought to give us insight into the performance and/or structure of the process. What factors can help us in deciding how to break down complex business information processes, and what is the rationale in each case?

6 Discuss the purpose of annotating DFDs and indicate how this technique can provide management with valuable information about business processes.

7 Comment on the purpose(s) of prototyping as a systems design technique and indicate the similarities and differences in purpose in protyping a new aircraft.

8 Explain why the design of an information system is so full of challenges.

BIBLIOGRAPHY   Avison, D.E. and Fitzgerald, G., *Information Systems Development*, Blackwell, 1988.

Benyon, David, *Information and Data Modelling*, Alfred Waller, 1990.

Beynon-Davies, P., *Relational Database Design*, Blackwell, 1992.

Bowers, David, *From Data to Database* (2nd Edn), Chapman and Hall, 1993.

Crinnion, J., *Evolutionary Systems Development*, Pitman Publishing, 1991.

Downs, E., Claire, P. and Coe, I., *Structured Systems Analysis and Design Method* (2nd Edn), Prentice Hall, 1992.

Skidmore, S., Farmer, R. and Mills, G., *SSADM Version 4 Models and Methods*, NCC Blackwell, 1992.

Teorey, T.J., *Database Modeling and Design* (2nd Edn), Morgan Kaufmann, 1994.

The information technology: challenges and potential for management

9.1 INTRODUCTION

The implementation of a new information system, or a major change in an existing system, may seem to be the specific responsibility of systems professionals even though the overall responsibility for the project may rest with general management. The benefits or problems that result from the introduction of the system are either benefits that management hope to gain, or problems that management have to resolve (or live with). In both cases there is strong motivation for managers to take a more than passive role in information systems development. In this chapter some of the basic business and technological issues will be discussed where changing demands for information and changes in the availability of technological resources are a constant challenge.

Some technological issues have already been introduced at points in the book where they have been relevant to the discussion. The discussion continues in this chapter but the focus is on the information technology not on the technicalities of it. We are more concerned to discuss, even at the risk of repeating some of what has previously been stated, basic considerations for the use of the technology from a management or decision maker's point of view. As essential background to the development of the technology theme a non-specialist's introduction to fundamental aspects of the technological resources used by computer-based information systems will be given.

9.2 AN OVERVIEW OF THE TECHNOLOGICAL RESOURCE BASE

A description of the major computer-based components of an information system from the perspective of their basic resource implications is necessary so that related management issues can be discussed. In fast developing areas such as computing and communications, tomorrow's high technology can soon become the outdated and inadequate technology of yesterday. This approach therefore will focus more on characteristics of the technology that continue to be relevant even when specifications of particular items of equipment change with unerring frequency.

The characteristics that are considered as useful background will develop the theme of this chapter, and can be grouped under three headings:

- computer hardware
- computer software
- communications.

9.2.1 Computer hardware

Under this heading we have included the physical components that facilitate:

- interaction with the computer, such as when entering details or asking it for information
- the presentation of information as reports, charts, meaningful sets of figures or the production of business documents
- the storing of details for future reference or consultation
- changing, manipulating or calculating details such as when details are kept up-to-date.

9.2.1.1 Hardware needed when we enter details or when we ask for information

Somehow it is necessary to be able to talk to a computer-based information system. It must be possible to ensure that details can be got into the system, that it can be asked for information or that it can be told what details need to be changed, etc. One common way of doing this is through a *keyboard*. The obvious advantage is that it can literally spell out exactly what details we want to enter, for example, the name of a customer whose account details we want to see. The main disadvantages are that not everybody can type well enough to use the keyboard to its best advantage; it is also very easy to make mistakes when typing. For both of these reasons the keyboard is considered quite a slow and unreliable way of interacting with a computer even though it is the most useful for general work.

Because of these disadvantages some other means of communicating with the computer have been developed. For example, bar coding is an approach which uses a *bar-code scanning device* to read the code which is printed on labels that are put on items such as supermarket products. Each code is associated with a set of details that relate to the item represented by the code. The advantage is that bar code scanning is fast and very accurate, but the disadvantage is that it is only appropriate for certain situations. The situations are clearly those in which the advantages of the approach can be used best; thus where speed and accuracy offer a significant improvement on a manual alternative.

Behind the scenes other aspects of bar-coding involve entering details that are associated with the code into a database; each time a bar code is scanned the details associated with it can be found. Only when there is multiple use of a specific code does the value of only entering the other details once into a database become apparent. For example, the bar code found on a can of baked beans will be the same for probably thousands of identical cans. The other details associated with the can, such as the description of what it is, the size and the price, etc., are only entered into the database/information system once, but the benefits are experienced every time one of the cans is sold in supermarkets up and down the country.

The *mouse* is another means of communicating with a computer-based system, but its use is limited to moving a pointer around a computer screen and clicking one of the mouse's buttons when the circumstances are appropriate, such as when the pointer locates something on the screen that will react when the button is clicked, or when clicking it has some other meaning in the context. Either way, using the mouse only has a function when its roles have been determined by the programs or software that it is used with. For example, an information system may allow options to be chosen from a menu by using a mouse such as asking for a list of customers who have accounts outstanding. A further option may allow the selection of a customer from the list in order to get further details of his or her account. The mouse/pointing device allows the selection of items and, therefore, there is no need to use the keyboard; typing is unnecessary, cutting down on the number of mistakes which might otherwise have been made. It is possible, of course, to click on the wrong part of the screen, choosing the wrong customer's name by mistake, but it is assumed that such mistakes can easily be corrected.

Some applications allow communication through speech but this use, while increasing, is still quite limited and specialised. No way of communicating with computers has yet to equal the versatility of the standard computer keyboard. A lot of research and interest has focused on making it easier for computer users to avoid the keyboard as much as possible, but for the foreseeable future it will continue to be our main way of communicating with business information systems.

9.2.1.2 Hardware needed to present information

The two common means of presenting information are the display of information on a monitor or computer screen, and printing the information on paper. There are two basic issues here, but there are many others also. The two basic management issues relate to the quality of the presentation, and the matter of quantity. Since there is concern only with hardware in this section, the monitor will be considered first.

Monitors can range from plain monochrome (single colour background with contrasting single colour writing or graphics), to monitors which can display a vast *range of colours*. The *resolution* of a monitor may range from low to high, and the size of the monitor's screen may vary from quite small to large. Obviously the most effective presentation of some information will use a good range of colours, using a high (clear) resolution, and will be of a *size* that is easily comprehended. Traditionally, information systems that are used by many people at the same time and are based on larger computers such as main-frames or minis, are only equipped with very basic (usually small and quite low resolution) monochrome monitors. The monitors used with PCs tend to have increasingly higher specifications and are usually capable of producing high quality, colourful presentations. Good presentation of information therefore tends to be associated more with PCs than with larger systems.

Printers again come in a range of types but, as they get better and cheaper, professional business managers are inclined to measure the quality of presentation against the best products rather than the poorer quality products of yesterday. Whether the traditional dot-matrix workhorses, the newer colour inkjets or laser printers are considered, it is necessary to assess the performance and potential of different printers in the light of the intended use.

Printers are measured in terms of quality of the printed product by:

- resolution;
- shades of grey;
- colour;

and in terms of speed of printing by:

- characters per second;
- pages per minute;
- how much they slow down for high quality or graphics production.

The quality of printing is important for presentation of information. The resolution of the printer will determine how sharp the characters or images will be, shades of grey can give more depth to a picture or figure, while colour can really enhance graphs or charts so that information stands out. The speed of printing can vary considerably from machine to machine. Faster and more robust machines usually cost more, but for many businesses faster machines are necessary because of the volume of work that has to be produced. In-house draft documents or memos may be produced on high quality dot-matrix printers, but now inkjets or laser printers are becoming the standard. The only good way to choose an appropriate printer is to see what sort of work it produces.

Printers can be a bottle neck in the production of information if they are too slow for the workload. There may be more than one answer to such problems; for example, faster printers may be called for, more printers may be necessary, or other strategies may help such as allowing more documents to wait in a queue for printing.

After assessing a printer's performance we need to take note of factors such as price of purchase versus price of leasing, cost of consumables such as paper and toner, the cost of maintenance, and the ease of maintenance.

9.2.1.3 Hardware needed for storing details

Computers have two main ways of storing details (or any other software, including programs) that they work with. In principle, the more permanent details are filed away and stored on *magnetic disks* or perhaps *optical media*, while the *memory* holds only the details and programs that are needed for processing at any point in time. The relationship between the permanent storage and the temporary memory storage, plus other relevant factors will be explained.

Although interest is primarily in storing data for use by a database, or perhaps a spreadsheet, in order to deliver information, virtually all applications software and data are stored on some sort of permanent medium. The software that runs the computer classifies application programs and data as different types of files, and it keeps track of where the programs and data are stored on the disk by reserving the first part of the disk as an index to the rest of it. It is sensible to use the computer's filing facilities to organise all the files into a sort of library so that it is possible to know where the files have been stored.

Storing details permanently

To permanently store software whether as data, program, or other special purpose files, it is necessary to use magnetic disks, optical disks or magnetic tape. Each of these has advantages and disadvantages which tend to make them suitable for different usages, but there are two characteristics which they all share and which are significant. Like all resources they have certain limitations, and so we have to recognise that:

- they have a finite storage capacity
- it takes time to locate files.

It is also necessary to remember that reliability is a very important factor. If the details are crucial to the running and management of a company, then their security must also be crucial.

Magnetic disks. It is not necessary to go into all the types of disks in common use, except to say that in terms of large mainframes, mini computers or personal computers(PCs), disks tend to come in different storage capacities and there may be differences in how long it takes for files to be located on the disk. A disk, like its cousin the record, needs a disk drive or the equivalent of a turntable for it to function. Sometimes it is possible to change the disk such as with large disk packs in mainframe computer disk drives, or with diskettes in a PC disk drive. Often with mini computers and PCs we have 'hard disks' which consist of a disk and disk drive unit which is mounted inside the computer casing. Not only do the hard disks and diskettes come in different storage capacities, but hard disk drives are often available with different access speeds, the faster ones usually being the more expensive.

Magnetic tapes. Hard disks can, unfortunately, fail; permanence can thus only be regarded with caution. *All business data held on hard disks should be backed up on a regular basis, and this is often done using special tapes.* Tapes are suitable because if a disk fails or the software has to be reinstalled, then the data on the tape which is stored in a linear sequence is simply copied back as a sequence onto the disk. Disks are good for constant access because any part of a disk can be accessed quite easily and quickly.

Optical disks. These are now emerging as a viable storage medium and are used extensively in situations where facts are recorded on the disks for consultation only, and the disks can be published widely enough to make their use economically viable. Encylopædias and other sources of useful information are now published on CD-ROMs, i.e. optical disks that contain material that can only be read but not altered. Although it is now possible for users to store their own material on optical disks, the limitations at the time of writing are the cost of disks and appropriate drives, access speed and possibly capacity, therefore they are not suitable yet for use in standard business information systems.

Databases by their very nature grow as more details are added, and in use the computer often has to search for details held in the data files on the disk. These two characteristics mean that both disk capacity and speed of access can be important considerations in the selection or upgrade of computer hardware. Clearly the choice of storage hardware must be related to the demands that may be made on it by the business context.

Storing details temporarily

Learner drivers who are about to take their driving test will probably study the Highway Code just before the test to try and keep the facts fresh in their minds in case they get asked some questions on it. A student who is due to take an exam may try to 'cram' for it so that he or she will be prepared to answer the questions with confidence; the crammed material usually does not stick. It is all there still in the books or notes, but much of it seems to fade fast from the conscious memory.

A computer's *memory* works a little like our own when we try to cram; it consists of electronic 'chips' which retain facts or programs for as long as the computer is switched on, and for as long as they are needed. Often, it is possible to increase the storage capacity of a computer's memory by adding more chips or by exchanging them for higher capacity ones. The amount of memory that a computer can handle can depend on a number of factors, some of which are related to the hardware, and some to the software. Nevertheless memory is a finite resource and from our point of view has to be seen in terms of how much is required for the database management system application and business context in which it is used.

The computer's processor(s) uses the memory to store the programs (or sets of instructions) that it is running, and to store and manipulate the data that they use. Usually there are also other programs running that manage the computer hardware and its resources and, if there are a number of people using the same machine at once, then there are programs running to manage the computer resources used by them as well as the functions initiated by them. All in all the memory of a computer can have a lot of work to do and, the more it has to do, the less of the memory resource is available for any one purpose since more of it has to be shared among the tasks that are competing for it. More people, more active database tables and so on, usually indicate a need for more memory.

Software application manuals often specify or recommend minimum memory capacity for optimum performance of the application.

9.2.1.4 Hardware for changing, manipulating or calculating details

The part of the computer that performs the processes that are contained in programs, or which implements all the instructions that users give it, is the *processor*. The processor (or processors, since some computers have more than one), like other hardware resources, has limitations on its performance. Two relevant characteristics of a processor can be identified: the speed at which it operates which may be expressed as the clock-speed (Mhz) or as how many Millions of Instructions Per Second it can process (MIPS), and the relative volume of data it can handle which is expressed in terms of bits (such as a 32 bit or 64 bit processor).

Technical advice can be sought to fully explore the suitability of a particular processor (or processors) for a given context but, as can be seen, the speed and power of a processor will clearly affect the performance of the applications that are run on it.

It should be remembered, however, that the performance of a database depends upon other factors too, some of which have already been noted. It is said that a chain is only as strong as its weakest link; the main hardware links that affect database/information system performance can therefore be summarised as:

- how long it takes for the computer to transfer details between the memory and the permanent storage
- how much memory space is available to the processor for running programs or processing data
- how much work the processor can get through in a given period of time

- how fast details can be entered into a system or how well and quickly information can be presented.

9.2.2 Computer software

Without software, a computer is like a car without a driver; nothing happens. From the moment a computer is turned on, software determines what we can get it to do and how it does the things it does. Software consists of instructions and procedures which tell the computer what to do and how it should appear to the user. For example, if I want to write a letter I might decide to use a word processing package. To use the package, I tell the computer in some way and it finds where the software is *stored* (say, on the hard disk), it *copies* the relevant word processing programs into 'memory' and then it begins to *run* (process) the package by *displaying* one of the package's screens (on the monitor) and it *waits* for me to start typing on the keyboard. If I want to print the letter, the word processing software has a 'driver', i.e. software with a specific set of instructions, to enable me to use my particular printer. All the hardware components are therefore controlled or used by software.

As the specifications of hardware components improve, software is developed to try and exploit the full potential of the hardware resources. For the software which controls the hardware it means for example that if a computer can have a very large memory capacity, then the memory area needs to be managed so as to get the most benefit out of it. For an application program, it means what features can be improved or added to make use of the improved hardware capability, for example, some high-end word processors now include sophisticated desktop publishing functions that use a lot of memory. In this way it is possible to get greater capabilities from software packages as they are written or rewritten to get more out of improvements in technology.

The down side to this is that as software products boast more features than their rivals they become more complex and they inevitably become more difficult to use; there is a lot more about them that needs to be learned – a word processing/desktop publishing package in the hands of a novice can be used to produce more effective bad documents. Also, many new versions of software seem to assume a higher-level of hardware specifications than the previous versions, thus machines already in use may find the newer software challenges the available resources. For example, PC users find that graphical interfaces such as Windows and the packages that work with Windows tend to need more powerful processors, more storage space on a hard disk and more memory to run the programs well. Larger and higher resolution, thus more expensive, monitors, also offer benefits for these more sophisticated and visually more attractive software products.

The fact is that competition between software producers drives them to produce software applications that have more and more attractive features. This software is often written to take full advantage of highly specified hardware and this tends to force businesses into considering frequent upgrades to their technology. New complex software does not always offer significant benefits to a business, and sometimes the rush to produce newer complex software means that it is not always fully tested or completely reliable.

9.2.2.1 Systems software

Software can be grouped into three main types. One type, sometimes called *systems software*, or more specifically the operating system, or network software, is software that drives respectively computer hardware and computer communications technology. It provides the functions that enable exploitation and management of the technology. Operating systems software provides functions that help us manage the storage resource(s) such as preparing the magnetic media for use, creating storage areas for applications and their data files, copying files from a hard disk to a diskette, and many other functions. It also allows general management and monitoring of the use of the computer, including the memory resource.

Many of the characteristics associated with certain types of computer are actually functions of the operating systems that drive them. If the same computer (hardware) was driven by a different type of systems software it would seem like a very different computer, for example, a high specification PC driven by the Microsoft disk operating system (MSDOS) would behave and operate completely differently if it were driven by the UNIX operating system. MSDOS was designed to run machines that are used by one person at a time, but the UNIX operating system could allow the machine to be used by more than one person at a time, and the system has to therefore provide sufficient management functions to ensure that there are no clashes, people's work is secure, and so on. Some types of computer have only their own special operating systems.

9.2.2.2 Applications software

The second type of software consists of a suite of programs called *applications software* that drives general applications such as databases, spreadsheets and word processors, or specially designed applications such as stock control or payroll systems.

In the case of a word processing application, the intention is normally to create documents and possibly illustrations. The set of programs which make up the application software is specifically designed to provide all the *functions* of the word processor and to produce *data* (such as letters and reports) which are documents or illustrations in the form of computer files. The data files can subsequently be used to print out copies on paper.

A spreadsheet application comprises a set of programs in a similar way to that of the word processing software. It too produces data as computer files (such as cashflow forecasts), and the software can be used to print out copies on paper. The advantage of all such data files is that they can often be easily amended if some of the contents of the document or spreadsheet change.

A slightly different kind of application is the database application package. In this case the software allows a person to create a database 'system' which must include programs to do things as well as data files upon which the programs act. In other words the database application packages are intended to provide users with the ability to create applications of their own for specific purposes, such as a stock control system, or a hotel reservation system.

The database application will use functions provided by the underlying systems software such as the file management facilities, and will supply others of its own. This special area will not be pursued further, except to say that the way in which the systems software manages the processor and the computer's memory, can affect the performance of a database application.

Database management systems software tends to be very complex, and the programs can take a lot of space on permanent storage. Relational systems can also demand a lot of space in the computer's memory in order to perform certain tasks. Without seeing software in action it is hard to know how well a specific product will perform on a given configuration of computer hardware (sometimes called a platform). Because of this it is wise to evaluate products first if performance is an important consideration.

9.2.2.3 Database data files: software that grows

Database applications produce 'tables' (or data files) in which business details are stored. Other files such as index files can also be created to make searching through chosen columns of a table a quicker process. As more rows of details are added to the database table, both the table and the index files grow larger which means more space is required and more time will be taken to search for data. Spreadsheet applications can also grow if new spreadsheets are added and linked to previous ones, say monthly, for some purpose. The issue here is likely to relate to the amount of memory space required and perhaps the time needed by the processor to do the calculations. Thus, it must be borne in mind that, while the hardware resources may seem perfectly adequate to begin with, after a period of time the limits of the hardware resources may be challenged.

The problem of the growing database table could be compared with starting a collection of records. At first a shelf for the records might seem enough space. The records could be sorted into some order such as music types and within types perhaps artist or group. If more records are collected on a regular basis, the shelf might turn to two shelves and eventually that too would be inadequate. It would probably take longer to find a particular record as the collection grows, and each time one is added more time would be spent shifting others around to preserve the order.

Computer software enables computer hardware to do the business tasks such as writing letters or reports, producing budgets, or storing significant data and providing information from them. Thus when selecting technology, in principle, management should first decide what they want to use the technology for, then they should choose appropriate software, and then finally they should decide what specifications the hardware should have in order to run the software and to produce the information products that are required.

9.2.3 Communications

Computers might almost have been designed to communicate as fish were designed to swim. But it is only recently that such a conclusion could have been arrived at and it would be true to say that originally communication was probably far from computer manufacturers' minds. In the last few years, however, technology has improved in response to the great demand to be able to harness the combined and varied capabilities of different computers in business applications, and also major communications companies like British Telecom have developed high quality communications links to support reliable interaction between computers at national and international levels. Data and information-intensive business applications can benefit greatly from co-ordinating the potential of distributed computing resources within a coherent network where both the benefits of localised computing and connected computing can be realised.

9.2.3.1 Communications in the context of a localised business

Communications in the context of computing suggests two issues worth considering in a text of this sort. The first has to do with viewing the computing resource not as being bound to a single type of computer system, but as an integrated set of computing resources in which different components can be used to provide the functions for which they are best suited. The other has to do with identifying how our patterns or types of use relate to typical patterns of computer communication.

Viewing the computer resource(s) of an organisation as an integrated set of technological components is now becoming a realistic possibility. Different types of computers tended to be seen as separate and distinct resources providing their own type of contribution to the running of the business. Different technological or computer 'solutions' were typically sold as providing a *better* type of solution than 'competing' technology.

Now it is possible to think in terms of using the diversity available more effectively. The essential characteristics of common approaches to computer communications will be considered.

Sharing a central computer resource

Before the advent of PCs as a serious business computer resource, computing in business was dominated by the use of mainframe or mini computers in which one central computer was made available to a number of users through the use of keyboards and monitors. Other, now antiquated, devices such as punch cards and card readers were used to communicate our intentions (as programs) to the computer. Mainframe and mini computers are still used but now it is not because of the lack of choice, it is often because they have an appropriate role within the business. The primary reason for using a significant or powerful central computer resource should be because it is important that a number of users can access a common resource, and clearly it is important that the resource should have appropriate specifications to meet the requirements.

A typical and good example of where it is important for a number of users to access a common resource is in the case of information systems where a central database is needed by a number of employees in different departments for the purpose of, say, creating new customer accounts, updating the accounts or other customer details, and producing information for managers, the customers themselves, marketing initiatives, etc. Ideally, a centralised information system provides information for people at different levels and in different parts of an organisation, and will need to pick up details of business transactions and so on from many different sources. For such a purpose the best technological solution would seem to be one which provides a central resource with which many different people in the business can interact.

From a technical point of view it should be asked, for example, how many people can interact with the system before the performance becomes unacceptably slow, and whether it can cope with the anticipated rate of growth in the database, etc. From a management point of view, its ability to provide management level information in a form which communicates well to specific decision makers at different levels and in different parts of the company could be questioned. In other words, is it a realistic expectation for a common resource to provide tailored information for all decision-making purposes? This is a question that requires considerable thought and management consideration (*see* Chapter 5).

Common computer resources tend to be better suited to large applications and can be very expensive to provide and to maintain. Specialist staff are needed to run and manage them, and in the case of databases to help deliver ad hoc requests for management information. Larger systems such as these tend to be quite inflexible to use and restrict users to a limited choice of information products (e.g. standard management reports, sales figures, etc.). Furthermore, the information products themselves do not usually have a high standard of presentation.

Linked computers on every desk

The virtue of all employees having a computer on their desks, the aim of some organisations, is that users have the potential to develop their own applications and to produce information that is tailored specifically for the chosen recipient or recipients. If the computers are part of a network it is possible to send the information directly to the recipient's machine or perhaps to a whole group at once. Memos and reports can be sent to colleagues, and the network may allow users to jointly contribute to the development of a common project.

Local area networks (internal communication systems) usually consist of a number (it could be less than ten or hundreds) of PCs. Special purpose PCs, called 'servers', in larger networks may:

- run special network software or a network operation system
- control and contain large storage facilities such as hard disks and CD-ROMs
- run a group of printers for network users
- run an external communications facility.

Networks (i.e. groups of computers) need to be managed by software just as a single computer does. Most networks have systems software that runs in conjunction with a standard computer operating system such as MSDOS. Users on such systems are usually allocated some private space on a large hard disk (on a file server) and access is gained through logging on to the network and through password control. Application program software is stored on a file server, and when a user wants to use it, it is copied into the memory of the local machine. Resulting data files are created in the user's private storage space.

The central storage of application software means that a consistent and controlled variety of packages are used across the business; it is also more cost effective to buy software for a network than to buy separate packages for each machine. Another advantage is that the PCs do not need to have their own hard disks for permanent storage of application software or data files. If the PCs do have hard disks, they will clearly have the potential to store other software.

From a user's point of view, a networked machine works very much like a separate individual computer. The machine is able to devote virtually all of its processing power to the person using it; its performance can be quite good, therefore. In some networks, users may also be able to create and use applications that can be jointly accessed, such as databases or where several colleagues contribute to the development of a report. Added advantages for the business are that efficient use can be made of printers by sharing a few (using the print server) among a lot of people who only need to use them once in a while. Similar efficient use can be made of other devices, such as external communications links (using an external communications server), thereby reducing the costs of the resource base.

It is said that we don't get something for nothing, and this is true of networks. Communications networks consist of a number of computers which are attached by some sort of communications medium such as a cable. The computers can be linked in different ways and by different sorts of cable. It is rather like a number of towns which are attached, as it were, by different sorts of road. At rush hour lots of vehicles pour on to the roads from the towns, and depending on how large the roads are and how busy they get, the traffic will slow down or speed up. When all the computers on a network are active, every time an application needs to access data on a file server, or if it needs to use another suite of programs which are held on the hard disk (in storage), the data or programs have to travel in small data packets along the cables. Depending on the number of packets and the capacity of the cables, the communication will either slow down or speed up. The choice of communications technology will often be decided on the basis of the potential volume of traffic and the sort of performance required, but it has to be borne in mind that once the value of such technology is appreciated, users may put it to greater use.

Also, like traffic lights on a busy main road, it is possible to find queues of work waiting for the use of a limited resource such as a printer or printers which can only process documents at a certain speed as complete items in a serial fashion. Bottle necks tend to occur when the options for processing are limited by the number or capacity of resources.

Another limitation on the use of networked computers relates to the people who use them. Even though there may be many application packages available for potential exploitation by users of the network, it by no means follows that most users are capable of using the packages well or effectively. Just as vehicles can be driven well or badly, computer software which is far more complex, takes training and practice to use well. Management not only has the responsibility for ensuring that adequate resources exist for delivering the products or services of their company, they also have to ensure that information systems exist to monitor the business activities effectively and that they and their staff are properly trained to exploit the technology to the advantage of the business.

Networks foster co-operative effort by colleagues but they tend to rely for their effectiveness on their users having sufficient sophistication to deliver the potential of which they are capable. When a centralised common computer resource is provided for users, the responsibility for its effective use is, by contrast, often in the hands of professional staff who may understand how to use the technology well, but who could not understand the information needs of every user, and in any case could not provide tailored information for all even if they did.

Communicating to take advantage of diversity

There are advantages to sharing a large common computer resource, and there are advantages to local processing, or having a network of PCs in which each user has a degree of autonomy. Mainframes (large scale centralised computing), minis (medium to small scale centralised computing), and PCs (single user or networked computing) used to be thought of as different worlds and representing different and separate approaches to providing computing resources for a business. It is now increasingly possible (although *be warned* not always straightforward in practice) to integrate different types of systems by using special hardware and software. Using different types of computer systems, however, requires users to learn new things and different skills, but at least it is becoming increasingly possible to see the advantage of using the strengths of large and smaller systems together to deliver high quality and effective information.

EXAMPLE

> In a large construction company there may be a database management system which stores details of major projects in which the company are principal contractors in different countries of the world. The information system, which is how the users see the database management system, classifies activities and summarises the details of projects to provide a breakdown of expenditure which forms the basis of a comparison of performance and cost between projects. The information can be produced either as paper documentation containing text, headings and many columns of figures, or as a data file in a choice of computer text formats. In an integrated system it might be possible for the file to be picked up by PCs in local area networks and for the text file to be modified by a computer literate manager or administrator who re-presents the columns of figures as coloured graphs suitable for their boss, charts that are meaningful for a meeting of top executives, or as well illustrated reports to convince a foreign government official of the company's good record in managing important development projects.

The main information system provides a large and rich data resource plus the ability to organise and process the data into a useful form; the communication aspect means that the data can be sent from one resource to another without anyone having to manually copy the details from one system to another which would waste time and possibly introduce errors. The PC is a flexible resource with which a large range of high quality application software can be used, and it is particularly well suited to producing information in visually attractive forms. While PC software is becoming more complex, it is also the case that because it is produced with the single (unsupported) user in mind, the software for it is usually easily learned by the average person.

9.2.3.2 Communications in a wider business context

Many businesses extend far beyond a single locality or context in which the use of computer resources can be restricted by location. For example, banks need to be able to communicate account details between branches, branches and banking centres and with institutions in other countries. Performance of individual supermarkets and regional performance can be monitored by head offices through the use of computer communications. One of the results may be that distribution of products to regional warehouses and to individual stores can be organised efficiently. Many business reasons could be found for ensuring that information systems have access to, and can be accessed by other external systems with which they want to exchange data or information.

To communicate in a wider context a company normally has to take advantage of the great networks of communication lines that telecommunications companies like British Telecom have established throughout the world. A travel agent in Sydney, Australia may want to book a seat on a British Airways aircraft leaving London the next day. The enquiry initiated from Australia and the response sent back from Heathrow, London may all take place in a matter of seconds. Transfers of funds from British banks to other European partners on the continent have to be reliable and fast. From a management point of view, it would now be necessary, perhaps, to make a case for exploring the potential offered by such a network but, in the not-so-distant future, it might, instead, be asked why the potential had not been explored and exploited.

The potential must be related to what business opportunities it opens up or possibilities it promises, and to what the telecommunications network can deliver in terms of scope, quality, types of services and at what cost. For example, a British company which has manufacturing partners in the Far East may want to monitor aspects of their partners' manufacturing schedules in order to co-ordinate advertising with the expected delivery dates of products. The companies may decide to exploit the ability of their computer systems to communicate with each other quickly and efficiently.

Business customers of telecommunications companies such as British Telecom can make choices from three types of communication services for data transmissions. One of them is the ordinary telephone line, while the other two are higher quality lines specially designed for use with data transmission, i.e. they are particularly appropriate for communication between computers. The latest Integrated Services Digital Network

(ISDN) communications network integrates the different sorts of lines and services that are available, but it is not clear that even this highly specified service will meet all business requirements as computer hardware performance – for instance, its ability to process and transmit data at high speeds – continues to improve. It is not intended, however, to enter into a discussion of the technicalities, instead the sorts of factors that can affect what services might be chosen will be focussed on.

Communications networks can be compared to road networks. Different types of roads tend to be designed to take different volumes of traffic, and how long a journey will take is often calculated based on the size or classification of the roads en route. Different types of communications lines are similarly rated as to their capacity to handle transmission speed and volume of data. These factors in turn are related to the way in which the data is sent through the networks. From a business point of view, it must be decided how much data needs to be sent or received, and how fast it needs to be transferred. Once the answers have been found to these questions, consideration of which telecommunications services best suit the business needs can then be made.

Costs will vary according to the type of line(s) used, the capacity required of it (or them) and the amount of use made of it. Sometimes large businesses find it more cost effective to rent a line for their exclusive use, while a small business may use an ordinary phone line for occasional transmission of computer data and fax transmissions. The cost of a service may be weighed against the measurable financial benefits gained by using one service rather than another. The overall costs of developing an effective communications facility and providing the physical resources may be balanced against the costs of exchanging data and information in alternative ways in a competitive and demanding business environment, as well as against the perceived value of the data/information gained.

It is hard to put a specific value on information even though good management would be impossible without it. Much of the data that is communicated from machine to machine (or system to system) is the raw material from which information is subsequently gained, i.e. one computer sends data to be processed by another. Communicating outside the boundary of a company can bring benefits to a business in other ways. For example, on-line business information services can play a unique role in providing intelligence about issues of interest or concern. News of change in the financial markets, change in the behaviour of competitors or change in the industry, can be used by decision makers such as financial directors, accountants and marketing specialists to support appropriate business responses to the environment, supplementing information generated inside the company. Computer-based communication allows a business to participate in an international information community which not only has great potential for business exploitation, but in the future will relegate to a backwater companies who have not seen the opportunities before them.

9.3 THE TECHNOLOGY IN A WORLD OF BUSINESS

One of the greatest challenges, wherever computer-based technology is used as a tool to help achieve our human ends, is that there is only a partial compatibility between the well-defined, logical and mathematical world of computing and the poorly defined and only partially logical world of humans. Business is essentially a human activity and businesses are human organisations in which the whole range of human behaviours, rational and irrational, logical and illogical, are to be found. Within this very human world we have to ask how technology, and in particular information systems can play a beneficial role and enhance the human desire to do things better.

One of the reasons that the language of systems thinking/theory is used as a foundation for understanding the monitoring dimension of business management is that it forces us to think in a clearer and more precise way about how an organisation delivers the information it needs to support decision-makers. We have tried, in this approach, however, to show that business process modelling can and should take account of more that just the logic required to account for the delivery of information. A holistic view of business recognises the complexity of different types of systemic hierarchies in which resources and some processes may be competed for in order that different purposes may be fulfilled. It is within this untidy complex world that the powerful yet relatively limited capabilities of technology have to be integrated.

9.3.1 Managing the resources

This has been an introduction to the basic elements of technology from which information systems are built. It can be seen that different elements have different strengths and limitations and that, in an ideal world, it is desirable to match the information needs of a company with an appropriately designed set of computing and communications resources. The real world however, tends to impose constraints and force compromise, but it is still necessary to be aware of what may be gained or lost through making certain kinds of choices.

For example, in a hospital laboratory in which tests are made which relate to patients, it might be decided that it is easier to create a database on a PC to record results than to wait for a centralised computer systems department to develop software on a centralised computer system. The pressure to produce data for doctors and the administration may lead to the adoption of, what appears to be, the most pragmatic option. But what would be lost, and from whose perspective? The invaluable benefit of experienced database designers who work in the centralised computer systems department might be lost. Time, which would be better given to the analytical activities of the laboratory, might be lost. From the hospital's point of view, useful data which is held in an isolated and independent system would be hidden, and it may be practically unavailable for management purposes, such as statistical analysis. The hospital might also lose if it is found that isolated pockets of specialists hold personal details of patients in contravention of the Data Protection Act 1984.

9.3.1.1 Managing the resources from the information users' perspective

Managing the technological resources cannot be considered in isolation from the information needs and the information generating processes of the organisation. Looking first at some basic issues relating to information provision, a lot of stress has been placed on 'information' almost as if the only role that information systems have is to provide neatly wrapped packages of information to assist in every decision that every decision-maker has to make. In Chapter 5 reference was made to the idea that, potentially, a business or organisation requires a 'world of information' in so far as a changing business environment is likely to cause new questions to be asked every day, which means that it is not possible to fully specify a complete set of information for a company; the reality is that it never gets anywhere near it anyway. Priorities have to be made and strategies have to be developed in order to ensure that decision-makers have access to the information they need but it is often hard to distinguish how great the need really is for many items of information, and it can also be hard to argue that some users should be excluded from receiving 'information' that is available but of marginal use to them.

One approach to providing information may therefore be to conduct a complete information audit in which all decision-makers are required to specify precisely what information they think they need. This way of tackling the issue is user-driven in that they decide what they want, and in principle it seems a good idea. There are, however, several difficulties with it. One problem is that it is unreasonable to expect a user to comprehensively describe and even prioritise the information they use to do their job. Even if the job and its requirements never changed it would be hard to specify *all* the information that would be needed for all eventualities. If it could be fully specified, the user would also have to know, by implication, what specific aspects could be addressed by an information system. It is known, however, that, in any case, jobs, their requirements and the information needed to do them change and consequently a set of fully specified information requirements produced today could be out-of-date in a week's time. This could be true of any or all users covered in an audit.

If there are difficulties specifying an individual's information requirements, then the problem becomes greater as the number of users increase. Another aspect, of course, is that the range or volume of different information 'needs' may prove an impractical target for a large centralised computer systems department to achieve, that is if it is assumed (which it shouldn't) that a centralised system should provide it all. The implication is that it would be necessary to classify all information requirements into those that would best be met through the use of different types of technological resources, but this raises important questions. Should an information system be developed, therefore, by auditing the information users in a company and attempting to meet their requirements, or should an information system be developed by basing it on an analysis of the existing manual or computer-based systems? The motivation for basing a design on an audit of information requirements provided by users is to develop an information system that should satisfy the people who need it. The motivation for using existing systems as a basis is that it would seem safer to move from the known to the unknown in incremental steps. Knowledge of current systems provides a base line of shared experience and understanding amongst users. Each approach has certain benefits for users: the first attempts to bend over backwards to satisfy their requirements, but gives them the responsibility to get the requirements right, while the second attempts to give them the comfort of some familiarity with what has gone before, and gives them little responsibility in the development process, but it also gives them a more limited choice of what information is provided.

Should it be assumed that the main core of information ought to be provided by centralised systems, or should an attempt be made to deliver a greater range of information and exploit the benefits of hybrid technological systems? These more technological questions are not unrelated to the sort of questions that have just been considered above. From a user's point of view a centralised information system usually provides a relatively limited variety of information or of limited quality. Users often see the responsibility of providing the right information as something that belongs to systems analysts and other specialists; the users could well feel relieved not to be more involved with what they see as technology, frustrated that they have little influence over the products, or resigned to working with inadequate systems. The technological resources are therefore managed by specialists on behalf of the users just as road systems are managed on behalf of road users. If, on the other hand, users are to reap the benefits of hybrid systems in which some high quality information could be the sophisticated products of PC software application packages, then the users may find that they are not just consumers of information but they may also have to play a role in the production of it too. As some of the responsibility for producing information shifts from specialists in systems to specialists in their own areas of business, new management issues arise.

9.3.1.2   Managing the resource from an information provider's perspective

An average information user's relationship with information systems in a large organisation is probably very much like an average telephone user's relationship with telecommunications systems. Most users will just assume that the service they see is the service they get, and for the most part they will expect information systems to be managed for them. From the information systems specialists', or information providers' perspective the management consists of providing an efficient and effective information service to all the business users who need it. Managing the technological resource should mean ensuring that:

- the technology suits the business environment in which it is used
- there is technical support to help people use the system
- there is training given to encourage people to make better use of the system
- there is maintenance available to respond to technical failures
- internal and external standards are set or adhered to.

The technology should suit the business environment

It has already been said that specific contexts within a business will suggest certain types of technological responses. Any development of a system needs to take into account the potential for change and growth in the business. The interaction or possible interaction with other areas within the business may also be factors to bear in mind. The tension between what is at any point in time and what might be, may often be resolved by practical limitations such as keeping down the cost of development and/or the costs of the technology.

Another factor relates to the skill and experience of potential users, for example, it would only make sense to provide a hybrid or PC-based system if the potential users have the appropriate skills and/or training to exploit the technology sensibly. Providing PCs with fully featured software packages to poorly trained users would probably result in either very few of the features being used, or else users wasting time and possibly support staff time through experimenting and getting lost in the software.

Technical support should be provided for people who use the system

It is not enough for the information systems provider to introduce new systems into a business and leave the users to it. No system or software packages are totally self explanatory; people will need help and guidance on how to use the software, and support has to be available when users make mistakes or do not know how to use the software properly.

Manuals should be available for different purposes such as for reference, for guidance on how to use the software in different work contexts, and, perhaps for new users who need an introduction to the system. If the information system software has been developed specifically for the business then the production of good documentation is the responsibility of the people who provide the system. Unfortunately, the experience of most users is that documentation or manuals often leave a lot to be desired. Documentation should be available to every user and so should the support of systems professionals, but the problem is that these can be regarded as extras or overheads rather than as a legitimate part of the ongoing costs and responsibility of the information provider(s).

Hybrid systems in which PCs feature widely provide a serious challenge to the providers, because to support users who have taken responsibility for producing some of the information themselves, even if it means using the products of a central system and then repackaging the information in suitable forms for specific audiences (e.g. for different levels of management), it implies that the support staff would need to be familiar with a very wide range of software in order to provide an effective service. There is a clear conflict here in that it could well be argued that technical support should only be given for software that is considered 'standard' or part of the planned provision in the business.

Training should be given to encourage better use of the technology

Some software that is provided for use on centralised systems is commonly used with operating systems supplied with machines manufactured by major computer companies. Some software may be one-off solutions that are designed to meet specific contexts; alternatively some PC applications development software such as database packages are sold in their tens or hundreds of thousands. Training is normally advisable in all these situations and it may be done in-house or given to training consultants.

Large companies may have a number of approaches to training users of systems. Sometimes the training can take the form of classes and practical work, sometimes special training software is available or developed for people to practice on when time allows, or sometimes individuals may be sent on a short course. As in the case of technical support any training costs money, the people being trained cannot be productively working, and the people doing the training are either training specialists or they may have to interrupt their other duties as, perhaps, analysts or support specialists.

Maintenance should be available to respond to technical failures

Technical failures relate to hardware, software or communications problems that are caused by the technology itself. Managers, decision makers or other users are more likely only to have discovered a problem than to have caused it, and normally fixing it will be a specialist's task. Maintenance in an information systems context is often associated not only with problems that arise, usually with the software, but with modifying it so that it can perform more functions or so that it can perform some of its functions better.

The problem of failure and maintenance is so serious that a common management viewpoint is that it is better to avoid it as far as possible than to have to deal with it. Maintenance for bad or large complex information systems is an ongoing drain on financial and human resources and, furthermore, the performance of business activities may be adversely affected; the user base may become very negative towards such systems.

Attempts to avoid the problem include: taking a strongly user-centred view and initially trying to ensure the right problems are being addressed; taking a user-centred view and trying to ensure all reasonable requirements for information are met by the system; taking a technically-orientated point of view and trying to ensure that the development process is well structured and managed; taking a view which says it might be better to look for a successful, proven system that looks like a close fit with the objectives of the business; or, perhaps taking an approach which would allow for more rapid and maintainable development possibly in the context of re-engineering working practices in conjunction with information systems development.

Managing the resources clearly includes the responsibility for maintenance, and it is not surprising therefore that some businesses have chosen not to develop their own software to meet their users' needs but rather have opted for buying an existing proven system to which they hope both their procedures and people can be adapted. To develop their own information system(s) could be seen as a risk and responsibility not worth taking.

Standards have to be set internally and external ones have to be adhered to

In larger organisations management of the resources is almost impossible unless control is ensured through the use of standard practice and standardisation of the resource base. Large centralised systems are easier to control because they are usually quite well shielded from abuse or inadvertent damage by the average user by the technical complexity or unfriendliness of the software, and by sophisticated means of protection. The facilities provided by the systems are usually developed by technical staff and the centralised control is relatively easy to enforce. By contrast hybrid and PC networks (or single PCs) can be harder to control unless there is standardisation of software.

Smaller networks or groups of users may benefit from a relatively autonomous status in an organisation, but with the potential advantages such as flexibility of response to demands, and the ability to respond quickly to change, also comes the potential for pockets of data or information being hidden, the possibility of pooled ignorance concerning the development of information systems, the adoption of non-standard software packages for which there is no technical support available, and so on. If small groups or clusters of users are to be encouraged then a set of standards concerning the components and use of the technology and how communication with the rest of the organisation is to be managed ought to be established and monitored. The temptation for local autonomy to become local anarchy has been hard for some users in business to resist.

The need for businesses or other organisations to communicate with each other also means that there is a necessity for most information providers to consider and adhere to international communications standards when establishing internal communications systems that will have to interface to external systems. By not considering the need for communication beyond the bounds of the immediate business, information providers can actively prevent their users from the effective or efficient delivery of the services or products for which they are responsible.

9.4 SUMMARY

The basic components of the technological resource that underlies most information systems have already been discussed. For the most part, the components are common to computer-based systems in any context. Aspects of the resources that will continue to have relevance even when the specifications of specific items change and improve have been focused on. As far as possible technical detail has been avoided and what the components bring to an information system, as well as how they can limit it, have been highlighted. The discussion of the technology provided the backdrop against some of the main management issues from the perspective of the users of information systems, such as managers and other decision-makers, and from that of the usually more technically inclined information providers.

QUESTIONS 1 Comment on the main functions of computer hardware in an information system.

2 Explain the nature of the relationship between computer hardware and software in the context of database management systems.

3 Compare and contrast the difference in roles between systems and applications software.

4 Database tables (i.e. data files) pose a resource challenge for planners of a system, and for managing the system. Comment on the nature of these challenges and on how you think they might be addressed.

5   Imagine some far-reaching ways of exploiting the ability of a business to 'plug in' its information systems/database management systems to world-wide communications networks (to which other systems are 'plugged in'), and then examine recent computer/communications literature (such as magazines and trade journals) and find out whether you are ahead or behind the times.

6   Discuss any tensions you see between what information users look for in a system and what information providers can reasonably provide.

7   If more managers and other users of an information system are given more flexibility and opportunity to take roles in providing information (or producing information products), say through the introduction of PCs, in a business, then what are the implications for the business if such a change is to be successful and effective?

8   Explain why 'standards' are a significant even crucial consideration for developers of systems.

BIBLIOGRAPHY   Stallings, W. and Van Slyke, R., *Business Data Communication*, Macmillan Publishing Co., 1994.

CHAPTER 10

The case study: a voyage of discovery

10.1 INTRODUCTION

One of the more common ways of 'teaching' information systems in business is to use case studies. A strong argument for this is that it is hard to convey the significance of both the analytical and the business dimensions of information systems without providing a business context or scenario in which they can be considered and explored. In this chapter what a case study is and how it is normally used will be explained, and then some worked examples will be provided. Different parts of the book will be drawn on in order to support the use of the case scenarios.

10.2 A CASE STUDY: WHAT IT IS AND WHAT IT IS NOT

The term 'case study' has been defined by Martin Gandoff (1989) as:

' ... *usually used to describe a problem 'scenario' that could provide the basis for several exercises and assignments. It is often intended for on-going effort by several students or groups of students and is usually designed to be 'integrative' in nature ...*' (p.4)

In the book *Case Studies in Business Computing* edited by Barry Lee, a 'case' is described as:

' ... *a written account of an actual situation which raises problems that the student must solve. It contains background information on the objectives of the system, its size and location, the people involved, etc. The problem may not be clearly defined, so that the student may have to determine what the problem is as well as the best courses of action for its solution. A case, though it may be disguised to maintain anonymity, is an account of an actual situation, though the solution adopted is typically not described in the case; rather the development of the course of action is left to the student ... '* (p.11)

Two points come out of the above definitions: one is that case studies are to do with learning, and the other is that cases often have something to do with actual situations in, for example, the business world.

Each of the points may cause some difficulty. Learning itself is an unsettling process because it means, in order to learn, not just to add knowledge to what is already known and understood, but also to change the knowledge base in the light of new information. The second, unsettling aspect, is that most scenarios which are presented in case studies are, at best, only portraying a limited view of actual situations. Very seldom do case scenarios include much detailed information and, if they do, the details are not going to be comprehensive but only representative of certain aspects of the case. In order to explore a case more fully, it may be necessary to provide missing facts and to make assumptions about which there may be uncertainty.

In addition to the challenges mentioned above, there is also the possibility that you have not been given as much responsibility for your own learning as in this type of situation. Not only is the lecturer or tutor likely to take a back seat rather than 'spoon feed' you, there may well be more than one possible solution and you will have a major role in discovering one that is suitable. Feelings of uncertainty can initially provoke a sense of frustration and anger, while others may from the beginning enjoy the challenge of the discovery process.

There is no doubt that many students gain as much from learning how to master the process of case study based assignments as they do from mastering the subject matter. The process will be examined a little more closely in the next section.

It may be worth emphasising that case studies are not, and could not be, complete accounts of actual business situations. A complete account would have to include information about all the processes, all the resources and all the documents that would be involved, as well as comprehensive views and opinions of all the affected participants, in order to build a complete picture from facts and human reactions to the situation. Formal business procedures and informally developed 'systems', communication patterns etc. would also be part of the picture. A case scenario will only pick out certain aspects of the whole situation, providing a skeleton upon which to build.

10.3 TACKLING CASE STUDIES

Case studies are used in order to work out a problem or series of problems that have been set by a lecturer. As with many problems in course studies, there will be some *given* information, some which is *implied* (by, for example, relevant course-related factors) and there will be some which has to be *deduced* or searched for. Let us start by looking at some principles for tackling a case study scenario. It will be assumed that the following factors are relevant to any assignments or other questions based on a case study; there will be:

- an overall purpose or focus that is provided by the subject of the course unit.
- a body of theory or academic ideas that are relevant to the course unit, to the case scenario and, in particular, to the aspects of the case being investigated.

- analytical techniques associated with the theory and subject of the course unit.

The case study scenario depicts some aspects of reality in the business world about which our studies should tell us something.

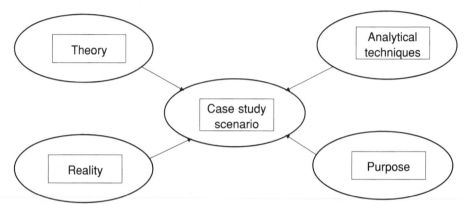

Fig. 10.1 Factors for consideration in a case study scenario

10.3.1 The focus for a case study exercise

The subject of course units should provide a focus and a starting point for the exploration of a case study. If, for example, the subject of your course has to do with economics then you should be looking at the case study with an expectation that economic issues are what you are looking for. An exercise on business analysis or information systems, on the other hand, should be looking at how the business operates or what information is needed to run it and how it is delivered.

At first, the greatest difficulty can be getting a clear understanding of just what the focus or purpose of the exercise really is. This is a particularly difficult and unsettling part of case study exploration since gaining understanding is often meant to be one of the products of the process and not something a student can be assumed to have from the start. Actively seeking clarification should, therefore, be one of the first priorities of the explorer and this is where groups (for all their headaches) can be useful in debating the issues. Bear in mind, however, that seeking will need to consist of testing the picture already made of the business, system, or even of what is thought important, against the 'reality' until the necessary clarity is acquired. This will include eliminating some possibilities and gaining a better knowledge of others.

10.3.2 There will be a body of theory or academic ideas relevant to the case study

One of the main purposes of using case studies is for students to gain insight into a scenario by looking at it from the perspective of one or more theories. Theories are usually attempts to explain how and/or why things behave the way they do, for example, the scientist John Newton developed the theory of gravitation to explain why it was that an apple seemed to 'fall' from a tree. From that one experience Newton developed his ideas and was later able to suggest a general scientific principle which he expressed in precise scientific or mathematical terms to account for the power of attraction that affects all matter. Later Einstein proposed a different theoretical model that seemed to account better for the phenomenon of gravitation. The point is, theories should be expressed in a way that allow them to be tested and, where appropriate, modified or allow better ones to be developed.

It is quite easy to see that the theoretical model of gravitation is relevant to physical behaviour of objects in real situations, but it is not so easy to start with observations of reality and come up with a theoretical model that is adequate to account for it. If you are given a case study to explore then, within your subject, there should be academic or theoretical ideas that are relevant to the case. The problem may be to discover how the theory relates to the case scenario and how it can be used to help understanding or thinking about certain aspects of it. If you have a constructively critical perspective in which you consider how successful the theory is at giving useful insight into a problem, then you should benefit from gaining a new perspective on a situation but, in addition, you may find that you can improve on the theory to give better understanding of such problems.

Theory does not have to be particularly profound or difficult to grasp but it should consist of a set of related principles which help to consistently explain and predict the behaviour or physical properties of certain things in given contexts. Some theoretical principles seem so obvious that they are hardly taken seriously, such as if to say that the laws of gravitation predict that if letting go of a china cup a few feet above a hard floor then the cup will hit the floor and may smash. Space scientists and designers of aircraft, however, need to know precisely how strongly the earth attracts objects to it in different contexts, and they rely on the laws of gravitation to provide the precise answers they need to design planes that fly and to plot the course of rockets and satellite orbits.

Information systems designers also usually need to know precisely what information particular business contexts require, and how it needs to be presented, etc. but to the casual observer at first glance it might seem obvious. This book contains a number of principles: principles of business and principles based on systems theory, as well principles related to analysis. These principles are relevant to, and help in the development of, effective information systems, providing a foundation for further and more detailed study should you wish to pursue it. Good theory should be expressed in such a way that it is possible for people to test it and improve on it; perhaps you can do this with the ideas expressed in this text.

10.3.3 There will often be analytical techniques associated with the theory or academic ideas

It is common for analytical techniques to be associated with theory or academic ideas because theory is often developed through identifying key elements in a situation and making hypotheses about how they characteristically behave or react in given conditions. To see whether the theory works or to understand better what happens, it is necessary to monitor or analyse the situation using relevant criteria, that is, criteria that test whether the ideas in the theory account well for the reality. For example, if it is considered that an information system should deliver management information, then a simple test is to ask for some and to analyse how such information is delivered or whether it is possible to generate such information from the data that are stored/recorded by the business. The analytical techniques should therefore cause a search for (i.e. use relevant criteria) those elements in the situation that are important to the purpose of the (sub)system that is being studied.

Information systems development requires analysis of how the business functions and how it is monitored and how information is provided for its management. Some basic techniques have been discussed in previous chapters and some guidance has been given on how to go about the analysis. It should always be borne in mind that techniques have a purpose and that when applied to a case scenario it should be remembered what it is that the techniques are trying to reveal about the scenario. It is easy to become preoccupied with the mechanics of a technique rather than to use it intelligently.

Analytical techniques associated with the development of information systems include business process analysis and modelling (*see* Chapter 8) and data analysis and modelling (*see* Chapters 6 and 7).

10.3.4 There will be some reality in the business world that we can assume about a case scenario

One reason that case study scenarios are given is because they are meant to bring some outside business reality into the classroom. By their very nature, case studies are limited and selective in terms of what they include and leave out, but they do inevitably include implicit information about a business. Implicit information is information that is not actually stated but which can be implied from what we would know to be generally true about something. For example, an implicit fact about police officers is that within their jurisdiction they have the power to arrest someone. Implicit facts about business could be that a company usually wants to make more profit, that records have to be kept of financial transactions, that resources need to be managed, and at a more detailed level that most invoices and orders include very similar types of details and so on.

It can be a good idea to check with your lecturer or with students in your group what kinds of information about the case can be assumed as implicit and what cannot. You may have to read textbooks or talk to people with experience to gain a clearer picture of the types of issues or business activities that could be contained within a case scenario but which are not mentioned directly in it. Quite often, as lecturers or business people, we leave information about business or theory or techniques and modelling as implicit because we forget that others may not have the shared experience that knowing the implicit information might be relied on. Part of your responsibility as an active learner is to learn to recognise where facts seem to be missing and to ask about those which are relevant to the scenario.

In summary, there are four major factors which can help you to tackle a case study scenario. First, the course that you are on should provide a general focus and purpose for your assignment. Second, more specific interest is indicated by particular theories and analytical techniques that you are required to use by the assignment or by lecturers. Third, by using the techniques you may discover what additional knowledge you will need to acquire about the business dimensions of the scenario in order to produce a suitable model, for example, what data need to be recorded, how they need to be organised, and what systems/ways the business has for producing information from its data resource. Finally, knowledge of business and the typical activities that are associated with business, can help supply some facts to supplement information given in the scenario and thus give a better understanding of the exercise.

Take care to apply *appropriate* theory and analytical techniques and remember to keep clear in your mind what the purpose of your analysis really is and how it fits in to what you want to know about the business.

10.3.5 Case studies can be used to develop different skills

Assignments or exercises based on case study material can be used to develop different sorts of skills.

Group discussion and brain storming can be a valuable context in which to suggest ideas and to get ideas from others. Of course, the down side to this is that group dynamics are unpredictable and negative aspects of group work may take considerable skill and time to overcome. If you find groups difficult then take an honest and pragmatic look at the role or approach *you* take and see if there is any way for you to grow through the process successfully. You may need to develop better negotiating techniques, you may need to listen better to others or you may need to find ways of standing your ground, such as getting stronger support from other group members when assertive personalities seem to sweep all before them.

Investigation is a necessary and valuable skill to develop. Investigation often consists of building up a picture much as a puzzle is built up from the pieces. Parts of the picture are usually provided in the case scenario, parts may be given by teaching staff and some you may have to find, but it is up to you to organise the parts in a coherent way. You may find several meaningful parts of the picture soon start to become apparent, but it is only when you have attempted to organise the parts that you will discover what aspects are missing and need to be sought. Not all your first attempts to organise the known material will necessarily be on the right track and you should regularly check your hypotheses with any new facts you discover.

The investigation will include consideration of the four factors mentioned above that affect how we tackle the case scenario. Organisation of the facts and spotting the relationships between them is as important as looking for more. Careful thought should help you to get more value from less questions and may help you to avoid pursuing hypotheses that are no more than red herrings, or which are not directly relevant to the assignment (*see* Chapter 8, section 8.3).

Problem-solving is both a skill and an art. Case study scenarios require you to solve problems rather than merely provide answers. Solving a problem may consist of suggesting a way forward from a situation; it may consist of helping to identify significant issues, or it may, for example, have to do with creating data models as a basis for the design of a data resource. Solving problems in the context of a case study will normally require you to demonstrate your understanding of the case and how your solution solves the problem(s) that has been identified.

Management of the processes of organising, investigating, and problem-solving is important. A common mistake is to assume, on the basis of a superficial reading of the assignment, that it can be left for a while until other work is done. The nature of case study assignments is that it takes time to develop ideas, find new information, and try out hypotheses. The rule is often 'little and often', in the sense that investigation and problem-solving are iterative. The problems and solutions gradually become clearer as the picture is built up. A late, ad hoc or poorly thought out approach to case scenarios invites panic as the deadline approaches and the picture still seems unclear.

Interviewing and interpersonal skills can be very significant if the case study exercise requires you to take the role of a consultant who is assigned to solve problems in the business, for example, if you are asked to investigate the potential for the introduction of a computer-based information system. As an analyst/consultant you will need to ask questions about the business: how tasks are carried out, what sort of information is required to monitor its activities or is needed for planning purposes, etc. You should make sure that the questions you ask will encourage the interviewee to give you information you do not have, rather than asking them to confirm or deny an idea you already have with an answer of 'yes' or 'no'. Good answers are elicited by good questions.

In the next section a scenario based on a real situation is provided and it will be used as a basis for a worked example of a case study. The guidelines on tackling case studies will be followed and the sections in the book will be referred to as they provide relevant assistance in the course of the analysis and modelling.

10.4 WORKING THROUGH A CASE STUDY

First a case study based on a real life scenario is presented, then some typical assignment questions will be given, which will be discussed in terms of the comments made earlier in this chapter, and chapters and sections of the book will be referred to where they are relevant to answering the questions.

The case study is a little unusual in that the business will be visited, as it were, at two points in its growth, to illustrate how changing circumstances provoke some new questions to be asked while others remain quite similar. The first growth or decision point will focus more on some basic business issues as Mr Spoke (*see below*) realises that his relatively amateurish venture into business has serious potential and requires a more professional approach. The second growth point comes at a time when he is in a position to look back at his past business performance and make some new plans for the future.

10.4.1 Case study scenario: Mr Spoke's first five years in the bicycle business

Mr Spoke used to work in the public sector but, when his employers equated efficiency with reducing staff numbers, the resulting work load on Mr Spoke and his fellow sufferers provoked him, after much thought, to trade the 'safe' future in his organisation for the uncertain but, potentially, rewarding future of a small-time entrepreneur (someone who risks his or her money in setting up and running a business). He decided to risk his future and his assets in opening a bicycle shop.

Our entrepreneur's job in the public sector and his main hobby, cycling, provided him with what he considered to be his most significant assets:

- he had experience of working with documents such as invoices and orders in a supplies department
- he had experience of frequently contacting and negotiating (albeit with the clout of a large organisation) with suppliers
- he has been a keen cyclist for many years and knows quite a lot about racing and off-road cycles
- he has quite a network of friends and fellow cyclists who have expressed interest as potential customers
- he was able to negotiate early retirement which included a lump sum just large enough to rent a shop premises for a few months, purchase essential stock and provide a small financial buffer to survive for a few months while the business would be in its early stages
- he is methodical and disciplined when dealing with paperwork
- his small pension would provide a psychological prop when trade is weak
- he is single and has few family responsibilities to worry about; his financial commitments are fairly modest.

Mr Spoke's cautious start, methodical mind, and love for bicycles were enough to see him through the early, tough months. His strategy was to build bicycles from good quality components for which there are several sources. The aim was to provide the best possible components for the lowest price to suit different classes of rider and, of course, he believed that he was able to provide a better deal than standard products sold at fixed prices.

At first, customers, a number of whom he knew through his cycling club and cycling events, were a little unsure about his hybrid machines, but his personal approach and careful matching of the machines to their buyers' requirements paid off. Respected for his knowledge and reliable products, he soon began to gain a reputation.

Not all of Mr Spoke's experience has been positive. He remembered how as a supplies officer he had approved payment to suppliers of goods or services only at the latest possible date, sometimes helping to put some of them out of business. He had tried to do the best for his organisation – for the tax payers. But now that he is on the receiving end (or not), having trusted some of his customers to pay the balance on cycles they had already taken, he realised how difficult it is to run a business when the money that should come in, doesn't.

Related to the problem of money not coming in was his realisation that his plans and hopes relied quite a lot on everything happening just as he thought they should. His working capital, that is to say, the money that he had to work with in buying new stock and so on, was not really as adequate as he expected it would be to ensure that he had a healthy choice of cycles in stock. In fact, if it had not been for a steady demand for services and repairs, he would have had very little stock to show when his income was affected by poor payers. He also found that chasing former 'friends' for the money they owed was quite stressful. Not having enough working capital taught him two lessons: the first was that he probably should do something about it, and the second was that he needs to ensure he has a clear policy on how customers pay, if for no other reason than to prevent his friends becoming foes.

The network of cycling enthusiasts and friends that he believed would form his main customer base turned out to be useful, though not as useful as he first thought. And after his experiences with (fortunately) few bad payers he discovered that dealing with friends can have its down side. Beyond that he had not really given much thought as to how to attract customers. In fact, if his prices had not been really competitive and his products good, then he might not have seen as much custom as he did.

10.4.1.1 First decision point: business plan/review at the end of year one

Mr Spoke takes stock of his position after one year, hardly believing he is still in business. He takes a sheet of paper and begins to jot down some thoughts, thinking that it was probably about time he went to see his bank manager about a small loan. These comments reflect the notes he made:

- What started as a desperate way out of a bad employment situation had become reasonably successful and rewarding.
- He felt pleased at having kept meticulous records of all his business and personal transactions.
- He had done better than he could have expected.
- Day-to-day trading seemed very unpredictable to him, except that he thinks it picks up a little after cycling events.
- He had had success, but hard lessons too, e.g. bad debts and a few sticky moments when he was offered stolen cycles as trade-ins.
- He realised things were happening that perhaps he should know about, e.g.
  - trends in customers' preference for components (fads ... follow the magazine hype)
  - amount of stock to carry ... could be better geared to typical usage
  - buying power beginning to become an issue
  - busy but can he afford help ... and what sort?
- He is struggling to raise enough working capital through trading to build up the range of cycles he would like to have available for sale.

Assignment questions for the first business decision point

Mr Spoke makes an appointment to see his bank manager. Still more of a competent paper-pushing public servant at heart than a businessman, he is nervous of the thought of borrowing money, but he cannot see a way around the problem without seeking investment. Encouraged slightly by his survival over the past year he arrives at the manager's office.

You have to put yourself in Mr Spoke's shoes as he finds out what he must do to move forward.

The bank manager sees good potential in Mr Spoke, but also sees that he needs a more structured grasp of business matters, and therefore tells him that before a loan can be considered he should submit a business plan which will form the basis for a subsequent discussion with the bank's business advisor. The following questions have to be answered.

QUESTIONS: PART A

1   Develop a reasonable mission statement and suggest two strategic objectives that you think would be appropriate.
2   State what you would understand to be the main business functions and how you would see these being handled within the business.
3   Indicate two action plans that you think would be reasonable and explain how they would help.

QUESTIONS: PART B

Assume that Mr Spoke is convinced that a PC would be a good investment to help him keep track of his business activities.

4   List four areas of his business in which you think he could benefit and indicate what sort of software would be appropriate to each (at least two kinds of software should be considered). Explain why you would choose the particular types of software.
5   Discuss what kinds of factors should be considered by Mr Spoke in choosing the hardware that he will need to run the applications you have indicated above.
6   Look through some advertisements and suggest a machine, packages and other equipment, such as a printer, that he could buy. List all the main features, include the costs of the products and any other factors that have influenced your decision.

Tackling the questions and finding answers: decision point one

If this were a real assignment there would be marks associated with each question, thus one of your first tasks would be to note how the marks are distributed and to ensure that as far as possible you do justice particularly to the questions that carry the most weight. This often means that these are the questions in which you are expected to comment on the theory or academic ideas that relate to the issue(s) and in which you may be expected to use or comment on any related analytical techniques if they are relevant.

High marks may be the reward for your ability to relate well and clearly abstract ideas to practical contexts. Do remember though that case studies are vehicles, i.e. they simply give you the opportunity to demonstrate your ability to analyse and apply ideas, and in one sense the details of the case itself are sometimes less important than your being able to grasp and reflect on the abstract ideas that relate to it. Some students get bogged down in trying to get more and more details about a case when, in truth, there are plenty of facts (given or that can be assumed) for them to use.

Question 1: *Develop a reasonable mission statement and suggest two strategic objectives that you think would be appropriate.*

Clearly a business-based question, it depends on knowing some specific terms, i.e. 'mission statement' and 'strategic objectives'. Text books and other popular books on management can be consulted to get a fairly good idea of what these terms mean and then they can be applied to the case study. In this instance take the simpler way of consulting only this text: in Chapter 1 it will be found that section 1.4.1 discusses the principle of developing a mission statement and section 1.4.2 discusses the principle of strategic objectives. Also in Chapter 2, section 2.5 factors relevant to strategic decision-making help to explain the types of objectives that are set as a result of making decisions at that level.

The mission statement is a very high-level statement that expresses what the business is setting out to achieve, but is not as vague as an overall objective which might be 'to make more profit'. The main purpose, or mission, of the business could be expressed in the rather quaint slogan 'Be-Spoke cycles for the serious cyclist: cycles built with *you* in mind'. It may be said that the mission is threefold:

- to build cycles to suit the cyclist
- to provide the best deals for the money
- to carve a niche business as a cycling retailer.

Bennett (Management, 1991, p 99) suggests that a mission statement '... is a concise summary of the fundamental *purpose* of the enterprise: what *exactly* it exists to do and how it wishes to relate to the outside world'. To show that you understand why there has been such interest in the idea of a mission statement in recent years you could comment on the expression, for example, you could note that mission statements can be stated in terms of a single sentence or a more comprehensive summary. You could also mention that some statements appear rather general while others are more specific. If you scan the literature and company reports you will find examples of all these possibilities. Mission statements have a valid role, but there is room for discussion. You could demonstrate through such a question that you see the reason for such statements and that there are several issues about them that are worth considering. Your answer and suggested statement then becomes your way of showing and applying your knowledge.

Strategic objectives should be market responsive and should be clearly related to, or at least should support the mission statement. In section 1.4.2 it was stated that, 'strategic objectives are specific measurable goals which should take the business towards greater success. The objectives are normally longer term and should be in line with the mission statement of the business'. Again the answer should at least reveal knowledge of what strategic objectives are and how they can be intelligently applied to the business in the scenario. The quotation from earlier in the book should prompt certain answers to questions as the objectives are considered. For example, what *time scale* might be involved, what *specifically* might the business goals be and, quite importantly, how should the goals best be measured?

Two possible strategic objectives might, therefore, be:

- *To become the regional centre for custom cycles and accessories in three years.*
- *To establish 'The Spoke in Your Wheel Programme' in local secondary schools within two years.*

The time scales are indicated, but the specific details of these goals would need to be spelt out more fully and the measures of success clearly defined. The first objective implies that the volume and profits of Mr Spoke's business will have to increase sufficiently to support the investment in a wider range of stock. Also implied is the type of niche he might want to establish in the bicycle trade. The second objective is a novel and challenging marketing theme which is intended to reach out to the younger generation of cyclists. The answers to Mr Spoke's business situation, however, are more likely to be judged on the grounds of how well you demonstrate awareness of the issues and how they can be applied, than on how well the hypothetical business solutions solve the hypothetical business problems. Always try to get clarification from your tutor in any specific assignment to make sure you provide what he or she is looking for.

Question 2: *State what you would understand to be the main business functions and how you would see these being handled within the business.*

This question also requires knowledge of what a fairly commonly used expression means, thus, using this text as a guide, section 1.4.3 introduces the 'main business functions', i.e.:

- **marketing**
- **production**

- **people**
- **finance**.

Good students would read around the area until they are satisfied that they understand enough about each of the functions to relate them to the case scenario. You would notice that consideration of the functional areas of business often occurs within a 'tactical' level of management, that is to say, a lower and more detailed level than the strategic issues discussed in question 1. The case does not contain a lot of details which means that some assumptions will have to be made which should, perhaps, be checked out with a tutor.

On the *marketing* front, Mr Spoke's awareness and use of a network of contacts showing a positive awareness on his part of his need to sell his products and services might be noted. He has, however, already recognised the limitations of this way of getting custom and realises he needs to do more. In answering such a question, however, beware that you do not merely suggest other ways of marketing. At the heart of many such questions is the real problem, recognised by the bank manager, that he has no plans or considered approach to marketing. If Mr Spoke is going to really succeed then he has to know where he wants to go and he has to plan how he intends to get there. Most ad hoc approaches to running a business limit its potential for success. There is enough evidence in the scenario to show that even though he is probably competent at administering and handling business documents, he still has a lot to learn about what makes business work.

Production in this context would include both the building of bicycles and the servicing and repair part of the business. It can be surmised that the way he would go about this work might differ considerably if he were producing bikes in volume instead of virtually hand-building to order. There are many questions that should be asked, but whether all the details which might be desired are contained in the scenario or not, the questions and your understanding of their significance are probably more important than whether you know precisely what procedures he uses, what his techniques are or what equipment he uses. Does he have any production goals, is there anything to suggest he has any quality controls or that he has any performance criteria, etc., and to what extent are these relevant to this particular business? These are just a small sample of possible questions about production that come to mind.

Each of these major functional areas should be discussed in answer to the type of question above. The specific business context, such as the one-man business of Mr Spoke, shows the relationship between, say, the principle of setting up quality controls in order to monitor production quality, and the possible irrelevance of such controls in a business where there is only one highly motivated and skilled producer has been taken into account. At least this type of issue might be debated in an answer.

Question 3: *Indicate two action plans that you think would be reasonable and explain how they would help.*

This question, like the ones before it, also has within it a significant expression that needs to be understood and explained. 'Action plans' are the subject of section 1.5 and constitute the plans that are developed in order to meet, often, strategic objectives.

Taking the two strategic objectives mentioned above, the action plans *should* take the business from where it is now to the desired states required by the objectives. The first action plan probably needs to develop a set or series of short-term goals to be achieved in stages such that each stage can be assessed with a view to possible further development of the business.

The circumstances would have to include factors internal to the business, and factors that relate to the environment. Internally, you might be looking at sales targets and maximising income while at the same time looking at ways to reduce costs. In addition and just as significant, it is hoped that the systems or ways Mr Spoke has of performing his business and production functions are both effective and efficient. Externally, he should be aware of trends in the demand for types of bicycle components and accessories. Whatever the steps and timetable, the action plan should take him from here to there.

The second objective may well have some bearing on the first, but again it is necessary to know just what Mr Spoke is aiming at and, perhaps, why he sees this as a strategic plan. If the idea of the schools programme is to stimulate interest in serious cycling that has elements of education, fun, challenge and reward then an action plan could be built around these related goals.

Actions plans tend to be expressed in terms of the major business functions, and thus require a look at what the implications are for marketing, production, people, and finance. In the case of the **first action plan** it is necessary to begin by asking what types of things it ought to address:

Marketing:
- How should he organise and develop his marketing?
- Who does he see as his main or prospective customer base?
- Where and how should he advertise?

Production:
- How many bicycles is he going to have to sell, thus assemble in order to achieve the growth he wants?
- Is there special equipment that he should invest in to improve his ability to assemble bicycles quickly and easily?

People:

- Can he cope alone or does he need more people, and with what skills?
- Is there some definable stage which suggests that the business needs would support additional help?

Finance:

- How much finance will he need to purchase the parts, possible extra equipment, and to pay for employees?
- Is there some point at which it would make sense to seek investment to finance the continued expansion of the business?

It would also be sensible to ask what knowledge and what systems he will need to develop in order to manage the new activities that come with increased business and possibly as an employer.

It is important to watch that in such an assignment you do not get so carried away with the business solution(s) that you forget that the exercise is meant to indicate your competence in understanding and handling the issues. The task is to communicate as clearly as possible that you know and understand what action plans are and how they relate to a business (any business) moving from its current state to a desired state in a given amount of time.

If **the second action plan** is related to the second strategic objective (i.e. to establish 'The Spoke in Your Wheel Programme' in local secondary schools within two years) then it will be necessary again to think in terms of what role(s) the major functional areas may have to play in achieving it. It will be necessary to be clearer about what 'the Spoke in Your Wheel Programme' is about, however, before an action plan can be devised for it.

Assume that it has been checked with Mr Spoke and that he has confirmed that he does have such an objective and that it consists of two six-week programmes of lessons for pupils in their first year of secondary school. One is an initial programme for 'Ace Cyclists' and the second one is for 'Super Ace Cyclists'. Topics in the first programme include facts about bicycles, what to look for in a good bike, basic accessories, riding in traffic, safety and handling emergencies, tuning your bike and emergency repairs. Topics in the second programme cover advanced riding techniques for the road, advanced defensive riding, off-road techniques and what to look for in a mountain bike. He intends to encourage off-road cycling to be taken as a serious sport by the schools and says he will offer a mountain bike and accessories as a yearly prize for the best finalists in his suggested inter-schools competition.

Mr Spoke is genuinely interested in safety and good cycling techniques, but he also sees an opportunity to promote his business interests. The strategic objective would probably fall within the realm of marketing, but each of the main business functions are affected:

Marketing:
- What should his main theme be, and how should he sell it?
- How can he maximise the opportunities if he gets into the schools?
- Should he plan to run his programme only within the one area, or should he extend it to others if successful?

Production:
- If he runs and staffs the programme himself, then when can he do it without drastically affecting his ability to assemble cycles?
- If the programme results in generating more business, then how might that affect his ability to provide services and assemble cycles to meet the increased demand?

People:
- Can he seriously think that he can just shut his shop and staff the programme, provide services, assemble bikes and sell his products by himself?
- If he decides to employ someone (or many people) should he be looking at part-time or full-time employment and what skills should he look for?
- Is there knowledge he should acquire about being an employer, such as to do with tax, social security stamps, etc. and what happens if his employees are sick? Is he meant to pay them?

Finance:
- Can he afford to consider such an initiative?
- What costs would be associated with the programme, such as if he has to employ someone to staff the programme, or alternatively, run the shop while he staffs the programme?
- What would it cost to provide literature or other material for the programme?
- What would it cost to close the shop while he staffs the programme (assuming he does not employ someone)?
- Can he take the risk of employing someone on the assumption that enough extra business will be generated (over time) to pay for him or her?
- Will he generate enough business to fund the prizes he says he would donate?

The questions above are not a complete set, but just possible ones that could or should be responded to in an action plan because they are some of the challenges that would have to be addressed by it. As you can see, even though the programme could well be seen as a sort of marketing ploy, there are serious implications for the other business functions.

Question 4: *List four areas of his business in which you think he could benefit from computerisation and indicate what sort of software would be appropriate to* *each (at least two kinds of software should be considered); also explain why you would choose the particular types of software.*

This question asks us to identify four areas of the *business* in which he might benefit from using a computer, and then it asks what sort of software might be appropriate. There are a number of discrete, meaningful areas of his business which consist of sets of activities which could or should be monitored:

- he needs to keep track of his income, that is, sales of products or services
- he needs to keep track of how he is spending money:
  - there are 'overheads', 'fixed', or 'indirect costs' such as Mr Spoke's salary, rent and utilities
  - there are 'direct' or 'variable costs' such cycle components or tools and equipment
- he ought to know his current financial position
- he ought to keep track of what components he is getting from suppliers
- he ought to keep track of what he has in stock
- he could keep track of who his customers are and what they are spending
- he might want to keep track of his service and repair jobs
- he ought to keep records of what correspondence he has sent (and received).

These are different aspects of his business that can or should be monitored if he is to know what state it is in or how it is performing. There are more than enough possibilities here to use in answering the question, but the next part of it means that thought has to be given to what sort of software would be most appropriate to the four aspects selected. The types of software to be considered will be limited to database, spreadsheet or word processing applications, although it should be noted that special business accounting packages are also used by many (even small) firms.

Some criteria will be needed to help distinguish between why the use of a database would be suggested as opposed to a spreadsheet software package because, to the uninitiated, they can seem to have overlapping functions and spreadsheets are sometimes sold as having database facilities. The criteria to be used in order to choose which type of software is appropriate and to explain of why it was chosen are as follows:

Factors that suggest the appropriateness of a spreadsheet:
- Where the details are primarily financial, e.g. looking at sales of different types of products for each month over a period, say, of six months.

- Where the details can usefully and meaningfully be arranged in rows and columns, e.g. where column headings can be the months (or other periods) along the top and product types can be listed down the side.
- Where it is useful to see the effect that changing one detail has on the rest, e.g. where projected costs and income are calculated and Mr Spoke might want to see the effect of paying an employee one rate as against another.
- Where graphical representation of financial or other numerically represented facts is a good aid to comprehension and communication, e.g. representing sales trends (by graphs) or the relative proportion of sales by, say, product type (by pie charts).

Typical business uses of a spreadsheet:
- cash flow forecasts
- profit and loss accounts
- balance sheets

Of course, the spreadsheets are not ends in themselves; they will be used for ratio analysis and such like which means that what is presented on a spreadsheet should be functionally well designed and well presented.

*Factors that suggest a spreadsheet may **not** be appropriate:*
- A spreadsheet may look ideal for representing lists of products with their related details in adjacent columns, if these lists frequently grow and may grow quite long, then using a database approach ought to be considered, e.g. monitoring what is being spent by different groups of people or on different types of product, such as bicycle components if it means adding another line every time more frames or saddles are ordered.
- If it is important to reduce the chances of mistakes being made on entering new details of transactions. Almost anything can be entered on to a spreadsheet, and few users know enough to limit the possibility of errors being made, or, more importantly caught. A database application may be more suitable.

Factors that suggest the appropriateness of database software:
- Where it is useful or necessary to keep details about different types of entities that are important to the business, e.g. suppliers, customers, orders (what has been bought from whom), invoices (who and what has been paid, and for what products).
- Where there are frequent transactions or events whose details ought to be recorded on a regular basis, e.g. payments for stock, payments to

staff, use of resources, etc.
- Where it is important to limit the chance of errors being recorded, or to limit employees' access only to details or views of the business that are relevant to them, e.g. it might not be necessary for an employee of Mr Spoke to know how much he pays for certain products, but the employee might want to know if there are any of those products in stock.

For further reasons why database software can be invaluable *see* Chapter 5 for more discussion of the sorts of facilities that they can provide.

Typical business uses of database software:
- Stock management
- Recording details of suppliers, customers, financial transactions to do with buying and selling, personnel, etc.
- Customer accounts

*Factors that suggest database software may **not** be appropriate:*
- While the details in a database may be represented on a screen or on a printout as columns and rows, and many calculations can be performed, a lot of accounting applications are better implemented on a spreadsheet (*see* above)
- Graphical representation is often hard to achieve using database software, but spreadsheets can have excellent facilities for this. Note, however, that it is often possible to use database software to record details, sort them, and then export them to a spreadsheet for final processing and presentation.

The above criteria should help you to decide about which software to put with which area of Mr Spoke's business. Let's say that he wants to keep track of how he is spending money, but in examining this it can be seen that there are possibly two sorts of expenditure. For the fixed costs a spreadsheet could be used since adding more details on a regular basis is not being considered, and he could even test out what his costs would be if he anticipated a rent increase. The variable costs arise because he is always having to buy more components and stock for as long as there is a demand for his bicycles and other products. This type of activity could be recorded on a database provided there is a sensible way to make entering the details reasonably painless; otherwise simple human resistance might result in the 'system' eventually failing.

If he wants to keep track of the components he buys from suppliers, then this again would be a candidate for database software because details of what he orders or receives from them would be added every time he needs more. Anything which required frequent updating is likely to be suitable for database software. The correspondence issue, of course, does not require us to consider either database or spreadsheet software, but rather his use of a word-processing package with which he writes his letters. Copies of the letters he writes, will be saved for future reference; however the correspondence he receives will be filed away in a filing cabinet (although he could scan them and store them as computer files).

Question 5: *Discuss what kinds of factors should be considered by Mr Spoke in choosing the hardware that he will need to run the applications you have indicated above.*

In Chapter 9, section 9.2.2 it was mentioned that it is often the software application that determines what minimum specifications are needed when choosing or using hardware. The question of hardware may largely depend on what software packages are used, and these in turn should depend upon what Mr Spoke thinks he needs (or likes). The software packages themselves will often recommend what the preferred hardware specifications ought to be.

Question 6: *Look through some advertisements and suggest a machine, packages, and other equipment, such as a printer that he could buy. List all the main features, including the costs of the products, and any other factors that have influenced your decision.*

Answering this question would be a matter of looking through magazines and making sure that the significance of the specifications of different systems is known, in terms of what would be considered relevant to this assignment.

10.4.1.2 Second decision point: a review of the use of information technology in view of changing business circumstances

An update on the 'Be-Spoke Bicycle Business'

Mr Spoke's business has not developed exactly as he had planned it, but it has developed. At this second decision point not all the aspects of the business will be discussed; only those in relation to the monitoring or management control dimension. The primary interest here is in what information he needs and how it is produced.

Referring back to the first decision point and the two strategic objectives discussed and explored above, you are in a position now to look back and see whether the objectives were met and also whether the vision provided by the mission statement looks like being fulfilled. The situation is that Mr Spoke has definitely carved out a niche as a cycling retailer; perhaps what could be called a 'value added' cycling retailer. He discovered through his contact with the school kids that they like to experiment with different components for their bicycles, as a result he operates a cycle clinic in the early evening from the back of the shop premises to which many youngsters come. Trade has steadily increased as they upgrade their machines, even though he allows trade-ins and he has begun to sell the second-hand traded-in products.

The school programme was a success in the schools in which it was accepted, but the heads of some local schools rejected it. Within the five year period Mr Spoke has become well known as a supplier of 'hybrid' bicycles and he is associated with good prices, good service and good quality.

His business now comfortably supports one full-time and two part-time staff, all of whom are keen cyclists. He has recently been approached by one of his cycling friends who has been made redundant and who would be willing to invest a significant part of his redundancy money in a similar business, but who sees that there may be benefits in buying in to Mr Spoke's business. The capital that his friend, Mr Phillips, is willing to invest would allow them to open another shop in Mr Phillips' home town about 30 miles away and to equip and stock it with only a small amount of help from Mr Spoke.

The agreement is that the shop trades under the same name as Mr Spoke's in order to capitalise on his reputation, and that he buys all the cycle components and accessories in order to increase buying power. In addition they decide to badge the bicycles as 'A Spoke's Hybrid', and agree a plan to phase Mr Phillips into the buying side of the business.

Until now, Mr Spoke has kept accurate records of all his business activities. He has a printed order book and receipt book, carefully files away all invoices and copies of his orders, but he has only used two types of software: a word processing package with which he writes business correspondence and a spreadsheet which he thought would 'do' for a business as small as his. He uses spreadsheets to record his takings, all the orders that he sends to his suppliers, payments for all his fixed overheads and his suppliers' and customers' details. The fact that he had gained some experience with both types of package in his previous job, and that he did not really understand how to develop a database application may also have influenced his decision. He has realised the limitations of the spreadsheet especially as trade grew, and considers the business factors that suggest a review of his use of the information technology as appropriate at this point.

Business factors that are relevant to a review of information provision

It has to be remembered that the purpose of providing information is to help Mr Spoke (and Mr Phillips) to know how the business is doing, to know how much business they have with the companies they deal with, to know which bicycle components sell at what rate and how that may be influenced by which others they may be combined with and so on. They will also want to know how much stock they have of the various components and other products and what it is worth, and so on.

Mr Spoke now deals with over twenty suppliers or manufacturers. He reckons that he makes out over one hundred orders a month on average, some large and quite a few small special orders, and receives even more invoices. It is not uncommon to receive only part of what was requested, the balance also coming in possibly many shipments. He reckons it is worth waiting for better components rather than getting poorer quality ones on time. The important thing for Mr Spoke is to recognise what sort of lead time is needed for different bicycle parts or manufacturers. Of course with the new venture the volume of this type of work will increase and other questions arise.

Assignment questions for the second business decision point

This decision point is related purely to a major event in the development of Mr Spoke's business, in particular, a restricted part of that scenario. Question 7 sets the stage for the next two questions by focusing on a specific management-motivated request for information; a decision or action depends upon it. As a result of the analytical and modelling exercises, something useful should be learnt about Mr Spoke's approach to handling some of his business activities, which, after all, is a desirable and practical outcome.

QUESTIONS: PART C

7 Using business process analysis techniques, create a model to show how effectively and how efficiently (remember that effectiveness and efficiency are not the same thing) Mr Spoke can *currently* produce information on how long it takes (on average) to get rear derailleur gear sets from the five manufacturers he trades with. All of the manufacturers produce good products but he thinks he might possibly deal only with those who deliver the best service. *He therefore wants information to help him decide whether to drop or keep his present suppliers.*

8 Produce a data model that is appropriate solely to the request for information specified in question 7.

9 Discuss why a database approach would be preferable to Mr Spoke's current system for delivering this sort of information.

10 Discuss technological issues that Mr Spoke and Mr Phillips ought to consider and how they relate to the need to monitor and manage the activities of the business.

Tackling the questions and finding answers: decision point two

We will attempt, as before, to give guidance in how to answer the questions rather than providing fully worked out solutions. There are, however, some clear indications of possible directions that the solutions could take, and you might find it interesting to sit quietly and work through them to gain a little more familiarity or confidence with the techniques.

Question 7: *Using business process analysis techniques, create a model to show how effectively and how efficiently (remember that effectiveness and efficiency are not the same thing) Mr Spoke can currently produce information on how long it takes (on average) to get rear derailleur gear sets from the five manufacturers he trades with. All of the manufacturers produce good products but he thinks he might possibly deal only with those who deliver the best service. He therefore wants relevant information to help him decide whether to drop or keep his present suppliers.*

First, look at what it is necessary to deliver for this question. One of the first tasks is to specify precisely what the information consists of; it is not enough to simply say that he needs information to help him decide whether to drop or keep his present suppliers. He will have to use some criteria against which he can measure their performance and he will have to look at those aspects of their performance that tell him what he wants to know.

Since Mr Spoke is concerned about how quickly each manufacturer responds to his orders for derailleur gears, and thus how quickly he in turn can respond to his customers, let us say that the information he seeks must include:

● when orders are made for these products
● when he receives the gears
● when the manufacturer wants paying
● which manufacturers and which gears are involved.

The time-frame of interest will extend to as long as it would take to get a clear picture of what is typical of each manufacturer's performance.

A diagnosis of Mr Spoke's business can be made to test its health in respect of its ability to deliver the sort of information that he wants. A business process model can help capture how efficiently and how effectively Mr Spoke's 'system' deals with the task of recording and processing the relevant business data to provide the information that he requires. In order to produce a reasonable model it helps to 'think through' the process(es) from a practical management perspective. Let us begin by representing this complex (because a number of activities are involved) process as *a system to provide information on how long it takes (on average) to get rear derailleur gear sets from Mr Spoke's five suppliers*. Chapter 8 discusses in more detail a 'systems' approach to analysing and modelling business processes although partial analysis to illustrate the application of the approach is included here.

The level zero or context diagram in Fig. 10.2 should capture the main purpose of the sub-system which you intend to analyse and model. In this case its purpose has to do with providing the information that we have specified. The diagram simply shows where the relevant data have to come from and where the information needs to go; these are a matched pair in that they account for the source of the 'flow' and its destination. The labelled flows imply that the sub-system has transformed the data into the required information.

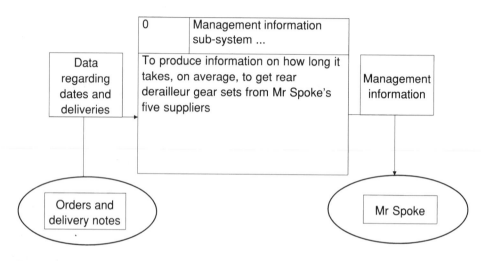

Fig. 10.2 Context diagram for Spoke's management sub-system

A second, level 1, data flow diagram could be constructed to show the processes that would be needed to pick up or process the data in the first place, to produce the information required by Mr Spoke, and to transform the former into the latter. In Chapter 8 some principles or factors are discussed that might help you to decide how to decompose complex processes such as what might be represented in a level 1 DFD, (i.e. processes that include a number of sub-processes such as the transformation process) into simpler but coherent sets of components such as might be represented in level 2 DFDs (i.e. (sub)processes and resources). Identifying (sub)processes and the resources that are needed in the business context to enable the processes to happen, you see how effectively and/or efficiently the business is set up to produce, as in this case, information needed to manage it well.

In this case, an annotated level 2 DFD might identify Mr Spoke as a significant resource spending valuable time ploughing through a file containing his orders and perhaps a file containing delivery notes in order to locate all the details that he will need to work out what it is that he wants to know or in other words to produce the information he seeks. Manually-based means of keeping track of business activities and transactions often show their limitations when their ability in terms of effectiveness or efficiency to deliver higher-level management information is tested. Unfortunately, early and poor quality computer-based information systems may not show much improvement in this respect over the manual systems they replaced. The contention is that the data flow diagramming technique can usefully reveal areas of weakness in business information management, can help managers to understand some of the problems better, and in doing so may provide the basis for practical improvements.

Question 8: *Produce a data model that is appropriate solely to the request for information specified in question 7.*

This question can be related to the previous one because there is a common interest in both the information that is required and in the data that have to be captured and kept in order to support it. Question 7 wanted to know what was involved in producing it, but in this question the interest is in discovering what sorts of details need to be kept by Mr Spoke and how they need to be organised in order to provide information of the type that is required here. If you assume that the purpose of this exercise would be to produce a data model as a foundation for the development of a relational database management system, then you might want to read the first part of Chapter 5 for an overview of how database tables are used to provide information. Chapter 6 should give enough guidance to develop a data model using the top-down approach. Once you have grasped the idea, you will discover that modelling is largely a matter of applying common sense.

The bulleted points used in the previous question give us a good start for the analysis. For our initial search for entities, i.e. the things about which Mr Spoke will want to record details (limited for now by what information is required in question 7), you could start by asking if there is a document entity that 'talks about' or 'refers to' or is used to 'record transactions related to' natural entities of relevance to the business. Such a document entity would be an *order*. The natural entities it refers to are the *products*, i.e. specifically the gears that have been ordered, and the *manufacturers* who would be specified on the orders. Two other documents are hinted at but not named. One could be the delivery note or whatever document shows the date of dispatch or delivery of the product. In this case let us assume Mr Spoke has a *delivery book* in which he records all his deliveries. The other document which is hinted at could be a *manufacturer's invoice* on which payment terms may be specified.

Note that the two 'implied' documents whilst not mentioned are suggested because we want to know 'when he receives the gears' and 'possibly when the manufacturer wants paying'; neither of these elements of information could be provided by details associated with the more obvious entities. The initial entity relationship diagram (the first stage in creating the data model) would represent the entities discussed above:

Document entities
  Order
  Invoice
  Delivery book
Natural entities
  Product
  Manufacturer

In order to model these entities it should be borne in mind that the ultimate goal of our modelling process is to identify a set of attributes for each entity that will be able to supply all the information that management and other employees need to know about them in the course of managing the business. Furthermore, in this example, it is common for documents to record events of interest – events which tell us something about the relationships between entities (often natural entities) which need to be understood. For example, the order records the commitment of Mr Spoke to buy certain products for a certain price, i.e. the exchange of financial resources for components with which he in turn expects to make money. The development of a data model is more than just an exercise in modelling; it entails understanding what managers and others need to know about these business activities. Figure 10.3 depicts an initial entity relationship diagram showing the five entities.

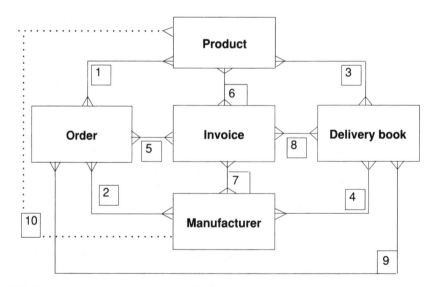

Fig. 10.3 An entity relationship diagram suitable for Spoke's management sub-system

Statement of the cardinal relationships between entities:

1   each order can contain many products/each product can appear on many orders (m:n)
2   each order is sent to one manufacturer/each manufacturer can receive many orders (1:m)
3   each product can be recorded in many delivery books (over time)/each delivery book records the arrival of many products (m:n)
4   each manufacturer can be recorded in many delivery books/each delivery book can record deliveries from many manufacturers (m:n)
5   for each order there could be many invoices/for each invoice there could be many orders (m:n)
6   each product can appear on many invoices/each invoice can refer to many products (m:n)
7   each invoice can come from only one manufacturer/each manufacturer can send more than invoice (1:m)
8   each invoice could relate to many delivery books/each delivery book will relate to many invoices (m:n)
9   each Order could relate to many delivery books/each delivery book will relate to many invoices (m:n)
10 each product can come from · only one manufacturer/each manufacturer produces many products (1:m).

Explanations for the relationships should come from the business context as far as possible. You will see in Chapter 6 that the most useful relationship in a model is the one-to-many (1:m), but this means that we have to resolve the many-to-many (m:n) ones and look carefully at any one-to-one (1:1) relationships. In the process of developing the model it is important not to lose sight of the meaning of the relationships in the business context. Unless their meaning is understood it may be difficult to determine the cardinality, e.g. in relationship 5 we assume that an order may be only partly filled by the manufacturer and that Mr Spoke could receive one invoice for the products sent initially and one invoice for the products that complete the order. In relationship 8 we make a similar assumption in that if an invoice covers a number of products that are delivered, it is possible that if the quantity of each product is recorded in the delivery book, say on a separate line, then the end of one delivery book may be reached and another one started while recording the arrival of products on one invoice. These sorts of considerations are common sense if one considers the context.

By following the analytical steps in Chapter 6 you should be able to continue the analysis of Mr Spoke's subsystem until it is resolved resulting in a model such as that shown in Fig. 10.4

We will explain some of the reasoning that took us from the initial entity relationship diagram to this data model.

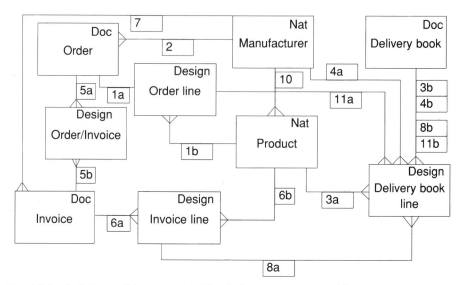

Fig. 10.4   A data model relevant to Spoke's management sub-system

Four design entities have been introduced to resolve many-to-many relationships:

● Order line (order/product)
● Invoice line (invoice/product)
● Delivery book line (delivery book/product/manufacturer plus invoice/order)
● Order/invoice (order/invoice).

You will notice that three of the four cases of many-to-many relationships have been resolved by the common technique of recognising that we can more precisely establish the relationships between the natural entity *product* and the document entities by recognising that each on the document line refers to a product that can be related to a specific order, invoice, or delivery. The other design entity would be needed to keep track of which invoice or invoices each order is associated with (and vice versa).

Note that the relationship between the invoice/delivery book and order/delivery book is indirect and assumes that we will be able to relate specific deliveries to products specified on specific lines on invoices and orders. In the case of the order-lines and invoice-lines they will be related to the documents on which they are found and are in turn related to the relevant manufacturers.

Question 9: *Discuss why a database approach would be preferable to Mr Spoke's current system for delivering this sort of information.*

In order to answer this question it would be necessary to know how the advantages and limitations of each approach affect the ability of Mr Spoke to make management decisions such as the one we have been considering.

Question 7 should have prompted a careful examination of what he would have to do to in order to produce the information. In this way, it is possible to discover not only that Mr Spoke will have to undertake a tedious examination of all the documents involved, but that because of the time needed to do it, *any* similar kind of information will require the same sort of time and search – a set of processes which incidentally are prone to error.

The answer to question 8 provides perhaps a less obvious insight in that the logical conclusion to our data modelling would result in the design of a data resource which could give all the information required.

Assuming that the entities are mapped to database tables then if the product table includes the columns *product-code* and *description*, then it should be possible to find out which product codes exist for the description 'derailleur gear set'. It should then be possible to find out which orders and invoices have contained those products by finding the lines that mention those codes (assuming, for example, that order line contains the columns *order-number* and *product-code*). By searching through the delivery book line we should then be able to tell whether the products have been delivered and when (assuming that there are columns for *order-number, invoice-number, product-code, date-of-delivery* and, perhaps, *quantity*). Through this rather simplified example we can see that in principle the information required could be obtained quite simply and quickly since a computer can rapidly search through appropriate tables and provide the information we want just as long as the data resource is designed well. The advantage of using database technology is therefore that a great deal of time can be saved when the information we require has to come from looking through past business transactions or other activities.

The paper-based system that Mr Spoke currently relies upon would be quite sufficient it all we wanted was to check on whether the occasional order had arrived or if there were a dispute over whether some invoiced goods had been delivered.

Question 10: *Discuss technological issues that Mr Spoke and Mr Phillips ought to consider and how they relate to the need to monitor and manage the activities of the business.*

We could reasonably start to answer this question by examining each of the main technological areas mentioned in Chapter 9, i.e. by considering hardware, software, and communications in the context of the Spoke-Phillips business. The situation at present seems to be that Mr Spoke uses a word processor for writing business correspondence and a spreadsheet package for recording financial transactions and other business details. The hardware consists of a PC with a keyboard and mouse, a dot-matrix printer and a telephone. Mr Phillips does not have any technology except a telephone.

In Chapter 9 we said that in principle the business should decide what it wants to do or what information it wants to deliver, then software should be selected that can produce what is wanted, and finally hardware can be chosen to run the software and to be used by managers or others in the company. Technological components are seldom exploited effectively, for example:

- Word processing software may not be fully used because the person using it does not have the time or training to use all the features it contains such as mail merging or desktop publishing capabilities. (human weak link)
- Word processing software may not be fully exploited because the printer that produces the documents is limited in resolution, to black/grey/white products, or even to certain kinds or sizes of font. (technological weak link)

Software considerations for the Spoke-Phillips business

Mr Spoke uses a word processor for very basic tasks. The technology is limited, but he hasn't had the time or inclination to explore its capabilities. He does not understand how to use mail-merge facilities, nor does he know about headers nor formatting documents other than setting out a standard business letter. In his defence, the package that he uses does not give him much encouragement to expand his control of it.

Mr Spoke uses his spreadsheet software for anything that looks like it can be set out as a list or in columns, or that involves finance. At first the spreadsheet looked as if it was just the right tool for the job, but now some of the 'lists' are very long, and the spreadsheets are becoming quite unwieldy to manipulate. From discussions that he has had with more computer literate friends he realises that he probably needs to master database, and possibly some accounting software to complement his use of spreadsheets particularly now that the business is expanding. *See* our earlier discussion concerning indicators for spreadsheet or database software.

If Messrs Spoke and Phillips are both likely to be using a computer, then they should both consider what sort of documents they want to produce; for example Mr Phillips thinks they could create interesting marketing literature to send to schools, clubs, and other potentially interested parties. Thus they should not only think about what 'functions' they want the software to perform, but they should also arrange to see competing packages to get a feel for how they relate to the way each works. The hardest type for them to assess will probably be the database software since it is harder to learn initially.

They should look at the physical documents that can be produced by the software and at what kind of printer they feel they think produces the standard of document that they want. Price, running costs, reliability, etc. are all factors in their decision-making.

Hardware considerations for the Spoke-Phillips business

One obvious consideration is that Mr Spoke already has a computer and a printer. He will have to decide whether he is going to be bound by the limitations of his technology or whether to invest in new equipment. The issue will be decided in part by the information products they would like and then by considering whether the current technology can produce them.

Assuming that they decide to purchase software and hardware to fit in with their business strategy then they will need to look carefully at *precisely* what information products they want, such as, numbered and headed orders and receipts, readily produced working and planning information, and up-to-date charts and graphs of their business performance. Sections 9.2.1 and 9.2.2 cover some of the basic hardware and software considerations. Messrs Spoke and Phillips will, for example, have to find out what the minimum or preferred specifications are for hardware components for using the software in the way they intend. They also need to consider whether their demands on the technology are likely to increase within its working life and to plan accordingly.

As has been noted in other places, careful thought always needs to be given to the input and output aspects of an information system, i.e. those areas that are prone to cause bottlenecks or potential human discomfort. Software packages that use a graphical environment usually require more highly specified hardware and can make more use of high quality printers. Probably most businesses now tend to buy or hire equipment that supports professional standard documents and letters.

Communications considerations for the Spoke-Phillips business

Since the business includes two shops which are separated by a number of miles the issue of communications must be a natural consideration. Earlier we noted that one type of equipment that they have available as a resource consists of telephones, or more exactly telephone points. We should find out, however, not whether they need to communicate, but what they want to achieve through communication. Mr Phillips needs to communicate what he is selling so that Mr Spoke knows what needs to be replaced or what should be ordered instead. Mr Spoke needs to let Mr Phillips know what is on order so that he can give his customers good service. In other words communication needs to exist in both directions for these and other reasons. Options available to them are:

● Each communicates by telephone, makes notes and updates his own system.

- They send each other updated files on diskettes, say twice a week.
- They communicate via a modem and the telephone network to update each other's system, say every weekday.

The choice they make should take into account the benefits and costs of each option. Some costs and benefits can be expressed in financial terms, but others in terms of service benefits or, for example, the time that would need to be taken to learn the technology.

10.5 SUMMARY

The important point to make about case studies is that you can identify the issues of relevance to your assignment and that you use the case scenario to explain or demonstrate how they fit in and to give you examples with which to show you understand the principles. Remember that many case scenarios could be used as a vehicle for you to communicate your understanding, but the principles usually remain fairly constant and are almost always more important than a perfect solution. Good lecturers will be more interested in how you arrive at a solution than in the solution itself.

QUESTIONS

1 Case studies usually contain 'given' information and some which is 'implied'. Explain what the difference is between given and implied information and what kinds of thing will normally be implied by your course context.

2 Discuss what kinds of skills can be usefully developed or improved through exploring case studies.

3 Make a list of factors that you think could be damaging or cause difficulties because of the groupwork aspect of case studies and discuss them in a non-threatening group of friends and devise some creative, positive, practical strategies to try if (or more likely *when*) you find yourself in a challenging situation.

4 Discuss the kinds of criteria against which case study exercises may really be assessed. You may want to rank them in order of importance as you see it, and you might want to test your understanding with your tutors whenever you meet this form of learning to check you are on the same 'wave length'.

5 **Scenario 1: Moss Electrical**
Louise Moss had just completed a degree in business and computing at a well-known teaching university. She was somewhat surprised when her father asked her to consider gaining some experience in his business, since previously he had regarded academic study as being irrelevant to the real business world. Her father, a self-made successful businessman had built a

medium-sized electrical wholesale company which sells electrical goods to the trade. Mr Moss used to handle the paperwork himself but now he shares the responsibility with the office staff. The office is basically a disaster in that priority is typically given to the problems needing the most urgent attention. Mr Moss is most worried at the moment because the business seems to be approaching a cash-flow crisis; most of the orders have been completed so that his customers requests can be met, but amid the chaos neither he nor his staff are sure which accounts are outstanding. Details of transactions with customers are kept in filing cabinets which are ordered alphabetically according to the company names. It is a system which seemed to work satisfactorily once, but now causes real problems. The only way to check whether a customer has paid is to look back through the bank paying-in book which records the customer's name, the cheque details and the relevant invoice number. Nobody has time to make a note on the copy invoices.

SPARK EMPORIUM

19 Spendmore Shopping World
nr York,
YO8 11HP

Telephone 0408 123445

ORDER: SE10336   **DATE:** 3/1/99

To: Moss Electrical
        Advance Industrial Prak
        Scunthorpe
        South Humberside
        DN19 4QP

PLEASE SUPPLY:

ITEM	QTY	DESC	UNIT-P	EXT-P
T3240R	100	40W Pearl	0.45	45.00
T3260R	100	60W Pearl	0.45	45.00
T3300R	100	100W Pearl	0.45	45.00
8KN652	5	Toaster	8.62	43.10
F8341P	25	SA Fuses	0.30	7.50

Our a/c no: SE313

MOSS ELECTRICAL

Advance Industrial Park, Scunthorpe, South Humberside

INVOICE: 545   **DATE:** ....

    TO: ....   **A/C NO**: ....

              ....

              ....

              ....

Item	Description	Quantity	Unit price	Amount
			Sub total	
			P&P	
			VAT	
			TOTAL	

(a) Assume that Louise needs to make a case to her father for investing in some technology and, in particular, that they should consider an information system to monitor and provide information about customer and supplier transactions. To help gain an understanding of how effectively and efficiently the business can deliver management information products, focus on the area of customer transactions and think of some management action(s) that the Moss's might want to make in the current circumstances and develop/specify a diagnostic request for management information to support or inform the action(s) that they might take.

(b) Produce an entity model based on the diagnostic information request you have just specified.

(c) Produce an annotated data flow diagram based on the diagnostic information request.

(d) Comment on whether you believe an information system (based, say, on relational database technology) would improve the ability of the Moss's to manage the business, and state your reasons.

6   Scenario 2: The Bader-Klein Clinic

The partners: Five years ago two Swiss physicians met at a medical conference on alternative medicine and subsequently set up a successful elitist clinic together. Dr Dieter Klein had spent ten years on the African continent and, apart from offering his considerable medical talents, had also been influenced by and collected much detailed knowledge of traditional healing practices in his work with minority cultural groups. Dr Klein's father had increased an already considerable family fortune with his interests in finance and pharmaceuticals. Dieter Klein's African experiences had been more than financed by his own inherited share of family investments. While no fool in financial affairs, Dr Klein's main goal is to contribute something to medicine and mankind. He cares much about his patients, and in particular about finding answers to some of medicine's greatest challenges.

Dr Ulrich Bader is considerably older than his partner, and grew up just outside Zurich. His father made just enough money from his business in the city to provide his son with the educational opportunities necessary for him to pursue his goal of practising medicine. After 25 years practising in the city, Dr Bader became bored and disillusioned with his work, his patients, and his family. He had left everything behind, except a small 'nest egg' from the sale of his father's business, and was living with a young New Age enthusiast when he met Dr Klein at the conference. Ulrich Bader had been wondering for a while how to exploit more profitably his medical training and at the same time keep the interest of his young mistress. The meeting with Dieter Klein seemed most opportune.

The Clinic: Dieter Klein invested what was for him a relatively moderate amount of his assets, and Ulrich Bader, all of his, in the purchase and refurbishment of a delightful property in the mountains. Although Dr Klein's contribution was in fact much larger than his partner's, the financial inequality did not seem to trouble him.

The clinic consists of 45 large single bedrooms, all of which have en-suite facilities. The decor has been chosen by a team of psychologists, colour consultants and for Dr Bader's benefit, New Age 'psychic dreamers'. The clinic is divided into three discrete units: one is for experimental 'long stay' patients, one is for 'medium stay' patients who are taking completely 'natural' treatments for common illnesses, and the last unit is for 'short stay' revitalising treatments based on individualised revitalisation plans.

Treatment at the clinic is expensive, and the specialist staff are well compensated for their dedication and expertise. There is always, day and night, a superbly qualified nurse-manager on duty, supervising each unit. The 'long stay' unit has ten bedrooms, and an experienced nurse per five patients during the day, and one experienced nurse plus one newly qualified nurse during the night. The 'medium stay' unit has 15 bedrooms, and has an experienced nurse and two newly qualified nurses during the day, and an experienced nurse and one newly qualified nurse at night. In the 'short stay' unit it is considered that a newly qualified nurse is sufficient during the day with a nursing assistant to help cover the night.

In addition to the nursing staff, other staff such as physiotherapists, chiropodists, psychologists, and other specialists visit the clinic regularly during the week. A full-time pharmacist with special expertise in natural remedies both develops new preparations in consultation with Dr Klein and is responsible for maintaining stocks of drugs and all ingredients, The pharmacist has two technicians to assist her in the lab and dispensary. Successful preparations are marketed to specialist clinics and physicians around the world once they are thoroughly tested.

A dietician and a nutritionist work together with a 'top flight' master chef in preparing and experimenting with new menus for the patients. The food and drink served to the patients are considered a crucial part of their treatment and thus the contents of each patient's meal is carefully measured and recorded. Not surprisingly the kitchen facilities seem more than adequate. There are three separate kitchens: one for each unit. The first kitchen caters for the 'long stay' patients and for staff. The kitchen has a chef and three trained cooks. The second kitchen has a chef and two trained cooks, while the third kitchen has a chef and four cooks. In each case the duty period for a team is eight hours, and there is a continuous 16 hour coverage each day consisting of two duty shifts.

Weekly multi-disciplinary conferences in each unit discuss the patients' progress in the light of the total treatment regime.

The financial management and running of the clinic is under the direction of a trained accountant and a team of three office personnel. The accountant, an old school friend of Dr Bader, liaises with him at regular intervals. Apart from a poorly used spreadsheet package, there is no use of computers at all in the clinic. The accountant, M. Dupont, keeps a lot of information in his head. and commits to paper only as much financial information as the law demands. He is touchy when questioned about anything unless by his friend Ulrich Bader. One of the nursing staff mentioned she thought she had seen them both leaving a casino in the early hours of the morning about a year previously.

A problem became apparent about six months ago. The fees for treatment at the clinic were originally costed so that if all 'medium' and 'short' stay beds were full, only half of the 'long stay' beds need be occupied to make the clinic comfortably profitable. The clinic has been continuously full. Dr Klein had deliberately intended that up to half of the 'long stay' beds could be offered to those without financial means.

Although only three 'long stay' places are occupied by those who do not have the means to pay, an accountant, who was brought in to cover the holiday period, asked Dr Klein if he was aware that the clinic seemed to be running at a small loss.

Over the five years the ratio between the legitimate costs of running the clinic – e.g. staff costs, maintenance, budgeted items for replacement, etc., food, and so on – and the fees has remained constant as realistic fee increases have been maintained. Dr Klein discussed the problem with his partner, but was concerned by his reluctance to talk about specific areas of possible irregularity. Dr Bader, who has always thought the fees too low for the very affluent clientele, suggested a moderate fee increase, and further proposed that if all 'long stay' patients were in future to pay the full fees, the Bader-Klein Trust Fund could redirect resources from support of poor patients to support of research.

The Trust Fund should have been in the black. The income for it comes from the profits from fees based on the full occupancy of the medium and short term beds and half occupancy of the long term beds. In addition the full fees of paying occupants of the remaining five beds plus Dr Klein's own salary go into the fund. The accountant and/or Dr Bader have discretion on how to use the reserves in the fund after poor patients have been subsidised. The fund is virtually empty.

After some discrete investigation, Dr Klein concludes that the clinic seems to be leaking like a financial sieve. He could see that sensible management systems ought to support the current approach which was to trust in the integrity of staff or key personnel.

(a) It may have crossed your mind that management control is very weak in this clinic. Consider some ways in which controls might be implemented: some might be best managed through computer-based systems, while some might be best managed in other ways. For example, it shouldn't be the case that M. Dupont keeps financial information 'in his head'; if it is relevant to the running and monitoring of the clinic's finances then it is probably best managed using a computer-based system from which Dr Klein can obtain up-to-date reports. On the other hand if, as good chefs often do, the chefs spend significant amounts of money on food in the early morning fresh produce markets, then it might be better for the chefs to agree budgets with relevant management rather than them being given a completely free hand, as at present, to present bills which might include hidden subsidies for local restaurants too!

Find examples of two different kinds of contexts in which management control could or should be exercised and explain the principles of control explicitly stating them in systems terms.

(b) Suggest some diagnostic requests for management information that you think would help Dr Klein in his present predicament. Be very specific about the information products he would require and explain how you think they would help him manage his way out of his problems.

(c) Do you think that the present management problems could in any way be related to the high level differences in outlook between Dr Klein and Dr Bader? Discuss what effect such high level differences might have on the way organisations are monitored/managed.

(d) Do you believe that the clinic would benefit from the introduction of an information system or systems? What reasons would you give for adopting a single or multiple approach?

BIBLIOGRAPHY   Bennett, R., *Management*, Pitman Publishing, 1991.

Edge, A., *The Guide to Case Analysis and Reporting*, System Logistics Inc, 1991.

Gandoff, M., *Systems Analysis and Design: case studies for business students*, Heinemann, 1989.

Lee, B., *Case Studies in Business Computing*, Hutchinson Education, 1987.

INDEX